A Shower of Warm Light

A Shower of Warm Light

Reviews and Essays on Canadian Poetry

MSc Miguel Ángel Olivé Iglesias

First Edition

Second Volume of CanLit Reviews and Essays

First volume: *In a Fragile Moment: A Landscape of Canadian Poetry*
Author: M.Sc. Miguel Ángel Olivé Iglesias

QuodSermo Publishing
QuodSermo@gmail.com

A Shower of Warm Light: Reviews and Essays on Canadian Poetry
Author – MSc Miguel Ángel Olivé Iglesias

Front and Back Cover Design – Richard M. Grove
Front and Back Cover Images – Richard M. Grove
Layout and Design – Richard M. Grove
Editor – Richard M. Grove

Typeset in Garamond
Printed and bound in Canada

Library and Archives Canada Cataloguing in Publication

Title: A shower of warm light : reviews and essays on Canadian poetry /
MSc Miguel Ángel Olivé Iglesias.
Names: Olivé Iglesias, Miguel Ángel, 1965- author.
Description: First edition.
Identifiers: Canadiana (print) 20210377666 |
Canadiana (ebook) 20210377674 |
ISBN 9781989786550 (hardcover) |
ISBN 9781989786567 (ebook)
Subjects: LCSH: Canadian poetry—21st century—History and criticism. |
LCGFT: Literary criticism. |
LCGFT: Reviews.
Classification: LCC PS8155.1 .O45 2021 |
DDC C811/.609—dc23

"The arts"–as we've come to term them–are not a frill. They are the heart of the matter, because they are about our hearts, and our technological inventiveness is generated by emotions, not by our minds. A society without poetry and other arts would have broken its mirror and cut out its heart. It would no longer be what we recognize as human.

Margaret Atwood
(Taken from her words in *Beyond the Seventh Morning*
(Poetry) (2013) SandCrab Books,
from the essay "Why Poetry,"
The Anne Szumigalski Memorial)

Dedicated
to CanLit
and all who write,
publish, read and support it.

Thank you for keeping
our Canadian voice alive!

Table of Contents

Special Acknowledgments

I thank God and the Virgin Mother for all the blessings in my life. I have prayed for me, my family, my friends, and I have been listened to. I have prayed for peace of mind, goodness, health, fortitude. He has always smiled on me, she has been always kind. That is why I live in trust, certainty and gratefulness. I cannot ask for more. Theirs is the best shower of warm light.

Gratitude is my best word to express what I feel about Richard Grove, my publisher, friend and mentor. I had unpolished poetry and an underdeveloped touch for writing essays in my heart but he made them blossom, showed me paths and encouraged me with affectionate words and generous actions.

A huge thank you to James Deahl, a CCLA asset, a champion of poetry and poets, as a mutual friend said to me about him. He seconded Grove in helping me and promoting my books. He prompted many poets to submit their poetry to me: without the source, poems, there is no offspring, reviews and essays.

I thank Amanda, my daughter, who lights up my life in so many ways. I still marvel how I could even breathe before she was born.

I wish to acknowledge my wife's contribution to this second volume and the previous one. Without her support, understanding of both books' significance to me and her realization of the concentration I needed and how much I exerted myself to bring them to fruition, it would have been impossible to finish them.

A Short Critique of Professor Miguel Ángel Olivé Iglesias' review book *A Shower of Warm Light*.

MSc Guillermo Ronda Velázquez
Head English Language Professor
Associate Professor, Foreign Languages Faculty
Havana University, Cuba

As a Professor of *History and Culture of the English Speaking Peoples* in the Havana University English Major, I was asked to write my opinion on Professor Olivé's previous review book *In a Fragile Moment: A Landscape of Canadian Poetry*, published in 2020 by Hidden Brook Press, a formidable material that aimed at paying tribute to Canadian poets and placing contemporary Canadian poetry on an even more prominent forefront in Cuban university curricula, given that "Canada has such a rich and diverse literary culture." (Taken from the review by renowned Canadian poet and reviewer, Ronnie R. Brown, on Olivé's *In a Fragile Moment: A Landscape of Canadian Poetry*)

His commendable efforts do not wane: I am honored to have been requested again to voice my views on his second volume, entitled *A Shower of Warm Light: Reviews and Essays on Canadian Poetry* (Hidden Brook Press, 2021). Echoing the publisher's (Richard M. Grove) comment on his opening note to the first book, I start by saying this second edition is "filled with insights and wisdom-filled observations."

Olivé's new passage across contemporary Canadian literature and poets brings us a scrutiny into poetry and prose books made public mostly during the last two decades of the 21st century, noticeably books published between 2010 and 2020, without relinquishing his homage to earlier, foundational classics.

True to his statements about the direction of his analyses, "… a literary-stylistic dissection of poets and their poetry. Readers will still pick my intrinsic efforts to connect with the authors through their poems, a correlation reaching out to reveal how they think, feel and view the world around them, from my standpoint…," Olivé offers a singular study of another equally significant number of authors who have left their notable imprint on Canadian literature.

In his Foreword he defines his role: "I have always attempted at acting as a humble bridge between writer and reader, as a translator from the language of poetics to clarifying analyses that would disclose fresh, unthought-of perspectives for the reader." Indeed,

Olivé becomes a gifted mediator, a versatile interpreter of other people's experiences; his cooperation comes to the aid and encouragement of readers as a medium they can access to take further steps in the understanding of what the writers mean.

I must note however that I do not see any imposing, absolute affirmation in his work. He focuses on presenting his unequivocally passionate views, supporting them with quotations from theoretical material to add scientific validity to his conclusions, and finally scaffolding them with examples from the original texts, which especially and practically illustrate his points.

His style evidently journeys more on an entirely acceptable, *licit* approach to literary explanations contributing a rather conversational, friendly flavor to them, typified in his well-received manner to end his reviews: "Thank you, (writer's first name)." About his particular penmanship, Brown said referring to his first review book: "At the end of each of his essays/reviews, Prof. Iglesias thanks each of his writers by their first names, so it is in that spirit that I feel all Canadians should say "Thank you, Miguel!" This refreshing tone still marks his work.

From cover to cover, this new book exudes tribute, acknowledgment and obvious proof of Olivé's extensive and intensive reading and studying of universal and Canadian sources to articulate a thoughtful, genuine product. His decision to include quotations from The Bible, Margaret Atwood, John B. Lee, Richard Grove, James Deahl, Ruth Latta and Elana Wolff, besides directing the readers´ attention to many other writers and scholars, like Shakespeare, Neruda, Al Purdy, Milton Acorn, Terry Barker and Malca Litovitz, along the whole text, speaks loudly and clearly of his preparation, charted contextual-mental bearings in his literary pursuits, and personal devotion to his objects of analysis and implicated subjects, which he constantly mentions.

But, most importantly, in reading all these excerpts, one comes to the realization of how deeply rooted poetry is in him – a fact that stands out too in his own poetry writing (Read his *Forge of Words* (2019) and *This Pulse of Life, These Words I Found* (2021), both by Hidden Brook Press), how much he values it and how substantial it is in his life. Canadian poet and professor, Antony Di Nardo, gives us a precise interpretation of Olivé´s work: "Not only is there an unabashed appreciation of the poetry he reviews, but there is evidence throughout this book that his insights into the broken line and the Canadian idiom speak of a genuine scholarship that stems from an intimate reading of the poets in question."

This second volume is reservoir and touchstone for giving poetry its most rightful station in humankind's culture and future, both threatened by excessive materialistic consumerism, selfishness, deviation from spiritual causes and ways of living, and painful disfiguration of the real goals of human growth and joy. This rightful station poetry must have, the role it must play in contemporary life, finds points of coincidence with Terry Barker´s comments on C. S. Lewis´s position in favour of salvaging "the life of faith, thought and the productive imagination" (Read *Continuing Chesterton*, Synaxis Press, Canada, 2015. Quotation taken from Barker´s Preface), a concern that holds up today.

There is also concurrence with Margaret Atwood´s profound words rightfully cited by Olivé in this book´s opening pages: "… A society without poetry and other arts would have broken its mirror and cut out its heart. It would no longer be what we recognize as human." (Taken from her words in *Beyond the Seventh Morning* (Poetry) (2013) SandCrab Books. From the essay "Why Poetry," The Anne Szumigalski Memorial)

Therefore, all in all, this new review book by Professor Olivé is a serious and intimate call – and an educational vessel – for finding "over-the-moon" enlightenment in poetry reading, one that will accompany us into a promising, brighter tomorrow, nourished and lit by the so-called *Belles-Lettres* style – which must sculpt in us an ever-developing aesthetic, cognitive and ethical perspective of life and the universe.

If Brown said, in reference to the first review book by Olivé, that "… this collection is unique," I am positive she will find this second one distinctive too in overflowing passion, original approach and noteworthy purpose.

For complete emphasis on and clarification of this book's ultimate objectives, and out of a conviction we are in the presence of a pure defender of poetry and poets and the preponderant influence of the arts in "humanizing" humans, I wish to cite Olivé's final words in his Foreword below: "We will rejoice in the never-ending appeal of the land and the boundless virtue of the souls writing to it…"

Rejoice, appeal and virtue are the key words. *Thank you so much*, Professor Olivé.

Foreword by the Author

In the months prior to the publication and launch of my book *In a Fragile Moment: A Landscape of Canadian Poetry* (Hidden Brook Press, 2020) by publisher and friend, Richard Grove (Tai), I was revving up my heart-brain-hand engines along more Canadian landscapes, so inexhaustible and luring.

Tai and I had already been entertaining the notion of a second edition for the book. He brought/sent me more books to read and study, we mentioned key names, started working on a new list and coincided on gold-leaf gilding the end again with at least two iconic figures. My priority – as I explained in *In a Fragile Moment: A Landscape of Canadian Poetry* – would be authors I was familiar with from my readings of Canada Cuba Literary Alliance (CCLA) issues and periodicals.

But my initial plans expanded auspiciously. James Deahl, a CCLA asset and Tai's close, valuable collaborator in promoting my first book, encouraged many of his poet friends within his vast geographical and influential scope to forward me their work. Their response was generous, immediate and bookshelf-overflowing! They were "first responders" to his call – a happy one; they set my reviewing wheels in motion. Thus Tai, James and poets/prose writers once more shared in the making of this second edition.

Based on Tai's keen artist eye, we decided to name this volume – which actually is the second edition of *In a Fragile Moment: A Landscape of Canadian Poetry* – *A Shower of Warm Light: Reviews and Essays on Canadian Poetry*. Tai liked it the very moment he saw it as the title of my essay on James Deahl in my previous book, and thought about changing *In a Fragile Moment: A Landscape of Canadian Poetry*, but it had already been "baptized" and this original title sounded wonderful too. I am happy we could crystallize his wish here. The new title is, in Tai's own words, "warm and gentle, and filled with profound light."

My *modus operandi* continues to be a literary-stylistic dissection of poets and their poetry. Readers will still pick my intrinsic efforts to connect with the authors through their poems, a correlation reaching out to reveal how they think, feel and view the world around them, from my standpoint, "written" – as poet Ronnie R. Brown wisely said in her review of my previous book – "in English, the thoughts… clearly Spanish-inspired." Thus the Cuban flavor is latent in my words again. In this sense, Ruth Latta's last lines of her poem ""Poetry Café" at a Retirement Residence," pertinently validate my endeavors to bring to light poets´ contribution: "What wisdom and what insight they have shown / as they affirm the value of a poem."

I have always attempted at acting as a humble bridge between writer and reader, as a translator from the language of poetics to clarifying analyses that would disclose fresh, unthought-of perspectives for the reader. All the authors consulted agreed I achieved that purpose. It is therefore more than relatable to mention the high-minded, extraordinary words for *In a Fragile Moment: A Landscape of Canadian Poetry* that John B. Lee honored me with. He said:

"… when we commune with the inner voice, the voice through which the poem flows from within the deep wells of the self, and from there onto the page." And proceeded, "The luminous writer and the illuminating reader join hands with the third reader, the one who returns to the original work carrying the light candling the mind. And in the fragile moments, we shine, however briefly, with understanding and communion in service of deep need. We are all the more human for the rarity of those complimentary voices. The original voice, and its radiant echoing when the critic and the poet sing in harmony, we hear perhaps the voice of angels as we join the choir."

Such euphony found, realization and fellowship attained, we may hold then the light candling our minds and visit once more in edifying alliance the enthralling, colossal landscapes of Canadian poetry. We will rejoice in the never-ending appeal of the land and the boundless virtue of the souls writing to it, for – let's borrow John Keats´ apt words in his poem "Endymion" – "A thing of beauty is a joy for ever:

Its loveliness increases; it will never
pass into nothingness; but still will keep
A bower quiet for us, and a sleep…"

Thank you, Tai, for EVERYTHING. Thank you, James, for your PASSIONATE SUPPORT. Thank you, Professor Ronda, dear friend, for your HEARTY critique. Thank you, Canadian poets, for your POETRY. Thank you, Canada, for your PERPETUAL BEAUTY *a mari usque ad mare*, which will grow in poets´ lines, as Shakespeare proclaimed in his Sonnet XVIII,

"When in eternal lines to time thou grow'st,
So long as men can breathe, or eyes can see,
So long lives this, and this gives life to thee."

Introduction Required:
My College Canada; My Sentimental Canada
A Brief Reflection on Canada
and its Influence on Canadians and Cubans

First Frames of Reference

My earliest recollections of hearing about Canada at all come from the friendly, close relation between Canadian Prime Minister, Pierre Trudeau, and our Commander-in-chief, Fidel Castro. I was a child but television images and newspaper announcements and pictures still flash in my mind, as well as when Fidel visited Canada to attend Trudeau's funerals.

The 70s, 80s, 90s and the 21st century brought to me Canadian music, mostly Anne Murray, Bryan Adams, Alanis Morissette and Celine Dion (and movies, with Donald Sutherland as most prominent star followed in Cuba).

Those singers coloured my high school and college years. I still play their hits as I scribble poems like "Oldies" to celebrate their music and its significance to me: "… Good old days boomerang / in names, melodies, singers, // oldies reminding us / that we lived — // still do." *(In my second full-length poetry book, This Pulse of Life, These Words I Found. SandCrab Books, 2021)*

Canada in the Canadian Heart

Outsiders, like me, will smile at Pierre Berton's reply when asked to define a Canadian, "Someone who knows how to make love in a canoe" *(Taken from Canada. Eyewitness Travel Guides. 2002. Dorley Kindersley Limited, London. Penguin Company)*, or melt before heartfelt poetic pieces like Nathaniel Benson's "Canada," from where I quote this vibrant fragment, "I have seen her in the quiet of the evening in the fields, / I have sensed her in the dusk-time that the star-decked prairie yields, / She has poised on purple mountains when my lonely step drew near, / And the North's green fires at midnight were her altar-lights austere."

We will also tremble with Audrey Alexandra Brown's loftily romantic "Take Beauty" where she praises Canadian natural scenery and its allure, convinced it is God-blessed: "Beauty's not far to seek… // Through meadows many-starred / With whiter flowers than snow… // Walk where the hare has trod / Taste where the moth has fed: / Take beauty for your bread / From the stretched hand of God."

Lampman's[1] arresting "Winter Uplands," including all that surrounds him as part of his vast Canada, was part of his poetic legacy that laid the foundation for contemporary poets´ bond with their nation: "… Like jets of silver from the violet dome, / So wonderful, so many and so near, / And then the golden moon to guide me home…; / And silence, frost and beauty everywhere." *(Benson, Brown and Lampman were taken from New Horizons, McClelland and Stewart Limited, Revised edition, Canada, 1965)*

Regarding this unique connection between Canada and Canadians, outstanding Canadian historian, Desmond Morton, referring to Canadians in general, speaks of "a kinship with nature." Morton also said that "Canadians have a sense of place." *(Both quotations taken from The Ambassador 06, the CCLA official magazine, words by Desmond Morton in his article "What Do Canadians Have In Common?")*

More poetic approaches to Canadian land and spirit come in fine poems by Richard Grove, like "Land of a Dream": "Before me lies / the land of my dreams. / Sprawling dense bush. / A canopy / of shimmering leaves / that purr…" *(Taken from Grove's book Poems for Jack. National Library of Canada, 2001)* or his "My Heart Grows Wings": "… brilliant sundrenched view… / vast wilderness panorama / unsullied, pristine… / Wing tips dip, / loon lances / silver mirrored sky"

This touching poem is included in his book *A Small Payback, Ode to Victoria Lake* (Hidden Brook Press, 2016). In his Preface he explicitly says: "The book is also a small payback to Victoria Lake for her pristine beauty." John B. Lee's Foreword to the book states: "In this book… you have the spirit of the place… A glimpse of grace. Rare and precious." The entire book is a visual-worded hymn to the beauty of a specific location that embodies Canada as a whole.

Another poet charmed by Canadian beauty is James Deahl. An example of how drawn he has been is his poem "After Coming to the North": "For miles around: only rock, / trees, these cold spring lakes. / And our tiny lives. / Ovid never saw this, nor / the Elizabethans, for all / their brilliance. Already night / has started to draw heat / from the day, its deep sky / searching, reaching ever deeper." *(Taken from Travelling the Lost Highway. Guernica Editions Inc., 2019)*

The impression left on him is obvious, and straightforwardly expressed in his mid lines: "Ovid never saw this, nor / the Elizabethans, for all / their brilliance." To the poet, there is nothing that compares to the Canadian scenes before him. Yet, his most eloquent "love affair" with Canada is the fact that U.S. born, he moved to it in 1970 never to move back to the United States. He firmly stated that "I never developed my own voice, my own vision, until I moved to Canada in 1970." *(Taken from Under the Watchful Eye, Broken Jaw Press, 1995)*

The epitome – one of them, to be accurate – of a sense of Canada is Purdy: "He is the Voice of the Land. He performed, according to Ondaatje, two of the most crucial

[1] In his essay Archibald Lampman: Poet on the Cusp of Modernism (Taken from *Canadian Stories* magazine, Volume 22, Number 129, Year 2019) James Deahl refers to Lampman – and Isabella Valancy Crawford – as "… key to any understanding of Canada and our culture." Later in the essay he says: "Lampman… could discern the land's spirit or soul."

duties of a poet: to map and to name; and that is what he did with Canada… Purdy brought not just the name of places to poems; he also celebrated the Canadian people, the Canadian flora and fauna, memories. His poetry sparkles beyond forests, valleys, mountains, cities." *(Taken from my Foreword as Editor-in-chief of The Ambassador 015, the CCLA official magazine)*

Two poems will be enough to exemplify this, "A Handful of Earth": "… our true language / speaks from inside / the land itself… // this handful of earth / for a time at least / I have no other place to go" and "Home Thoughts": "And our mountains… // Moving from east to west the land / rises… like prairie billiard tables / where players of sufficient stature / can't be found in the immediate vicinity…" *(Taken from Beyond Remembering. The Collected Poems of Al Purdy, 2000. Harbour Publishing)*

Canada and Cuba

Based on previous findings I have published[2], Cuba and Canada have been amicably connected for years. They have had interactions of some type dating as far back as the 18th century when "Vessels from the Atlantic provinces of Canada traded codfish and beer for rum and sugar." *(The following sources were consulted and quoted in the essay mentioned in footnote 2: "Consulate General of Cuba in Toronto." Embassy of Cuba in Canada; "Consulate General of Cuba in Montreal." Embassy of Cuba in Canada; "Canada Cuba Relations." Government of Canada; https://en.wikipedia.org/wiki/Canada–Cuba_relations)*

In 1945 Cuba was the first country in the Caribbean selected by Canada to locate a diplomatic mission and official diplomatic relations. Canada, along with Mexico, was the country on this side of the Atlantic Ocean which did not break relations with the island in the years after the Cuban revolution of 1959. As it goes, "Canada and Cuba enjoy a broad and diverse relationship built on a long history of mutually beneficial engagement, important and growing economic and commercial relations, and strong people to people ties across a wide range of sectors and interests." *(Idem previous quotation)*

Canada has also recognized Cuba's strong dedication to economic and social rights, with relevant achievements in education and health. Cuba is the third most popular overseas destination for Canadians (after the United States and Mexico) and Canada is Cuba's largest source of tourists: "Canada has maintained consistently cordial relations with Cuba, in spite of considerable pressure from the United States, with the island being one of the most popular international travel destinations for Canadian citizens." *(Idem previous quotations)*

Knowledge of Canada, its history, geography, policies and programs, is also promoted through Canadian Studies Centers located in universities across Cuba, and the

[2] Read my essay The Canada Cuba Literary Alliance. An on-campus and community activities cultural exchange. An essay about the influence and contribution of the CCLA to friendship and culture, in my review book *In a Fragile Moment: A Landscape of Canadian Poetry*. Hidden Brook Press, 2020.

country is part of the curricular map of the English majors in the Cuban universities. Academic cooperation represents one of the most important aspects of the relationship between Canada and Cuba, with expanding networks of academics and researchers from both countries working together in a wide range of disciplines. Cultural, literary and interpersonal ties do contribute as well to strengthening people to people relations between Canadians and Cubans.

The words of the Canadian Prime Minister, Justin Trudeau, in his 2016 visit to Cuba clearly summarized Canada's supporting and firm state of mind regarding the island in terms of foreign policy: "Pourmoi, les résultats de l'élection aux États Unis ne changeront pas les relations étroites entre le Canada et Cuba, basées sur l'amitié et le partenariat" ("To me, the U.S. election results won't change the close Canada Cuba relations, based on friendship and partnership").

Despite any changes on the political diplomatic map, the Cuban and Canadian peoples, writers, poets, friends, will continue to respect each other and share peace, culture and life.

Curricular Expectations

College provided varied references of Canada from a bird's-eye-view cultural-literary approach as part of my curricular pursuits but it fell short of really fanning out for me the wealth, depth, width and prominence of Canadian literature[3]. I had been captivated by English and American classics so much that I even memorized many of their poems. It proved very useful later in my professional career, as I would present excerpts or whole poems to my students: Shakespeare, Byron, Shelley, Keats, Blake, Wordsworth, Marlowe, Elizabeth Barrett Browning, Poe, Whitman, Hughes, Emily Dickinson, etc. Canada and Canadian poets had less presence on the curricular map at the time. I never really registered names of Canadian poets or prose writers, except Margaret Atwood and Alice Munro.

My two review books, my role as VP of the Shakespeare Center – a Holguín University cultural organization inclusive of all the Teacher Education English Major faculty and enrolled students, aimed at promoting English-language literature and arts – and my status as Cuban President of the CCLA, associated with the Holguín University's Canadian Studies Department, are instrumental in channeling further studies of Canadian culture and keeping it in our curricular pursuits.

[3] Read in this same book my essays/reviews: Architects and Epitomes. A Word about Three Canadian Poets: Richard Marvin Grove (Tai), John B. Lee and James Deahl Comments on poetry they have published in The Envoy, the CCLA newsletter (Poetry) (2019); No Stranger in These Lines. Leonard Cohen's Sweeping Lyricism in *Stranger Music: Selected Poems and Songs* (Poetry and Songs) (1993) McClelland and Stewart Ltd. Canada; and Nature-won Poetry in Pauline Johnson. An Analysis of Two of her Poems (Poetry) Taken from https://www.poemhunter.com/emily-pauline-johnson/biography.

Personal Glimpses

I have had memorable encounters with Canadians. As a student of the Teacher Education English Major, eager to learn the language and use it, I would go to Guardalavaca beach, a forty-five-minute-drive tourist resort north-east of Holguín city, to meet Canadians on the beach and talk with them.

My first Canadian friend was Patricia Lucelle Verbeke, from Dartmouth, Nova Scotia. I met her in 1984. After thirty-seven years her name remains with me. She was very kind and we kept an unstoppable exchange of letters for many, many years. Another name I remember affectionately is William A. McDonald, Bill, whom I met in 1989 and saw for the last time in January 2012. Bill was a friend in many senses. He taught me English, was generous both in word and action, and introduced me to other lasting friends: Daniel Barnhart, Robert Watson and Calvin. All of them used to come to Cuba on a yearly basis and we would meet in Guardalavaca to share for a few hours.

Robert has stayed in email touch with me since around 1998. He has played a significant role in my life both professionally and personally, mentoring me from the point of view of language but also splendidly contributing to my family's welfare, especially my daughter's, during a notably extended period of time that reaches into today. Sir Watson, as I jocosely call him, has been an unstinting hand helping me and my family in many ways for more than twenty years.

Somewhere in 2005 I met Polish-Canadian poet Lala Heine-Koehn. I did translation work for her and we grew as friends. The first poetry review I ever wrote[4] in English (I had written one in Spanish years ago about Roque Dalton's poem "Desnuda" ("Nude") and one in English about Ambrose Bierce´s short story "The Boarded Window") was about her poetry books (which she gifted me with and signed) out of profound gratitude for her openhanded, bighearted support during difficult years in my life. My daughter was lactose intolerant. Lala would systematically send me heavy packages with a special soy product for my daughter, who kept taking it until she thankfully overcame the intolerance. Lala wired remittances too so I could buy my daughter other kinds of foodstuff here in Cuba.

My connection with Canada gathered momentum when I met Richard Marvin Grove, Tai. We were introduced by my friend/brother, Jorge, from Gibara, Holguín, who had been friends with Tai for a few years. Tai is the Canada Cuba Literary Alliance (CCLA) Founding President. He founded the CCLA in 2004, along with other Canadian and Cuban supporters, to bridge both nations culturally.

Tai is the reason, source and future of numberless publications in and outside Cuba to honor both countries´ artistic, poetic and literary potential. And he is *the* key player in any inch of evolution readers might notice in me as a writer, and in all these essays and reviews, poems and stories I have written and published.

---

[4] Read it in my review book *In a Fragile Moment: A Landscape of Canadian Poetry*. Hidden Brook Press, 2020.

Without him and Jorge, I would have never gone beyond my humble words about Lala. Tai is generosity by definition. He has helped so many friends in Cuba in so many ways. I am one of the latest and luckiest ones: since 2017 up to 2021, I have found motivation, support and foundry to write and publish/republish more than a hundred and fifty poems, seven short stories, articles, over sixty-five reviews and essays on Canada, the CCLA, Canadian poets and prose writers, and milestone anthologies.

I remember my commentary in my Foreword to my first review book: "I always thought of the CCLA as where it all really started, where I found matrix and end... Without the CCLA, and Tai, there would have been only two, perhaps three, essays idling around, fading into actual "never-writtenness." It holds up today, almost five years later.

Yet the best point about the course I was led to and have charted since 2016 is suitably expressed too in my words in that Foreword: "But what makes the difference is not my writing and publishing. It is the people I have come to know; in emails or in the flesh. It is human social perspective and redeeming moments of sharing with so many generous poets what colours my existence within and without, and turns it into a worthy instant of creation."

The sentimental aspect wondrously counts as much as the historic and curricular analyses I may outline here. I will summarize it with my closing lines in my first book's Foreword: "In my profession, I am a university professor; contents to be taught must relate and be passed on one way or another to our students´ life experiences and sentiments. If this is not achieved, there is no education, no imprint left to transcend and influence. The sources I used and the poets I read influenced me. A regal bonus is that along the journey of reading and writing there was also friendship and humanity and what makes it even more worthy is having quoted them, having found coherence and place for my own writing, and having accepted the honorable proposal of being a CCLAer." A wonderful example of that human warmth is *The Divinity of Blue*, a 2020 Hidden Brook Press anthology of Canadian poets who visited Holguín and the Holguín University in early 2020, and Cuban poets who shared with them.

As closure, a poem I wrote to Canada, which reflects my view on what I have discussed in this necessary introduction. It was published in the CCLA The Ambassador 015, 2018, and in Devour: Art & Lit Canada, issue 004, 2020. Canadians will forgive my humble piece and will focus on its sincere message! Thank you, CCLA people. Thank you, Canada and Canadians.

O Canada

To Canada and Al Purdy
Al Purdy tells us of a place…
about people… Patrick Connors

I know you, O Canada,
thanks to books, singers, films, friends,
poems, writers and "friends-of-kin."

A golden maple leaf brooch
(Kim's present)
sleeps on my wife's chest of drawers.
She treasures it. Next to it

Al Purdy's collection of poems,
Beyond Remembering, mapping,
O Canada, your heritage of names,
places, people, memories.

Al, "The Voice of the Land,"
crosses his land, contemplates its vastness
and immortalizes it in his poems.

And in those poems,
O Canada, you'll always live!

The soul that moves the hand
John B. Lee

My heart grows wings
Richard M. Grove (Tai)

I decided that I needed poetry in my life…
If I could find a way to speak to people…
James Deahl

What wisdom and what insight they have shown
as they affirm the value of a poem
Ruth Latta

I want this word to last
Elana Wolff

How We Wonder Who We Are
A Review of Six Poems by Eva Kolacz in
Whatever We Are

(Poetry) (2019) Hidden Brook Press. Canada

When I laid my avid hands on *Whatever We Are* I had already finished my review book *In a Fragile Moment: A Landscape of Canadian Poetry.* Canada Cuba Literary Alliance Founding President, Richard Grove (Tai), forwarded it asking me to consider it, a John B. Lee Signature Series Book, for reviewing in a possible second edition. I was honored so I promised I would read it and write about it. I kept my word; here is what Eva Kolacz made me feel.

The first sign of high-quality material ahead of me was the quotation Kolacz uses to introduce her poetry, Octavio Paz's "... and this our life, when was it truly ours? and when are we truly whatever we are?" It is a preamble to an intense search into us, an exploration, a deep-water immersion and a reflective scrutiny into our lives and destinies. As well, it becomes a fulcrum towards a construal of our existence and our fates. Canadian poet Henry Beissel's poem "If I Had Known" touches upon this issue: "… you cannot comprehend / what is what and where and why and who you are." *(Taken from Fugitive Horizons. Guernica Editions, 2013)*

In a skillful array of semantics and syntax, the poet invites us in "Life," poem 1, to an intangibility zone, "let us have dreams," for a fleeting second, paused by a simile, "ripen like fruit," that appeals to a concrete object. Metaphysical interplays emerge in the second stanza blending/opposing reality, "… pastoral life farm…" and "virtuality," "animals are hardly seen // only their shadows dance, jump & shine with ease," as the piece unfolds. These forms waft about in the poem's transient status, as transient as life itself.

The philosophical import of "The beginning leaves time behind" is outdone by "This is what poet & mystic can define / effortlessly." Once more, Kolacz points at the spiritual and the supernatural, at the two sources capable of defining the invisible borders of time.

Somehow, one of the poets´ roles is outlined here, like Neruda described his: "Me dicen: perteneces a la sombra. / Tal vez, tal vez, pero a la luz camino". *("They tell me: you belong in the shadows. / Perhaps, perhaps, but I walk towards the light."(Taken from Neruda, 2004, pp. 34-35)*

The last stanza returns us to earth yet there lingers the fragile human presence/pertinence in the natural world: "… crows sampling air under their wings / &

swearing in harsh tones / at my unfamiliar face." Personification achieved in "swearing in harsh tones" supports my statement as human qualities are transferred to the birds. How much does the "ex-urbanite" element fit in? How "unfamiliar" is the face in that context? – What or who is she?

In "Life," poem 2, a picture-like image is offered with "Mad mad heat put August on the grill, / fields of corn exploding with fire, / dry exhausted sky / days shrink and disappear." The nature scene, depicted using personification again, "Mad mad heat put August on the grill," and vivid metaphors, "fields of corn exploding with fire," evaporates in the built in phrase "Last night I cut photographs."

Outwardly unrelated to the previous line-meanings, the phrase serves as a bridge between outdoor and indoor events, marked by the intimate "Departing has the taste of sadness," which by the way activated Shakespeare's line "Parting is such a sweet sorrow."

The three noun phrases below, essentially metaphorical, are further elaborations to stress the significance of departing: "the thread broken / connection lost / a filament of ash." There is a visibly wide separation between each of them in the same line, what may be interpreted as an intentional resource to create a sense of protracted time, of a slowness eroding our minds in crescendo.

The exploration of life and its meanings are clearly seen in the poem "Places Beyond Words." Superb metaphors abound, imagery at its highest, "Here at home the winds / don't have wings / but they are rushing down the hill / in the manner of a flashing hawk." Inquisitive, introspective/extrospective looks to try at discerning the riddles posed to humankind: "Life can be a weathered motionless boat / lying on the back of the sand, / to be turned upside down / in a desire to know what lies beyond."

This inquiry is coincidentally and unavoidably addressed by other poets, iconic Al Purdy among them: "… in the autumn of our lives to deal with / some of the questions that have troubled us in our leapfrog / trip thru the Universe… // … for which there are / really no answers except at this tranquil season of falling / leaves watching then a kind of jubilation." *(Poem "Red Leaves." Taken from Beyond Remembering. The Collected Poems of Al Purdy, 2000. Harbour Publishing)*

Kolacz's poem crosses temporal/spatial/mental barriers and speaks of surrendering to the context: "Move to the rhythm of / the stream that leads us along the trees. // That's a real possibility to taste the sun." Finally, a religious anchor giving the strength – cryptically the answer – to tread on: "… evoking God's wish for us to go / against the highest tide / & saving nothing for later."

Optimism rounds up the poem at the end, with an urge to cast behind and charge forwards: "Having come so far, be ageless. / Behind you a curved horizon, / grid of light furrows like spoken words."

A poem where Kolacz *continues* to address the questions of living is "Continuity." Another titan of Canadian poetry, Milton Acorn, also put thought and heart into a theme that poets cannot elude. Acorn wondered about the "keys of being" and acknowledged their complex, quasi enigmatic character: "More intricate than ferns…" *(Taken from In a Fragile Moment: A Landscape of Canadian Poetry, Hidden Brook Press, 2020)* Like so many, he wondered too, human and mortal, at the cosmic questions before him.

Kolacz lays it down this way: "every moment / has its own sense / of continuity / charged by philosophical questions / concerning / purpose of existence." The poet acknowledges the ups and downs, the challenges and rewards along the road: "… every moment / driven / by primal instincts… / & sometimes / will lure you into a spider's web / sometimes / will lift you like a bird on the wing." She also tells us that time neither pauses nor waits.

This is a central message in the poem, graced by fine imagery, a simile: "when we pause to refresh our minds / the moment continues / like a stream moving / in the channels of the body, / never looking for an exit."

The notion that time does not stop for anyone is revisited in the poem "Pause in Time." The poet resorts to personification, which we have enjoyed in her previous poems, bestowing time with human traits: "Time is clever —cynical perhaps…" A sprinkle of irony, probably a tinge of criticism, is felt in "… engaging us in dialogue / with words of wisdom," as she handles the idea of opposites, "combining familiarity / & *the other* unseen."

A welcome allusion is picked *(Possible reference to film and song "Singing in the rain," starred and sung by Gene Kelly)*, "… allowing us to sing with rain," as opposed to "… or walk through a wall of fire," both elements giving us the two sides of existence.

A singular poem where we find a remarkable convergence and balance of themes that have always tempted poets is "The Blueprint of a Lake." Kolacz addresses the matters of life and death, reality and fantasy, nature and beauty, physicality and spirituality dovetailing them into a fine construct that sings to those labyrinths we enter and tread in circles, sometimes in awe, other times out of curiosity or courage to confront them; fumbling along their walls, succeeding to come out (life) – or not (death).

From the quotation the poet uses ("Your happiness to be alive And sorrow that your life is closing," by Czeslaw Milosz) we notice where Kolacz is leading us. The first stanza defines the lake, "It is a place where air stops suddenly / and changes to a silver tone, / then rides toward the horizon…," and the poem's tone. The poet describes the place and by doing so she reveals her acumen at observing and crafting into words. Thus A. F. Moritz posits in his comment on the book's back cover that the poet shows "her delight in the immediacy of nature" and Travis Lane sees her insightful words as "serious poetry… inspired and informed by observation, experience…" *(Lane's comment also on the back cover)*

The stanza's last three lines punctuate the notion of fantasy, "making us feel / that we're here only half-present / and the rest is left in a dream-like state." The lake mesmerizes her, a trance she is willing to go through and renders for us a metaphorical "time that is faster than our thoughts / circling the shores of the lake." Moritz sees this poet-reality nexus as her "truer way of seeing existence." *(Idem, previous Moritz quotation from the back-cover comments)*

As Kolacz transitions across the poem, we are carried too from a lyrical first part to a direct narration of worldly events in mid-poem: "I see a school of tiny silver fish at play, / shining like shards of broken glass. / They jump into the air, / then try to hide in the waves. / Effortlessly, the hungry seagulls collect them / bite by bite." This directness is reckoned with by Moritz as "lyrical intensity… North American directness…" *(Idem, previous Moritz quotations from the back-cover comments)*

As forthrightly descriptive as it is, it includes expressive means of the language Kolacz is skilled in using, a simile in this case: "silver fish at play, / shining like shards of broken glass" and prepares the reader for a new "evolution" in the poem, which justifies the first segment and the quotation opening the piece: "Their performance a reminder / that everything comes to its end." Getting down to brass tacks, the poet gives us the black-and-white of life and death: "everything comes to its end / often in the hungry throat of predators / as a vital source of energy / for the need of species to reproduce."

Loyal to the Canadian legacy of honoring nature and writing about it, the poet opened her poem with beautiful images and now ends it with factual statements: "Nature is the force that carries the acts. / She explains her actions, / but will never ask us for forgiveness." Kolacz has surveyed the cycle of life, its mystique, in this special poem.

Eva Kolacz entitled her book "Whatever We Are" in what I now distinguish an open request to *decide* what we are. Alternately, her poems have made me shudder at the thought of infinity and uncanny worlds hanging upon my head or flitting beside me, imbued with human characteristics, ready to whisk me away through a dimensional portal. I also nervously smile at the plausible realization of the mere puppet role we play, unconsciously or not – or are ushered to play.

All in all, the poet has provoked us by hitting the probing poetic ball into our earthly reader court to see how we react. In a nutshell: we cannot allow ourselves to be stagnant, we cannot forget that, as Kolacz posited in "Continuity," "the moment continues / like a stream moving / in the channels of the body, / never looking for an exit." We will have to look for an exit, "surf against the highest tide," "save nothing for later" and "be ageless." Optimism surfaces, determination saves. These two virtues, among many others, led Kolacz to make pivotal decisions in her life.

I remember a paper I wrote years ago aimed at explaining the inner strings setting in motion our questioning everything and our motivations, which helped us outstand as a species: "The seeds of motivation go a long way back to the existence of humankind and the attempts to adapt… Deeply rooted in the platform of human need, interest and stimulation, human beings have evolved… Why does history record such progress…? Why was humanity compelled to transform reality…? What invisible strings pulled at brain and hands to urge them to sow, build, create, write, love and reach beyond the stars? What "*furnaces of Heaven*" pushed into the adventure of Life?"

The answer to all these questions – and the ones Kolacz poses in her book – might very well have an explication in our motivations, in our unending proclivity to explore and grow anthropologically speaking, in letting go of what constrains us and our free will. We owe to Eva some of these answers – and, fortunately, more questions about the adventure of Life.

No wonder John B. Lee said in his Introduction to the book that "The big questions we ask, the ones we ask concerning the possible absurdity of human existence and the spiritual realm of divine contemplation are here in glorious relief." Eva has opened a door to pursue further into that spiritual realm. Thank you, Eva.

Reader Profoundly Taken
An Essay on Don Gutteridge´s
Point Taken

(Poetry) (2019) Hidden Brook Press. Canada

My life has been filled with books since I can remember. My parents were avid readers, a gift they fortunately passed on to me during my childhood. I read almost everything they would put in my hands: stories, novels, poetry, biographies, historical treatises, etc. Teen age however saw me take a turn towards poetry reading – and writing.

Years after, my cup of tea continues to be poetry, a pleasure I have been able to expand and enjoy in more than one language. I have read poems in Spanish, English and French. I have reveled in their magic to expose the world to me; space and time compacted and served as no other genre has done for me. Canadian poets have largely contributed to that way I have felt, especially during these last four years in which the Canada Cuba Literary Alliance (CCLA) and its Founding President, Richard M. Grove (Tai), have given me the opportunity to read their poetry and fall in love with it.

The book I am reviewing here, *Point Taken*, by Don Gutteridge, is a huge, welcome undertaking that puts together most of his previous work. I must say that those early years in his life when he was "consuming the small library there (at Point Edward and nearby township) and writing both his first poem and his only play" *(Taken from Gutteridge´s Bio)*, were such a strong influence for his career, and a reminder of my own childhood.

Those were actually career-defining moments: "… he spent his first eleven years in a childhood enlivened by schoolyard chums and summers spent sunning on Canatara beach and paddling in the chill waters of Lake Huron… pristine days of his boyhood… There he spent three idyllic years…" *(Idem)* that furnished Don´s budding formative period and left marks on what would be his exceptional style and ability to recreate the past and lay it down freshly, strikingly and kindheartedly. It also built a foundation for his gallant, brave and confident attitude towards today and his being at peace with tomorrow.

This book has the rare touch to make me travel. While on my spatial-temporal voyage, I have been led into my own soul, my own memories, dusting many of them out of an almost forgotten past. I thank Gutteridge for it. It unveiled gently, completely, a universe of shimmering words and images to replenish the soul. In Gutteridge´s statement: "poetry is both bliss and consolation, a way of speaking to the world that subsumes both shy and defy." *(Taken from his poem "Defy" in the book Home Ground).* Jack Magnus tells us of Don's craft "in making his images sing…" *(Taken from back-cover comment on Home Ground, a previous book by Gutteridge also included in Point Taken)*

The book is divided into self-standing yet mutually-cohesive titles and dates that feel like sections, hand-guiding the reader across its over seven hundred pages. Despite its length, Gutteridge has succeeded in collecting poems that will stay with us long after we have finished the book. John B. Lee tells us about Gutteridge and his poetry: "we might carry these poems with us where we go…" *(Taken from back-cover comment on Home Ground)*

We will put the book down with a mixture of states and feelings wafting about us: a bit of fatigue from the long, edifying journey, a generous pinch of satisfaction for being witnesses to the extensive high-polish oeuvre the author has compiled throughout his prolific writing career, magnificently displayed here, much pride for sharing in the message and scope of his work, sincere acknowledgement to the merits of the book and the poet, and a sense of belonging to that group of people who are now in possession of an extraordinary volume. On *Home Ground*'s back cover too, Jack Magnus's impressions about the poet's work cannot be more commendable: "… instilled in me a sense of wonder and presence at his memories…" and he goes on to say: "the reader can't help but be affected."

In my view, this book is to be approached with spirit and an open will to walk down the roads Gutteridge paves for us. You will need time, which you can profit from alone, or in the company of beloved ones. The poems in the book are heartening, inviting and embracing. John B. Lee best coincides about the effect of poetry when he says: "kissing the darkness / when the pages are closed / and silent / as a dreamer's mind…" *(Taken from Lee's poem "Kissing the Darkness When the Pages Close").* The book gives us a latent past, a defining present and a future that may well be anyone's future. That is how I felt regarding this book and its lingering aroma after reading it.

The book's parts are The Way it Was, Tidings, Peripheries, Inundations, The Blue Flow Below, The Sands of Canatara, Inklings, Cameron Lake: a Suite of Poems, Home Ground, Night Skating, Days Worth the Telling, The Breath of My Being, The Star-Brushed Horizon, Foster's Pond, Mara's Lamp and Inking the World. A review of this intense-extensive compendium of colourfully-varied images and aesthetically-carved proposals must attempt at revealing its straight-to-the-heart poetic vision and stylistic precision, masterfully evidenced by the poet. To this end, I will make reference to some of the poems in some of the sections. It will help me illustrate my analyses and clarify my criteria for the readers.

Gutteridge presents his formidable book in a chronological arrangement of his literary production, 2014 through 2019, fanning out his most intimate nexus with syllable, word, rock-solid meanings and indelible metaphors, which are finely expressed in his poem to John B. Lee in *Home Ground*: "… the inheld breath / before we say the syllables / to ourselves and dream / them onto the page."

In The Way it Was section, the author embarks on a trip to his early reminiscences, and he gives us a free ticket to follow him. His poem "Blue-eyed," for example, abounds in tender phrases that depict moments and scenes familiar to everyone, thus creating links that we cannot break: "and me, / at five, hopping in a one-footed dance at her side," or "we breathe easy in the April / air, crisp clouds / clustered above: her glance / a blue-eyed barometer / of her love." The two instances settle comfortably in our mind's innermost recesses, playfully activating our personal experiences, positively connecting us to this and the next pieces.

"Letters" follows up in the trail of the previous poem. Earnest lines worth quoting for the reader, where Gutteridge displays his seasoned skills to give us his grandfather – and bring us ours: "I try again to catch / that fleeting face in the prism / of a poem, to see it / again with the clarity of crystal." The poet knows the role of poetry and the power of metaphors in eternalizing what is precious to us: "and feel that benign smile / in the serendipity of a simile, / knowing that he will survive / as long as these letters / linger and thrive." I could not avoid recalling Shakespeare's "When in eternal lines to Time thou grow´st."

"Dunes at Canatara" shows us a poet of deep thought, of concerned meditation about time and land, which he gracefully blends with his own life. The poet does not detach himself from the land; he rather admires such creation and paints himself, and peers, into it: "It took a million years to sculpt these dunes, grain by grain of wave-washed sand whipped / by seasoned winds into / voluptuous curves / and bevelled runes. / It took my pals and me / an afternoon to put / our imprimatur upon / the shimmering concavities…" I pick Purdy echoes in this poem: "I lay with my ear flat against the monstrous stone silence…, listening to the deep core of the world – silence unending and elemental, leaked from a billion-year period before and after the season of man." *(Fragment by Al Purdy taken from Al Purdy. Essays on his Works. Edited by Linda Rogers. Essay by Stan Dragland)*

We enjoy sound humour in "Career": "Oscar and I boxing / in the home-built ring / suddenly my chin… / too close to the gist / of Oscar's toxic fist, / and down I go, sprawled / on the cellar floor, knocked / here and everywhere / at once, and contemplating / the demise of my illustrious / career." We smile in half-closed-eyes gratefulness with "Nightfall" as we roll back to our childhood: "When night came down / upon the village verge, / we gathered around / the intergalactic glow / of the streetlight like / marauding moths …"

In the section Tidings I was deeply moved by "The Way Home": "The way home is thru / the heart, every blood-beat / hums with remembrance." This is a recurring leitmotif in Gutteridge, sweetly handled and firmly setting in our minds. Then again in "Home-grown" those Purdy vibrations that speak of the land, how Gutteridge mentions places of special connotation during his growth: "… the curve of Canatara's bountiful beach, / the infinite surge / of Huron Lake, the marshes / below the angular Bridge / spanning the blue cadence of our River, / while meadows bounced / with bobolinks near a park / where we played until / the evening evaporated / – these were all of God's /

geography I would need / to track the terrain of a story / or the swerve of a poem / with my cartographer's eye…" This is continually singularized in the poems "The Lake of my Childhood" and "Pleasure."

One particular poem of endearment is "For my Grandmother." This poem reaffirms Magnus's axiom: readers will be affected by Gutteridge´s words. So does "Allies": "Nothing abides like love: / for fifty-odd years / side by side… / satisfied… / riding out our last days, / we smile and, knowingly, / nod." These lines confirm my assertion about the poet's attitude in regards to what is ahead, his confidence and mature stance. He portrays his life poem after poem, his family, his fears and joys; and we gently ease into them and feel on our skin what he has felt.

Peripheries is a section of little jewels as well. "Letters" speaks about the emotions stirred inside the poet. He enumerates them slowly, as if to imbue all the homesickness they inspire, as if to re-live the past that now passes before his eyes: "It's a long way home / to the place where the heart lies: / the village that superintended / my birth, that gave me space / in its eyes to grow under / its lavish light... / a place where the heart lives, / etched in perpetual Spring, / unravished by Time." The last line tells us of the durable tie between poet and place.

Gutteridge is loyal to the Canadian tradition of writing about nature and the elements. In his poem "Gloaming" he impresses us with a splendid, eye-caressing feat of images, similes and metaphors: "… floated / like a drunken dolphin / … as the dark / deftly descended and the moon / lurked aloft, a-glimmer / in the gloaming…"

This is equally valid for "Eternity," a brief, passionate and nostalgic poem I quote fully: "My Lake was bigger than the / salten seas with no / horizon but a blue blur / where the sun would sequester / each evening, with a / kaleidoscopic squeeze, / and when we dipped a toe / into its chilled solemnity / and felt its heavenly breeze / upon our chastened cheeks, / it was as if we were touching / Eternity." I praise the poet for his delicate, well-outlined images and epithets: "kaleidoscopic squeeze," "chilled solemnity," "heavenly breeze," "as if we were touching Eternity."

"Unsayable" closes this part with the poet's musings about poetry writing. John B. Lee seeks answers to the mystery of writing: "… to feel the fertile germination / of a sentient breath / transforming / tight-packed syllables / of interlocking words…" *(Taken from Lee's poem "Kissing the Darkness When the Pages Close")* whereas Gutteridge explores possibilities and offers explanations: "I've spent a lifetime / seeking the reason for rhyme / in pursuit of the perfect poem / where dactyls dance until / they make indelible sense / in the midst of metrical meaning…" He does not give up ("I've spent a lifetime") and certainly does persist in the act, "in pursuit of the perfect poem," while his metaphors waltz: "where dactyls dance…"

Yet, "Silence" epitomizes this quest towards the why and the mystery of writing: "For sixty-odd years / I've been a wielder of words, / my pen propelled across / the page, metamorphosing / into three-beat iambics / enmeshed in metaphor / and circulating into sense; / when I can no longer be / a purveyor of poems, / I shall leave it all / to God and silence." We see the deeply religious man, poised and assured. Few poets spend so much time and sculpt such excellent pieces of poetry in dealing with this topic, and few achieve such heights in their attempts.

Inundations is a section that recaptures the scenes the poet so adores: family, context and childhood memories, sprinkling these with poems to nature, seasons, places and experiences like falling in love. Seasons, for instance, reverberate miraculously in his "Dappled": "When I die I want / it to be in the Spring / when the crocus erupts, / tulips tantalize / the sun, my maple's / leafage abruptly / levitates and the hedgerows / are hung with berries ripened / by light, when apple blossoms / blow blizzard-white, / and I may lie in some / dappled shade and dream / of being young." A sense of belonging and a bond with nature are noticeable in this poem, as much as in "Birdsong" – and many others.

The notion of poetry writing is revisited by Gutteride in this section too. Here we find "Wit": "Once more I sit / down to compose, / amazed again at the / limned linkage / between the ink-dark / word and the flush of feeling / induced… / dazed with knowing: words / are both weapon and wit;" "The Game": "I'd like to write a poem / to take your breath away / but words have a will of their own… / they may / be read in a dozen different ways…," and "Rhymes": "In my advancing age / let me still be the one / wrestling with words to wield / the world anew, to send / them dancing on some / distant dais, sylvan / with simile: the page / where all my rhymes ring / true."

The Blue Flow Below, The Sands of Canatara, Inklings, Cameron Lake: a Suite of Poems, Home Ground, Night Skating, Days Worth the Telling, The Breath of My Being, The Star-Brushed Horizon, Foster's Pond, Mara's Lamp and Inking the World will show the reader a Gutteridge nurtured by his past, charmed by his present, and in concord with what the future holds for him. We must heed John B. Lee's advice on the back cover of *Home Ground* about Gutteridge: "… he gives us the gift of something we might well carry with us into the future."

A more detailed analysis of Don's penmanship can be understood with a look at *Home Ground.* He opens this section with "Black Lake." There is light in the poem, quietness and peace: "unruffled, silvered surface," "ravishing red dot," "a pair of loons undulated," "sunny butterfly fluttering." The poet praises the painter, Gerald Parker ("so you added…," "to subvert the scene you…," and adds his personal poetic "strokes" by meticulous descriptions for the reader. While the title includes "Black," there is overwhelming beauty beyond blackness achieved by painter and poet.

As a professor of Stylistics, I could not help but notice flashes of the device known as alliteration: "lustrous light to lavish on Black Lake's…," "silvered surface, so," "loons ululated on the cusp of lust and the little stream…" Alliteration builds a melodic effect into the utterance and creates an emotional atmosphere, very much in line with the poet's purpose.

"Moon Over Monk" shows instances of alliteration: "Mara's lamp… mellowing its light along…," "gently gendered," among others, plus other stylistic devices that embellish and give emotional connotation to the poem: a simile, ("the moon sits in the horizon") "like a serene replica of Mara's lamp." The moon is a theme in Don's poetry and imagery, and it accompanies his memories. This time it reminds him of Mara – both lights will now show the way, together or alternately. The poet reminisces of his childhood games and "the sacred place where we play."

My father smoked a pipe and long cigars when I was a little boy. He quit many years ago, more than forty-five, but I still remember the aroma of cigar and smoke and I still keep one wooden box where he placed his cigars. It is deeply registered in my emotional memories. "Helm" made me remember how essential and transcending scent/sound are for people. In reading "a lozenge of elm or oak" I instantly felt wood scents coming from a carpenter's work-shop, and I was transported back in time. Gutteride then blends scents with sounds: "through the burr and bite of the band-saw." There is a floating sense of onomatopoeic echoes, direct and indirect, in the combination of the sound "b" in "burr… bite… band." Alliteration escorts the scene: "a particle of the puzzle he was perfecting piece by filigreed piece."

I realized of the gentle balance between the heavy work carried out in a work-shop: noise, sawdust, probably the logical mess of a place like that, and the child's full involvement ("I nuzzled in closer") with his grandfather's work, finely ended with "knowing I would be cherished and thrive here with this man at the helm" and preceded by "the unspoken tousling of my cowlick." It was a heart-caressing memory where the poet does not remember his exact age; but he does remember wood names! It is an unforgettable experience.

Gutteridge serves us fond memories in "Apostasy." Feelings and human values are kindled in the furnace of human connection. From there emerge convictions and attitudes for life. Gutteridge praises his grandmother for her devoted undertaking of pie preparing and baking. As I read, I feel like I am right there, watching her "put all her love and out-sized ardor into the gentle kneading of her dough… while we feasted on her pastries and praised the Lord." Gutteridge relives two experiences: unique home-made food and religion. One is a body-provider; the other, a soul-provider.

"Rare" offers another touching memory for us, and awakens our own. Alliteration is present ("on the sand in his Sunday suit," "even dove under like daring dolphins"). Gutteridge leaves behind no memory/experience/anecdote to be forgotten. This time it is the beach, a place most children adore – as they adore the Zoo in Glen Sorestad´s poem "Stanley Park." *(Reference taken from my review "A Taste of Life and Love. A Review on Glen Sorestad´s A Thief of Impeccable Taste (Poetry)." (2011) CCLA SandCrab Books. Canada)* I understand the sensation of water, of being "perfectly safe" in the hands of my father, of "venturing up to our waists and even dove...," of "(he) smiled at us and we smiled back at him." Happiness made ripples, splashes and adventure in the beach.

I have gone back on my own life, as I have been mirrored, so closely, in Gutteridge´s *Point Taken.* His collection of poems has brought happiness and homesickness to my mind. Even when Point was taken, it was me, as a reader and admirer, who was taken too into the glorious poetic knitting Gutteridge has done for us in this book.

As he hoped in his poem "Eternity," I can state Don has been able to memorialize his life in this book and leave for us a recorded legacy thus touching eternity. His book is poetry and autobiography, one that will reach out to people and remind them their own lives. John B. Lee has said that Gutteridge´s poems "partake in the light." I agree without hesitation.

His *Point Taken* should be among the top recent poetry books a reader must have and hold, go to for inspiration, for enlightenment, for pleasure, for the sheer elation of reuniting in time and space with family, friends, remembrances then place back on a treasure-keeping bookshelf feeling complete, always willing to return to the book for feedback and spiritual enrichment. This is a masterpiece – point taken! Thank you, Don.

Rainbows of Remembrance and Love
A Review of Graham Ducker's Poems in
Bridges Series Book I, Taste of the Rainbow

(Poetry) (2011) SandCrab Books. Canada

In 2020, I published a book of reviews and essays I wrote about Canadian authors, mostly poets. Graham Ducker, a well known and accomplished Canadian writer, teacher and poet, was one of the two prose writers I approached. My acquaintance with this author had been actually through his poetry, chiefly published in the Canada Cuba Literary Alliance (CCLA) flagship magazine The Ambassador. However, when his collection of short stories came to me and I read the first one, I decided I had to say a few words about how I liked his style.

Today I am returning to his poetry. I have enjoyed a selection of his poems taken from The Bridges Series Book I, *Taste of the Rainbow*, a 2011 CCLA SandCrab Books issue with four volumes to date; a fifth one in the pipeline.

The Bridges I Editor, and former CCLA VP, Manuel Velázquez, was insightful when he said in Graham's bio that the poet writes with "a clean treatment of daily themes that he colours with the veneer of very human feelings." In reading his poems compiled for *Taste of the Rainbow* I could not agree more.

The poem that opens his section in the book, "Castle Tower at Night," might at first contradict Velázquez's quotation as it seems to be set in *olden* "daily themes" rather than in contemporary life the way we know it: "The castle's flagpole," "… a knave and a princess." Nevertheless, the characters´ psychology and their actions prove to be as present-day as can be. No wonder Shakespeare's works have transcended into our times: his understanding of the humankind and his treatment, like Graham's, of human themes are timeless.

The poem starts with a stanza-metaphor, "The castle's flagpole / spears / the full moon," and another stylistic device, personification, in the second, "Silver-backed clouds / survey / the night." These two stanzas display the scene to the reader, a nature-focused one we can view as either a painting or a film. From there the poem centers on the human – "mental" –events: "The observer / sits and waits / as mental scenarios abound."

Thus "… skullduggery is intended," "… an evil deed is commissioned" and "… a knave and a princess / are sharing / a tryst," for example, are unavoidable human traits and behaviors belonging to 12th- as much as to 21st-century individuals.

The last line, "It is / a typical night / in the realm," made me recall a popular French singer, Francis Cabrel, and his song "Samedi soir sur la terre." (Saturday Night on Earth): « ... après c'est une histoire classique… une histoire normale... pas la peine que je précise d´où ils viennent... c'est une histoire ordinaire, on est tout simplement... un samedi soir sur la terre » *("... then it's a classic story... a normal story... no need for me to specify where they come from… it's an ordinary story, it's just… a Saturday night on earth." Taken from Cabrel's 1994 Audio CD « Samedi soir sur la terre,» recorded at Studios Polygone, France).* It is obvious that both authors perceive the universality of human life and the recurrence of how we act and feel, regardless of epochs and mores.

It also signals a romantic element in Ducker, as is noticed too in our next pieces. The "very human feelings" element is heightened by Graham's use of rhyme conferring a sweet musicality to his work. Nonetheless, what best appeals to me as a reader are the themes he chooses, the tenderness he is able to pen in "Christmas Memories."

Interestingly, the poem shifts from a possessive determiner, close connection, "**My** mother…," in the first stanza to the definite article, more detached relation, "… **the** mom" in stanza three. It also changes from active ("My mother **scanned** the crowded shelves… / she **fingered** tabs… / Across the shelf the mom **progressed**…") to passive voice ("Periodically her **purse was checked** / And **contents counted** slowly. // Finally, a simple **doll was chosen**") constructions.

Passive voice plus an impersonality hue is distinctly observed in the following lines: "A finger caressed it slow, / Last Christmas´ paper wrapped it up…" The poet seems to feel more and more distant, less and less a true participant, as if images were fading as irreversibly as he tells us in the last stanza: "Irrevocably time moved on / And removed my family." What keeps his feelings afloat is foretold in the stanza before the last one, "My lovely Jenny (The doll's name) helped me contend / With life's adversities," which develops into "We shared sad times and the good, / And treasured memories," and in return we read the poem's reassuring final lines: "But Jenny smiles from my bedroom shelf / And beams their love (Dad and Mom) at me."

A previous essay I wrote about another Canadian poet, Ronnie R. Brown, commended what mothers stand for when I read her poem "A Mother's Dream": "In my experience, being a mother is top priority for almost every woman I know. The expectations and plans many women blueprint long before they actually conceive and give birth is outstanding. Their commitment to a child and their sacrifices in unfavorable – or the worst – circumstances are worth-praising." *(My analysis taken from To Sleep or Not to Sleep. An Essay on Four of Ronnie R. Brown's poems in Night Echoes. (2006) Black Moss Press. Canada).* Graham's next poem, "A Mother's Silent Wish," corroborates my assertion.

It also made me reread A. Tennyson's "Home they Brought her Warrior Dead": "… Set his child upon her knee… / Like summer tempests came her tears / "Sweet my child, I live for thee"." *(Taken from Exercises in Stylistics, Editorial Pueblo y Educación, Ministerio de Educación, Ciudad de La Habana, 1984)* In a fortunate convergence of thoughts, Graham bequeaths to us another heart-caressing, rhymed piece full of tenderness, as only a mother can inspire.

It speaks of a mother's inner desires to partake with her son, "Would you mind if I tagged along / on your adventures today?" as she knows she "may not always be around / to mend life's many bumps." Especially touching is the line "… but if e'er your heart gets broken, / so will mine, I fear."

I strongly feel that rhyme yields ear-pleasing rhythm to the poem, which is a "mighty weapon stirring up emotions whatever its nature or origin, whether it is musical…" *(Taken from Stylistics, 1981, Moscow Vyssaja Skola, by I. R. Galperin)* thus rhyme and rhythm combine to create lulling sensations interwoven with the image of a mother singing to her child.

The poet exploits other expressive means of the language, such as euphemism, considered a "word or phrase used to replace an unpleasant word or expression… producing a deliberately mild effect." *(Idem, previous reference)*: "'I may not always be around," which softly hints but does not make a direct reference to dying as the mother is addressing a child. A gratifying metaphor comes to us with "… take some feathered kisses / to put upon your lumps." Its semantic power steps beyond a physical allusion of pain or actual wounds to spiritual/sentimental "bumps" mothers, overtly or not, wish to keep their offspring from.

The end lines, "I can but hope your future roads / will hold some thoughts of me," finally do telltale – Ducker uses periphrasis, "the use of a longer phrasing in place of a possible shorter… form of expression" *(Idem, two previous references)* – the mother's apprehensions. These lines also contain metaphorical/metonymical substance. Especially suggestive is the word "some": The mother is unsure; she just clings to hope. Although the poem's title reads about a "silent wish," it is highly evocative and eloquent.

I finish my analyses with a sustained metaphorical composition from the very title, the poem "Stitches." It hands over to us, deeply poetical and seriously thought out, the true foundation of marriage – and life in its entirety. The two initial stanzas are solidly explanatory and clarify before hand for the reader what marriage must be about.

Metaphorical expressions support the whole poem: "… what stitches / the invisible fabric / of a couple…, // What strong / intertwining thread / weaves its network…" The piece is an invaluable *vade mecum* for those who are married, for those who will get married; yet above all it is a chant to love and the gravitas of marriage as an institution, not just in formal terms of social convention but also in terms of looking at marriage as "the / textures and colours contributed by each…," "commitment / and dedication."

No wonder the poet gives us as answer to his questions – the opportune The Beatles´ "All you need is love, love is all you need…" echoing in my heart (and surely in Graham's too) – the best argument ever: "Love, my friends, / love." Thank you, Graham.

Land, Water, Skies and Emotion in Ed Woods
A Review of Seven of his Poems in
Poems One

(Poetry) (Poet's manuscript) Canada

In a whole-hearted interview with Malca Litovitz, Elana Wolff commented "You can only write from the depth of an emotion if you've been there." *(Taken from an interview made by Elana Wolff to her friend and poet Malca Litovitz, included in their book Slow Dancing (section Duologue). Guernica Editions, 2008)* What an aptly-spoken phrase to define the life of a man who has been here, there and everywhere, and has gotten deeply involved with living against all odds, Ed Woods.

He has been a globe trotter. He knows the world, has tasted land, sea and air, has held their essence in his hands and carried them in his heart, fully. He has plunged headlong into the act of living. Such experiences fortunately combined with his insight and gave him one-of-a-kind material to start writing poetry when life decided it was about time we heard from him.

A pilot by profession, Woods has performed all sorts of jobs and crafts. Now we take delight in his creative writing, expanded into topics that have forged him poems published in magazines, websites, anthologies, etc. A direct, uncomplicated, open and handsome style signs his work that limns nature, creation and everyday things his "trotting" has furnished him with. Many are his themes, yet I see love, hope and contemplation as the foundation of his work.

In a manuscript he generously sent to me[5] entitled *Poems* (separate typed collections from *One* to *Seven*) out of encouragement by poet friend James Deahl, he shows all of his emotions as they soar and land, sail free and seek safe port. In them, his responses to manifold experiences become words and his words reach us in simple, highly appreciated, lucid pieces, some of which I want to refer to here.

I am taking my examples from *Poems One*, a forty-seven-poem compilation which, as the author himself, covers land, water and air venturing, besides, into social and heart

---

[5] The poems I read come from a manuscript Woods kindly sent me. It should be noted that in the anthology *Tamaracks: Canadian Poetry for the 21st Century*, book's section Contributors, his bio specifies, and I quote: "... *Poems One*... All from Frozen Foot Publishers." No publication year is mentioned.

affairs from a reflective, sometimes humorous touch I appreciate in, for example, "Falling."

The opening poem is "Envy." Such title made me think of interpersonal relations. However, even when it still addresses an unquestionably human-related – and much a human fault – aspect, the "plot" is based on evident environmental criticism.

Many Canadian poets have touched upon or explicitly written about environmental issues and the damage our neglect of nature is causing to local and beyond contexts. I remember poets I have reviewed: Marvin Orbach and his mature critic to the excessive and unleashed drifting of man and "civilization" from what is natural and edifying to the soul; Katharine Beeman and her baring the never ending dilemma of killing for survival or profit; Norma West-Linder and her poem "Alewives;" Sarah Richardson and her piece "Woven;" Margaret Atwood and her "The moment," which "surprises for its direct frankness, but above all for its recognition of who was here first, of how important land and fauna and flora are in this world;" and many others. *(Examples of poets and quotations taken from In a Fragile Moment. A Landscape of Canadian Poetry. Hidden Brook Press, 2020. Reviews and Essays by M.Sc. Miguel Ángel Olivé Iglesias)*

Ed Woods sprinkles irony in "Envy" by pinning the blame of "this beach dirty and smelly" on nature itself. He finds refuge in the past when the beach was clean and surely scents of algae and salt wafted in the air. The second stanza brings us a lover's lament accentuated by the things he won't have: "no more urges to walk barefoot on soft grains hand in hand or caress your hair…"

Woods handles opposition well to reveal contrasts between the beach he remembers and the one he has before his eyes, "I will check out old photos." He emphasizes the photos are "old," "faded" and "creased" yet the images they show "may create envy." The poet finds refuge in the past of the beach for this one he sees now motivates him in no way.

So many poets have been inspired by beauty, happiness and tears. Musings about these themes are addressed by Woods in "Tears." The poet rejoices in a woman's beauty – and the beauty of life, which he acquiesces entirely despite the "mishap sprawls" he refers to in another poem, "Falling." This latter poem is revelatory of the poet's positive state of mind to face life. Its humorous spin, reached in the dénouement, makes it worth-quoting whole, as the poem is brief: "a mishap sprawl / upon the sidewalk // slightly hurt / I rise and realize / cement has a taste / of its own / and not that / of fine wine."

In "Tears" he is exposed through both his physical and spiritual sensors, he maximizes touch, movement, sight, "touch of skin… / sensuous in motion / river of tears," and plays with them to close the poem with a hyperbole (already anticipated in the phrase "river of tears"), "a love that will never end." The use of this expressive means exudes optimism and faith in Woods.

Handling with ease again his comical angle, Woods presents "Sunday." Even when he speaks about reflection, "time to rest / recreation / reflection," he introduces a key phrase that annuls his assertions, "let's cancel…" The poet dissects human expectations one by one charging the lines with in crescendo amusement, and my own expectations of what will come out of the poem escalate as I read. In the end, he detonates with a solution to the riddle he has created: "better yet / let's cancel Sundays."

My first impression with the poem "Our Future" was the feeling of slow motion, not only in the way Woods organizes the stanzas syntactically, but also semantically in the thoughtfully chosen words (each one carrying a specific shade/weight of time-suspended or time-decelerated action), stylistically handpicked to produce that contextual effect: "step by step / up to your loft / stairway // tea aroma fills the air // quiet stare // quietly / admire / bonding thoughts and snowfall."

The atmosphere the poets stages for the reader is enhanced by phrases such as "stairway candles," "tea aroma," "my gloves brush off snowflakes," "bonding thoughts and snowfall," "last night still feels great." They refer to shared moments, to a passion that endures, all of which stay with the poet long and persistently enough to foresee tomorrows, as he titled the poem "Our Future."

Slow-go perception is treated by Woods to eternalize pleasures he is able to put down in simmering wording. I instantly visualized scenes to follow thanks to the title of our next poem under analysis, "Lovers Ballet." The first stanza is a fine prelude to what follows, as the unfolding stanzas propose a sequential performance.

We progress from a start suggesting foreplay ("we dance around / as two beams of light…"), coloured with a strongly appealing, sensual metaphor (derived from a previous simile, "as two beams of light"): "… who criss-cross / the night sky / in search / of a mutual target." This is an obvious well-knit poetic allusion to lovemaking remindful of these lines "… hold eternity in our ultimate cry / and be on the verge of faint / clinging to chunks of breathless words, // closeness of the lips and hands translating // into this poem // what we feel," and also evocative of "tremors in harmony with / the Universe, // a river of two surging / towards the finish." *(Taken from the poems "Moment" and "Rivers" respectively in the poetry book This Pulse of Life, These Words I Found, by Miguel Ángel Olivé Iglesias)* The "ultimate cry" and "the finish" are the target lovers seek, together.

The scenario leads then to suspenseful, provocative instants of "time and wine / slow us down / to embrace // passion explodes / through celestial ceiling," intoxicating the couple towards *afterplay* in "until contentment / in deep slumber." But the lover does not forget it all "started by a kiss" that seasoned the setting, nor does he fail to trust that "this one solitary kiss / may be the prelude / to lifelong commitment." Ed Woods is brimming with faith and hope in the future.

The last poem to comment on is a soft, quietly eloquent piece entitled "Your Hand." I like the way Woods opens the poem, "hand in hand," indicative of a physicality that calls to mind closeness, connection between lovers, awareness of belonging and reciprocated support marching them through life and before everyone: " (friends) they see our contentment / and sense of love."

The second stanza naturally results from the first one, especially from its last line, "sense of love." A transit from public settings to a more private context that offers a stirring ritual in an ambience of intimacy provided "when darkness falls / and "quietness rules earth": "we touch and caress / and light up the night sky." There are compelling metaphorical symbolisms in the phrase "light up the night sky" as opposed to "darkness falls" and the nuances of meaning hinted by "light up": to illuminate, to display liveliness or joy. Both apply to the moment and the connotations the poet has tried to unveil for us.

Sensuously and wondrously laid, the poem insists on the hand element in the title (notice the detail "Your" reinforcing what *her* hands can make him feel), in the first stanza, "hand in hand," and implied in the second one, "we touch and caress."

This is Ed Woods writing from the depth of emotions he has felt, keeping them fresh and warm to turn them into poetry. Thank you, Ed.

A True Gift in a Throbbing Womanheart
A Review of Six of Elana Wolff's Poems in *Birdheart*

(Poetry) (2001) Guernica Editions. Canada

Canadian poet Elana Wolff surprised me one Friday morning when the postman called out my name: a package from her with seven books and a warm letter! As a privileged soul with my heart leaping out, I devoted Friday night – no better merriment for the soul – to skimming her books, so I could get to know the poet more.

In my thank-you e-mail I let her know I had been fascinated by many of her poems in my first "reading round." But, to write about her poetry, I'd need to read again and again. I chose six poems. It was so hard to leave out other poems. The ones I chose cover those she wondrously carved in cooperation with her beloved friend Malca Litovitz, poet and teacher, in *Slow Dancing* (2008), Guernica Editions, and many others from *You Speak to me in Trees* (2006), Guernica Editions, which I am already reading.

All of them speak decidedly in a voice of artistry and style, of their devotion and love for life, of their joy and constancy above pain. Both are poet-teachers; both poets dedicated to others – unstinting givers who have turned me into a joyful recipient of their work, touching me with their throbbing womanhearts.

The book *Birdheart* is Elana's first one. What a start! From her fifty-two neatly-carved pieces, I marked twenty-four in my first read! Elana's poetry and I clicked that fast and extensively. She dedicates the book to her parents, evidence of what they meant to her and the fact that it was them who took her on the trip that gave birth years later to the poems therein.

In talks between Malca and Elana they approach the notion of dance connected to poetry *(Taken from an interview made by Elana Wolff to her friend and poet Malca Litovitz, included in their book Slow Dancing (section Duologue), 2008, Guernica Editions)*. Elena says "… there's a life-affirming vitality to both" following up on Malca's assertion: "… there's rhythm and a sort of flesh in both." I picked this in the opening poem, "Dance."

It is a ten-line poem divided in three three-line stanzas and a closing one-line sentence with a to-the-point status I will discuss later. The first stanza gives us a metaphorical expression, "bags… to be carried into summer," and for a moment I felt as a reader that the poet is sort of detached from the scene (probably not willing to travel?), a passive onlooker at what is going on around her. Use of passive voice ("to be carried" – someone else will be doing that), opening the poem with objects rather than people ("the bags") and two closing descriptions of what comes ahead of her giving a sense of distance, vastness and separation: "Cross country, down the divide."

The second stanza emphasizes this notion with the phrase "Away from true north," plus the use of the adjective "another," which implies repetition, recurring vistas (fields) for the traveller. However, this same stanza already anticipates a change in the poet's mood: (field) "raises its ***bright*** head."

From here, a poetry-nature-dance-poetry-dance sequence takes over the poem – and the poet – beginning with the hyperbolic "a thousand," to reinforce a notion of immensity and quantity. From there then colour comes to stage, "canola-yellow," and finally movement, "waving in the wind." Has the poet been captured by the scenery? I believe so. The poem's progression exquisitely conveys that thought.

Last sentence, as mentioned, has an epigrammatic rank, a revelation – besides – of what the poet has been able to take in and embrace in realizing what "the open field" has to offer to the soul: a dance, that is, extended spirituality that intertwines poetry and dancing creating a monument of pleasure. Even when Elana closes the poem with "Dance in service of the open field," I am positive the dance also "serviced" her eyes, lightened her spirit and heightened her mood.

The poem grows in poetic intensity as it unfolds. It enjoys rhythm, the flesh Malca tells us about, and the vitality both Elana and Malca agree poetry pulses with and passes on to the reader. Ellen S. Jaffe has stated *(Taken from the Introduction by Ellen S. Jaffe to Elana Wolff's book Implicate me. Guernica Editions, 2010)* that "a poem is not a static, inanimate object, not just words on a page, but a living thing inhabiting a living space." "Dance" is irrefutable proof. I was implicated by the poem and the poet.

Fresh metaphors and fine hyperbolic contributions are a constant in Elana's poetry. This is transparent in "Blackberries," from the very start: "Weeds in bloom for miles, a train / of bushes by the path." The word "train" adds not only quantity and length to the image the poet wants to create but also a sensation of movement, as she is travelling.

The experience flashing into the poet's eyes is enriching. Once more, a Canadian poet illuminates me with her flair to describe nature. The gift is not just an inspired typing away of words; it comes from within the poet's understanding and involvement with what surrounds her. Malca Litovitz ("... the depth of the emotion") and Elana herself explain this to us: "You can only write from the depth of an emotion if you've been there." *(Idem, the first quotation)*

The involvement does not stop. Elana celebrates nature with a conjunction of visuality and taste, plus an untold suggestion of unavoidably present scents wafting in the air, fondling the mind: "A single ripe... / ... bidding me to pluck" (Do I hear onomatopoeic echoes in *pluck*?). It all happens even amidst the discomfort at some points along the trip: "... a rocky / drop / my muscles yawning. Heat can make you swagger too / and that's how I arrive – / reeling, / scorched and thirsty."

Such poet-context connection reminded me – a more dramatic situation, of course, but the message strikes as similar to me – of Leo Buscaglia´s passage in his book *Love* about a Buddhist monk who is running from a hungry bear. He comes to a cliff he has to jump from. He does, grabs a clump of wood in the fall and discovers a starving tiger at the bottom of the cliff waiting for him, plus two gophers nearby hungrily gnawing at the wood… but he sees a bunch of strawberries and a "giant, red, ripe, juicy one facing him… He plucks it and puts it in his mouth… exclaiming, "How delicious!"" *(Taken from Love, Ballantine Books, 1972, by Leo F. Buscaglia).* Buscaglia´s message is to live the moment; not live for the moment but live ***the*** moment. Elana indulges in it.

She relates to the positive stimuli around her and revels in the detailed depiction of what she sees and rejoices in, the berries, placing aside (still being a part of the context) heat, scorching and thirst. Her closing lines – gentle, in-crescendo sensuality implied – support my assertion: "I'll bring you back to pick / and eat when all the berries ripen, to / watch your lips / and fingers / blue to bijoux." Elana wants to share the moment, reenact it watching how that important "you" also partakes in the experience.

Savor this fragment from one Al Purdy classic, "The Cariboo Horses" *(Taken from Beyond Remembering. The Collected Poems of Al Purdy, 2000. Harbour Publishing)*: "… whose hooves were thunder… horses battering thru the wind / whose names were the wind's…" Elana's piece "Wild Horses" brought Al's poem back to me in a flicker of related images.

Elana takes delight in wild life, both flora ("Snapdragons, yellow-tulips, half a dozen / Gerber lilies") and fauna ("wild horses / cut like flowers standing in the morning"). She is overwhelmed by natural beauty, a constant in her work, in the way she absorbs the view before her and lays her apprehension of that view down in words: "All the pretty bodies tilting east into the sun." The line clearly evokes a painting – one that is definitely **not** frozen though.

The poet integrates into the scene glimpses of other natural elements and phenomena to round it off: morning, sun and rain. Most significantly, she *paints* a vigorous, bright, motionful instant she feels compelled to combine with – and fit in: "And I'm the fellow-traveller, riding stem- / back where they carry me. Petite now, / nearly weightless. / Hoofless as a flower too." She *is* part of the scene.

Her will to merge with the space/time she portrays, and her surrendering to its magic, is splendidly summarized in her last lines: "I close my eyes to bar the dazzle, / trusting where they canter, / silent petal, can't be wry." The poet is that much involved, that much committed to the sentient rush of delight engulfing her: I perceive a glorious intensity in her ride, an indelible imprint. This is, in Elana's own highly illustrative words, "… what I felt to be dwelling between the lines, and behind and beyond…" the poem. *(Taken from Elana Wolff's book Implicate me, 2010, Guernica Editions. Author's Afterword)*

In informal colleague debates I have always *jocosely* toyed with a "theory" (not legitimately validated) on how far ownership rights on what we write are fully ours, or balanced, or scales are tipped when we dedicate a poem, for example, to someone – or when we write a personal letter. Elana's "Round" revisits this idea for me. The first stanza reads: "All the words I sent / you are now your words / more than mine." She closes with: "Maybe they / were your words from the start."

The second stanza proposes a series of rhetorical questions addressed at the receiver, questions that seek to explore and activate an intimacy, a dialogue – duologue! – between poet and recipient of "... the words I sent." There is an obvious romantic layer in the stanza and, while the questions were "technically" meant not to be answered, an underlying longing in them claims for a response as romantic and intimate as the questions are.

The coda – a single, self-standing gem – corroborates my opinion as it reads "... we are rounder than a ring." Whereas the title is "Round," the poet finishes with "... we are rounder," building in an extra emphasis on their roundness.

The word "ring" ignites in me a couple of feelings I want to share as a reader. Firstly, one of the meanings of ring (Noun: "circle of metal worn on the finger" *(Taken from digital Babylon English-English. Third definition (noun))* – May I point out the circle may also be made or plastic, wood, thread, etc? Of course, the metal one bears a solemnity other materials might not qualify for. Secondly, I, human and a hopeless romantic, tend to associate it with engagement and/or marriage: in other words, with commitment in a couple, with an intimacy, closeness and perfection that is sealed with a ring, entirely above the social or conventional connotations it has, and more a spiritual attachment the poet conveys at least for me.

To complement the previous note, the comparative "rounder" (from the adjective *round*) still retains its meaning of "circular" – in context: more circular) – yet we can think as well, and be comfortable about them, of other extended and figurative meanings: richer, fuller, mellower, more complete, entire, whole *(Examples taken from digital Babylon Concise Oxford Thesaurus. Entries 3 and 4 (adjective)).* All of these confer myriad hues of meaning to the word, by extension to the poem. The poet is confident in the relationship, and is willing to freely share and give away her words to the person in the poem.

If in "Wild Horses" Elana hints her eagerness to merge with the scene she is describing, "Birdheart," the eighteenth piece in the book, bares a fully willing poet to blend: "On days like this... / I'd gladly be the yellow finch..." No wonder this is the poem to title the book. Underneath the skilled, finely metaphorical and lyrical writer is a woman who is "Tenacious as the moss / and rocks and water." Once again, the poet summons the elements of nature into her creation, sings to their exuberance and diversity, commonplace but still beautiful *per se*, and endows human features ("tenacious") to them purposely identifying with all that is naturally virtuous.

The poet wishes to avoid a moment that weighs on her ("On days like this, heart / heavy as a vow") and shape-shift as the "yellow finch." She praises the bird, a colourful songbird, and his *heart*, a word that I'd relate to passion and enthusiasm, as well as to his cheerful character due to his singing trait. That the poet wants to rid of a bad moment, and nature will comfort her soul, is evident in the excellent closing: "A birdheart so compact and small, / it leaves no room for sorrow."

To bring my modest analyses to a conclusion, I recall commenting once to Elana that some of her poems had a superbly distinct Emily Dickinson flavor in brevity and compactness, both in the rendering of the full poem and in the closing lines, which carry that epigrammatic aspect I discussed in "Dance."

Let's remember Dickinson's "1732"´s end: "Parting is all we know of heaven, / And all we need of hell" *(Taken from The Literature of the U.S.A. (1983) Concepción Prieto, Alfonso et al. Editorial Pueblo y Educación. Ciudad de La Habana, Cuba).* I value these characteristics in poetry, being a fan of Dickinson's poetry, Shakespeare's sonnets and other greats. Later I wondered how she would feel about being compared, but her reply was reassuring indeed and proved I was not wrong: she had been told that before.

Malca Litovitz tells that "… poetry compresses so much into a small space." *(Idem, the first quotation)* In her capacity to pour out so much swirling inside her and do it with elegant briefness lies one of Elana's many gifts as a poet. Her piece "I Know Too Much" is a masterpiece in this sense.

From the outset, syntax and significance are short and simple; with a tint of humor I welcome ("Enough for even blackmail"), in the form of a dialogue: "I know too much, you say..." Nevertheless, as in Dickinson, the last seven lines are the epitome of shortness and conciseness of a kiloton of substance condensed like a white dwarf star's density: "But what I know / is lighter / than a speck / for me to carry // And dearer / than epiphany / to me."

Elana is proud of "what she knows," rightfully positing knowledge of any sort is always good to possess, "… lighter than a speck for me to carry," and never a nuisance or a burden. The highest peak in the poem comes with the polished finish, like the bijoux she cherishes in "Blackberries": knowledge is "… dearer than epiphany to me." A profound religious allusion closes the poem with my grateful appreciation for what Elana has shared with me and has made revelatory and inspiring.

The trip from Toronto to the West Coast and back left such a lasting impression on Elana that she eternalized it in *Birdheart.* Gratifyingly unforgettable and shimmering with outstanding pieces, her first book is a little jewel of content and form majestically knitted by a poet who knows her craft. Canada is vividly reflected, the heart – human or bird – made to beat in synchronicity with poems that pulsate and a poet who edifies.

In my introductory words to a review I wrote about James Deahl I said: "Poets have a gift: they provide light, a different one. They craft words and images in ways no one else can and lay them down for us to marvel at a world that had been there but we hadn't noticed" *(Taken from In a Fragile Moment: A Landscape of Canadian Poetry (to be published in 2020) (35 Essays and Reviews about 31 Canadian poets) by M.Sc. Miguel Ángel Olivé Iglesias. Review: A Shower of Warm Light: A Review of James Deahl's Even This Land Was Born Of Light*

(Poetry) (1993) Moonstone Press. Canada). They aptly apply to Elana Wolff, and to all the poets I have read.

Allow me, please, a finale for my review quoting the last words from the interview Elana had with Malca *(Idem, the first quotation).* They define, like nothing else will do, what we feel and share in reading *Birdheart* and poetry in general, what we feel and share in writing poetry, and what we feel and share in living, overcoming pain, fear and challenges:

"EW: Is there anything you want to add, Malca?

ML: Just what marvellous experience this is.

EW: Yes, it's truly a gift."

Thank you, Elana (Thank you, Malca).

A Straight Word about Sidewise Angles
An Essay on Elana Wolff's Poem "Sidewise" in *Swoon*

(Poetry) (2020) Guernica Editions. Canada

You can know and get to admire poets reading one single poem, or you can follow up on their evolution and maturity when you are privileged to have a collection of their craft spanning decades. In Elana Wolff I enjoy all privileges: her first-step poetry, with *Birdheart* from 2001, her progression, and her latest book, *Swoon*, which will be published in 2020: almost two decades of fine poems. Today I would like to talk about "Sidewise," one of the poems from *Swoon*.

I have pleasantly seen Elana remain faithful to a syntactical arrangement, sometimes longer, sometimes shorter proposals, which has become her signature and object of interest for the reader's attention. The way she handles sentences, allowing enjambment, stanza breaks or continuity to pause/flow creating stylistic effects – plus visual amusement once you ease into it – tells us we are witnessing a sustained poetic style evidential of the map of thoughts, involvement, insights, meanings, feelings, subtleties, pain, fears, teachings – and learning – urging the poet's turmoil of visualization: observant, keen poet eyes and active mind in full poetic labour.

Formidable succinctness of expression is captured in her poem. An heiress of Emily Dickinson, Elana juggles with detached construction, cliff-hanging sentence structure, variation, conciseness and precision, elliptical explorations, meanings and messages veiled and demanding. In a review of her poetry, I said her poems "have a superbly distinct Emily Dickinson flavor in brevity and compactness, both in the rendering of the full poem and in the closing lines. In her capacity to pour out so much swirling inside her and do it with graceful briefness, lies one of Elana's many gifts as a poet." "Sidewise" is no exception to those elements – to rhythms, sudden turns, vertigo, shortcuts and sleight-of-hand skills she displays so comfortably when writing. Let's read below:

"Parts of a poem kept knocking along

my thoughts

like a cart on a slope. Spinning,

quiv'ring, veering over"

The act of creation is apparent in the poet's disposition of the first sentence. It is not her thoughts shaping up poetry; it is the other way around: "Parts of a poem... knocking along (her) thoughts": reality troops in, the poet is but the vessel that tries to contain it, but it overflows in a million codes. Then the rest of the psychological sentence with the break in sentences appealing to the senses and serving the meanings she wants to convey.

Notice the abrupt halt after "my thoughts," a full blank-space line down – a void – conjuring a sensation of falling, unsteadiness anticipatory to the precipitous "like a cart on a slope." The poet accentuates this notion through words denoting spiral-like meanings: Spinning, / quiv'ring, veering over." Here we have a truly engaged poet who sees beauty (a leitmotif in her pieces) and inspiration in what exists outside her but connects to her trains of thought. How Elana beholds a particular, everyday object and elevates it to a transcendental status transpires in the poem: "Remarkable yet ordinary— / glass in a wooden casement. / One I have in mind is sitting, looking inside out..."

The first sentence provides the significance of the object for her ("the glass"). However "ordinary" – placed second in the sentence – it may be; its "Remarkable" impression appears foremost. That is how the poet sees it, how the poet *sees* things from her gifted perspective. Lines three and four fan out for us the poet's mental bearings and a class-one metaphor: "lapidary shadows." The poet moves to lines five and six, introducing touch ("Handy how it let itself be tapped") to enter the realm of sound: "... the clarion quality glass has," and metaphorically contributory (personification) in empowering glass with will ("let itself be tapped").

After this comes the creative upsurge discussed in the lines analyzed at the beginning; later we are offered the likening of object and bird (nature always present in her poetry), gravitas implied in both, and finally a proclamation dénouement, "Only a poet can pen like this: // heart & hand commanding contradiction. / I'm trembling before such sweetness & disruption; I touch them..." This last sentence builds on the idea of touch: gentle/passionate/enigmatic, as a poem can be; deep and utter, as an implication can sweep her away and make her quiver.

Stylistically speaking, the line "I'm trembling before such sweetness & disruption" is worth looking at, as antithesis clinks in it – or flaps wings! The two words put together strike me as a feeling of both wish to approach (sweetness) and step away from (disruption). That seems to be, indeed, the poet's state of mind, that ambivalence she is experiencing yet cannot shake off.

Carried away by the torrent of excitement overwhelming her, a throbbing Elana plunges into the act of writing the poem with "heart & hand commanding contradiction." Such heart-hand conflict cautions her to be wary not to let her poet brittleness overshow, or her sensitiveness trespass: "I touch them // with as little fondness as possible. Not to seem too see-through, / too invested." One element to bring to analysis is that glass does reflect – might the poet see herself (and her life) mirrored in the window, being such torrential harvest a result of that impression? After all, it all happens *sidewise*... Enjoy the poem; it will positively tilt your world-view. Thank you, Elana.

To Sleep or Not to Sleep
An Essay on Four of Ronnie R. Brown's poems in *Night Echoes*

(Poetry) (2006) Black Moss Press. Canada

Nights have invariably been a source of inspiration for writers, artists, poets, lovers and film makers. If we uncovered the material that sparks off those dreams, a whole new realm would open up to mesmerize, shock, frighten and lure us.

U.S. born Canadian poet, Ronnie R. Brown, slips into – and tunnels us through – nights, dreams and wandering, piquant thoughts, exploiting them as favorite themes in her poetry. She explores with underlying sensuousness those dark places/states we enter when we close our eyes, and pulls us in through words and images that will stay with us. In a mixture of themes, well-arranged and eerily narrated, the poet puts *on our bed* forty-seven dream-poems in her book *Night Echoes.*

The back-cover comment says it "explores the parts of the self that are inaccessible only during sleep. Like dreams themselves, these poems deal with human hopes and fears, as Brown moves effortlessly between the darker side of human nature and the joy and relief that dreams can offer."

The assertion is one-hundred percent true. Readers will be wading in all sorts of emotions crackling, sound off or on, in the bottomless confines of the mind, oozing and shaping up human feelings: angst, desire, disappointment, delight, frustration, aspirations, suppressed conditions, love, lust, etc. In the process, they will be witnesses to the piercing descriptions of a poet who touches/discloses a wide spectrum of latent human fibers of parenthood, eroticism, flings, loss, pleasure, longings, humor and remembrances, all of which are unleashed, seemingly safe, within our sleep walls.

Take "Back to Nature," for example, where an ordinary excursion, "A Sunday nature drive, / and the kids´ heads are / filled with storybook animals…" develops into nightmarish anticipations. An ironically sad twist in the poem comes when "the youngest spots fur–a tail / loosely connected to a flat matted mass / flaps as cars speed by. Silence…" Then the father's lame excuse of "modern natural selection" turns the drive into "the horrors tonight's dreams will bring," especially for the kids.

Sensually rousing is "Going Down." The pretext for the elevator scene lies in the woman's line: "Let me tell you about a dream I had." From it, the fantasy, the "virtual" affair: "… her voice a near whisper, / about a man and a woman / in an elevator, / about blouses and belts, / flesh and nipples…" The poet heightens the mood of the poem using phrases and words such as "others enter… / but the intruders exit…", and escalates with "… until finally / she whispers, her breath, / her mouth, only millimetres from / his ear, "… and then and then…"" I was pleasurably unsettled by "then and then," as it gives me freedom to think and add, almost as a participant, what my stimulated mind elaborates.

Uniquely moving is Brown's poem "A Mother's Dream." In my experience, being a mother is top priority for almost every woman I know. The expectations and plans many women blueprint long before they actually conceive and give birth is outstanding. Their commitment to a child and their sacrifices in unfavorable – or the worst – circumstances are worth-praising.

Take the opening lines, this is the mother's fantasy: "Standing at the door of her child's room, / she watches as he sleeps, moves quietly / to him… / brushes back his hear, smiles… / She wants to stay, stand there / forever, but she knows she can't." Such dedication is nurtured even in early childhood, as Brown tells us in her poem: "Ever since she was small / she'd dreamed of being a mother."

Even when sadness envelops the poem, the mother's determination and above all her capacity to dream and be optimistic against all odds, save the poem and bring some peace to the reader. The line "Some nights she dreams / he is with her…" is reinforced by the closing lines: "… she thinks she sees / a flash of recognition / in his eyes, the hint of a smile. / The doctors tell her this / is an impossibility, but / after all, a mother can dream."

Clangs of futile attempts at resignation echo repressed emotions and cravings in a woman who *still feels* and dreams back in "Dream Envy." The title, aptly chosen, helps the reader understand the needfulness expanding and populating her mind – and her aging body. As quoted at the beginning, dreams offer relief, acting as an escape valve for the woman.

Brown uses "inner represented speech" – a stylistic device used to recreate the "thoughts and feelings going on in one's mind and reflecting some previous experience… (It) expresses feelings and thoughts of the character which were not materialized in spoken or written language…" *(Taken from Stylistics, 1981, Moscow Vyssaja Skola, by I. R. Galperin)* – to reveal the woman's innermost thoughts, which are presented in italics: "*Close your eyes* / she tells herself, *just close your eyes* / *and let go.*"

To me, these words in her head are a plea, a bit distressed, in an effort to adapt and conform to a present status, as is corroborated in the following lines: "She knows the where, the when / she longs to reclaim, wills herself / back to a warm afternoon…" Her endeavor is in vain: "... But, // try as she may / she cannot direct her subconscious. / Like her reality, her dreams remain trapped / within the years…"

My initial reference to painful resignation in "Dream Envy" is confirmed in the poem's next lines: "… Restless, / she rolls over, sighs and…" The word "sigh" re-introduces my assumptions on her conformity. Brown elegantly manages to balance and partially heal the apprehensions the woman is going through by giving us a romantic visualization in the man's own dreaming: "Murmuring, / he pulls her closer, holding fast / to the girl he met long ago / by the lake."

On the back cover, Gary Geddes says *Night Echoes* is "a strong, confident and at times moving book..." Yes, I see strength and certainty in the book, and it is definitely *disturbing* and inspirational! Even when the settings are a dream territory, Brown depicts believable characters and situations, surely because our dreams are reflections of realities and experiences we undergo – or forcibly/shyly withhold – which urge us while we are awake. Shielded in the hazy fortress of sleep, she handles the poems with resourcefulness and emancipation to say what she wants to say. After all, a poet *can dream…* Thank you, Ronnie.

Meta-Worlds in Michael Mirolla's Poetry
A Look at Three of his Poems in
Light and Time

(Poetry) (2010) Guernica Editions. Canada

In the poem "Naked Fifth" *(in Startled Night, 2011, Guernica Editions)* Elana Wolff calls light "the lip of time," a metaphor suggesting there might be an entire entity – made of substance only poets can knead at will into some sort of corporeality – behind it breathing, even talking; or devouring anything standing in its way. The title under analysis today gives us that much and more. Michael Mirolla himself describes his writing as "a mix of magic realism, surrealism, speculative fiction and meta-fiction." *(Taken from his bio)* *Light and Time* lives up to his characterization.

After reading *Light and Time*, I'd describe his style as Wow-poetry. Entering the book is entering a grid of images, those that may well hand you a key to a post-realm of words and syntax, a semiotic pathfinder I was challenged – and hooked – by. I see Mirolla's poetry as a voyage to, I dare call, a "back-into-a-yesterday-future" experience. I also sense the novel and story writer in his poetry: his poems flow like dream-stories that need to be told.

A perusal of the poem "August: The Landscape Without You," makes the reader think of an dream-inside-a-dream state where events and images happen in the poet's head. From a sheer stylistic viewpoint, the use of epithets to boost such images and leave drill-deep impressions on the reader´s mind is called for, impressive and unavoidable.

Take "cruel light," "dead afternoon," "laser-blue petals," "cryptic sky," "choked meadows," "emaciated mushrooms," "insipid stream," to mention a few. The reader will be confronted with personification/ technology/murky qualifying nouns all in once. The skein of epithet-charged realities bestows words with multi-dimensional portal-meanings.

The scenes´ "viscosities" limned by the poet seem to be "for a second… / for a split-second…" done away with; but such assumption collapses in the last two lines making the reader feel uneasy, wary and vertigo-trapped: "to swallow // himself." Webbed in this state of self-swallowing, the previous hazy worlds return; foreboding *cycles* resumed in the poem and capturing the reader. One might pick loneliness leading to a supra-creative stupor-like state where the poet oozes lines away to startle the reader.

Another maelstrom piece is "February: Entropic Vistas on a Winter's Day." The very first line, "like a stutter in time," is interplay of recurrence and fleetness, that is, repetition of an act conjugated with ethereal occurrence: two supposedly opposed realizations *in time*. The second line, "footsteps form themselves," floods the atmosphere with eeriness and suspense.

From lines four through nine the poet bombards the reader with no-verb sentences in a sheer free fall denoting multiple realities and forging them into convergence.

To me, the poem reverberates in static, stale, out-of-context immaterial instants, which in line ten shift dramatically when "A swan bursts" in and disrupts the metaphysical ambience. Factual reality, what is real and "normal," is entropy in this parallel universe where "the skeleton of a ghost slips by… over the drone of atoms… cleansed of flesh." I would ask Salvador Dali to paint some logic out of all this. The word *cleansed* implies purification, purging, thus hinting nuances of interpretation commingling with theological approaches in which flesh is deemed sullied and the spirit – the ghost? – needs to be rid of its material carcass so it can prevail.

Furthermore, is it an outer-space nature? A figment of a surrealist intense mind? Glimpses at a reeling, precipitous infinitesimal micro-cosmos anticipated in the film *The incredible Shrinking Man*? Another interesting perspective is the handling of nothingness related to motionlessness and to whether this is really happening. What is really spoiling the winter's day?

One of my favorite pieces is "May: The Carelessness of Resurrection," which peeks at a future that occurred in the probability of the past. The poem is an omen, deposited in flashbacks onto a series of pre-happening events. The last line, in simple present tense, "…walks with a swagger towards the deadliest stretch of highway" is premonitory and brings us back an imminent truth – to happen in the future...

The poem unfolds with precise description, a time-scalpel slitting the present in which the poem is told at a temporal divide when "Infinity goes both ways, from the fading moments of yesterday / to the endless days of tomorrow, / she slowly unfurls and settles; / but for a fleeting second, / in today." *(Taken from the poem "Infinity's Stopover," Hidden Brook Press, 2018, in the Bridges Series, Book IV, Where the Heart Lies).*

Plenty of asyndeton to contribute to giddiness in orientation, generous input of epithets – a feat Mirolla excels at with conscious stylistic penmanship – colouring the moment down to the minutest poem-pixel, short sentence breaks, simple and dotted with periods to mark a change in time or perspective or even mood, stand out in the narrative.

The sentence "But the creek continues to flow beneath, fearful of confrontation. The trees disavow all knowledge. The birds croon and paint their nails," is classic personification, which in this case unleashes a magic, unfathomable sweep overtaking the reader: realism-surrealism at its best. Dali, or René Magritte, would have loved to eternalize on canvas "The birds croon and paint their nails."

Conrad DiDiodato stated that "Michael Mirolla looks into his art as into a language prism: light glances off many sides of the ´object´ at once, and time… is what attempts to hold it still." *(Taken from the book´s back-cover comment by Conrad DiDiodato).* I have felt this overlapping mystique of light and time in Mirolla's poetry. His meta-world creative writing floats in a crystal capsule that resists the test of time, and can be visualized thanks to the light he is able to deflect from black holes into his poems.

This is how he sees our reality, crisscrossed by that reality he generates – bubbling inside him – one we can neither see nor feel unless he unveils it for us. Thank you, Michael.

One Life across Four Seasons
A Glimpse at I. B. Iskov's Poetics in *Sapphire Seasons*

(Poetry) (2010) Aeolus House. Canada

Canadian icon poet John B. Lee said about Iskov's *Sapphire Seasons*: "… these poems illuminate… who we have been, who we are, and who we might become with hope…" *(Taken from the book's back-cover comment by Lee)*. Lee looks into Iskov's poems and sees hope as leitmotif, substantial, undying and closely related with her life.

Lee also speaks of illumination in her poetry. Most of Iskov's poems include the word sun, or series of sun-related terms. From the first poem, "Almost Perfect," where she gives us an "amber sun," or in "Sweet Spring Welcome" with "After the trembling moon disappears / in the glimmer of morning," or "soft sunlight" in "In the New Year," to the last one, "Spirit Woman," with "sun-shower dreams."

From Terry Barker's knowledgeable words "For Ms. Iskov… is evidently writing in the tradition of Jewish Humanism" *(Taken from his Introduction to Sapphire Seasons)* – humanism viewed as "thought which values human dignity and achievements" *(Taken from digital Babylon English-English Dictionary)* – we can construe such tradition ebbs and flows powerfully in her Jewish-Canadian world-view. This is interestingly transparent in "Praying" where she says: "I pray, / remaining close to my faith; / muse ancient passages / mirrored in English," or in "Looking Irish" where Iskov tells us, "Growing up, I considered myself Canadian."

Maturely existential and deeply reflective, Iskov addresses her own life in her poetry. She goes to her roots, as far and high as those roots can make her leaves and flowers grow into the sun – into the future. Her pieces brim with hope, without giving up veiled/unveiled criticism of ugly truths, as John B. Lee affirms on the book's back-cover: "… she refuses to shy away from the hard truths…"

Iskov molds fresh metaphors that elevate yet do not miss nor forget their down-to-earth duties. Her line "Somewhere / on the other side of sky" in her poem "In the New Year" reveals hope, a possible re-birth, re-instated in the last stanza when she claims that words will "be born in the new year." Iskov looks into the year to come with levelheadedness, noticeable in her line "Dust scatters on tarmac," conferring a pause for the reader to linger on the image, silently.

The poet puts her confidence in words – poetry – and grants them a human trait, that of screaming: "Words / more composed than I / scream to be born / in the new year."

Words will do for her what she can't – or would do worse: be calm before such trepidation of ideas.

Hope recurs in Iskov, what is obvious in her poem "Praying": "Hope surrounds me, like a stole under the hammock heavens." An intense, *hopeful*, finger-pointed-at phrase in the poem is "I want to believe / in institutions; / feel safe amidst broken stars." The poet has a strong will, she intends to survive, and shares with us one way to do it: "I pray, / remaining close to my faith…"

Her poem "Sweet Spring Welcome" is an open, firm position adopted by the poet. She enumerates all that is to be left behind resorting to an expressive means, repetition of a phrase or structure, "After," which reaches stylistic force as it aims at emphasis, "an emphasis necessary to fix the attention of the reader on the key-word of the utterance." *(Taken from I. R. Galperin. Stylistics. Moscow Vyssaja Skola. 1981).*

This key-word adverb by extension creates suspense – its "main purpose is to prepare the reader for the… logical conclusion of the utterance," *(Idem)* which ends with a line full of resoluteness and hope, again: "I will expose my icy smile and / welcome spring with a sweet embrace." Between the lines, the reader can try at a whole fabric of interpretations beyond the natural element described by the poet: the poet will expose her icy – social? – smile, which will melt in the spring. She had to be *icy* in a previous harsher season – context? – now spring will soften her attitude, and she accepts it, sweetly.

Fine Canadian poet Katherine L. Gordon referred to Iskov's poems as "a gem-stone of verse polished into four facets of life experiences... the language earthy… poignant with the ring of truth." *(Taken from the book's back-cover comment by Gordon)* This is the Iskov I feel too, committed, high-spirited, remembering where she comes from and seeking out the harmony that develops with time, maturity, insight and mastery of her words, which will always want "to be born in the new year." Thank you, I. B.

A Poet's Dance of Words, Colours and Emotions A Look at Some of Marion Mutala's Poems in *Ukrainian Daughter's Dance*

(Poetry) (2016) Inanna Publications and Education Inc. Canada

Marion Mutala's book, *Ukrainian Daughter's Dance*, arrived weeks ago. It was part of the openhanded inflow of poetry books reaching my home in the last months, thanks to Canada Cuba Literary Alliance Founding President, Richard Grove, and our mutual friend, James Deahl. Their tireless promotion of both my essay-writer skills and my review book, *In a Fragile Moment. A Landscape of Canadian Poetry*, to come out soon in Canada and Cuba, published by Grove's Hidden Brook Press, has reached many Canadian poets who, in return, have reached me and sent me their poems.

My poet eyes quickly picked up a world of movement, sound and colour in Mutala's poetry alongside the deeply-rooted sense of belonging to her traditions, and her will to honor and remember them, intensely floating in her poems. Ukrainian by birth, Canadian by choice, Marion enraptures us with her musical poetry. It is all motion, hues, pain, hope and refuge in nature, close images neatly and sincerely outlined for us.

The poems I chose for comment here will show us a poet whose soul is richly gifted and in return it gives us memories, rainbows, winds and snow, depicted with passion and expressive control. Through the veil of nostalgia and remembrances Marion holds for us, we discern a poetic source emotionally linked to her country of birth and her "foster" country, natural beauties, recollections of childhood years and places she grew up in. This is especially felt in "Memories," ("Visiting the old farm house, a flashback...") where moments of both joy and sadness/fear coexist in her mind: ""Flying paper dolls... / Playing in the old grey caboose / Jumping in bales / Riding pigs... / Running scared to the outhouse... / Sleeping three to a bed... / Hiding under bed covers..." It also throbs in "Old Farmhouse" and "Grateful."

Syntactically speaking, the poem operates on an array of enumerations. Enumeration is an expressive means by which separate... phenomena... actions are named one by one so that they produce a chain," thus revealing "some kind of relation between them: "dependence, ... likeness, dissimilarity, sequence, experience (personal and/or social)..., etc." *(Taken from Stylistics, 1981, Moscow Vyssaja Skola, by I. R. Galperin).* Besides, we see no commas at the end of the lines plus and present continuous tense, to accentuate the sense of uninterrupted occurrences in space and time: "Flying paper... // Picking rocks // Swinging water bales // Playing... // Jumping..."

In addition to these feelings of nostalgia, constant flashbacks and allusions to past experiences, the poet finds emotional connotations that stir her mind and heart in specific objects. "Washboard" is an example. The first two lines in the poem, "Hanging on the wall in my bedroom / Momma's washboard," inspire the poet's reminiscences so strongly that a long poem comes out of a seemingly ordinary object in a house.

Sentimentally, I found so many coincidences between Marion's poem and one I wrote, "Flight," connected to finding an object that would bring memories flashing back to us. In my case, an analog watch I found in a drawer, a gift from my grandparents when I was a little boy. In her case, the washboard, associated to her Momma: "I found it last month / Sorting through boxes in the attic… // I forgot I placed it… / many years ago."

Thus the poem develops marked by two touching lines repeated in the first and the last stanza respectively, with a small variation in the latter to emphasize the poet's innermost, major wish: "What I'd give to see her use it once more // What I'd give to see her use it one last time."

Movement, taste, sound and mostly colours are leitmotifs in Marion's "Rainbow." The poet invites to the edifying act of imagining a rainbow: "Imagine the rainbow / Magnificent colours / Subtle, certain tints like pink hues…" Hyperbolic expressions help the reader grasp the significance of a rainbow to the poet: "I crave coloured tastes like ice cream in 1,000 daily flavours." In the phrase, also a simile for a more meaningful comparison.

Movement and colour inhabit the poem: "Magnificent colours," "Pink hues," "Soft shades," "Bright, boisterous sensations," "Coloured jets…," "Yellow, vivid changing auras," "Vibrant boomerang," A chameleon." The best image, however, is the poet's full identification with the scenes she has invited us to – and that is how she closes her poem: "I am the rainbow / Watch me." While "promoting" the beauty of the rainbow and disclosing it for us, the poet has created a fine resemblance between it and her. The end line is highly suggestive: "Watch me."

Mutala sings too. Her poem "Freedom" speaks, and dreams, of an open liberty she craves. The poem carries a distinctive feature, rhyme, built masterfully in along each stanza. It endows the lines with an especially evocative and cadenced flow. To the purpose of rhythm, she uses "tree," "free," "me," "sea," in the three stanzas. She also uses repetition as an expressive means with the phrases "Like a bird in the tree" and "… the waves on the sea."

The poet resorts to nature, "Like a bird in the tree…" // Like the waves on the sea," to word out her longing and add weight to the contrast between their freedom and her being "Tied to this old life / Move along these days."

The poem "Snow," comes to us in words that reflect the poet's state of mind and her connection to what she sees "Through the windowpane." From her apparently advantageous position ("Inside"), the beholder/poet is in an almost dreamy state: "White, pure, powdery flakes / Mesmerizing / Magical crystals…" The moment is so powerful it traps her and "Its beauty tricks me / into opening the door / Cold snow." Upon "awakening", the poet *feels* the cold snow. Back to reality; but the trance she was in for a few moments does stay with us in the lingering images she crafted.

The notion of winter – and immigration/adaptation – recurs in the poem "Embrace." From her mother country, Ukrainia, to her welcoming nation, Canada, she is poignantly evocative of her roots and new contexts: "Saskatchewan… / Fresh air, clean water / Lakes… // Grabs your heart tight / Embrace / My home / always…" She closes the poem with the suggestion: "Then comes *winter*… Marion embraces and lets herself be embraced by the new reality she is in: "Grabs your heart tight / Embrace." The thought of acceptance and being accepted feels good to her, and to me.

Enjoy these poems – and her book – my friends, as I have. Mutala is a poet of deep feelings and stirring emotions. Canadian poets continue to win my heart and my essay writer´s modest skills. Thank you, Marion.

Loving the Poems
A Look at Three Poems by Laurie Kruk in her Book
Loving the Alien

(Poetry) (2006) Your Scrivener Press. Canada

These last three years, especially the past four months, my bookshelf has felt so proud to act its role to the top of its capacity. Richard Grove (Tai), Founding President of the Canada Cuba Literary Alliance (CCLA), has been bringing me Canadian poets´ books on a yearly basis since 2017, and has encouraged others to do so, which they have. Thanks to James Deahl too, I am receiving almost monthly packages from poets and scholars. This week I was "visited" by Laurie Kruk.

Canadian poets enjoy a remarkable connection with the land and identify with nature and wild life. They have a rooted sense of belonging to Canadian geography with a solid social awareness; a feeling of proud nationality/nationhood; freshness and versatility in the use of expressive means and images; etc. A particularly salient and heart-warming feature to me is their commitment to family and values – values to champion, besides, what is true and what is moral beyond and above family contexts, and transcend, lofty and spiritual. Add to these the poets´ reminiscences of childhood, growth, and their recollection of friends, friendship and love.

In the words of Jeannette Lynes, Kruk "bears witness to the multiplicity and elusiveness of the self… The poems… dance with ancestral shadow and light." *(Taken from the book's back-cover comments by Lynes).* Kruk's poetry does honor multiplicity and elusiveness, and overflows with ancestral flashbacks. Take "Cousin Allie's Garden," "Charlie and Elsie," "Baba's Donut Shop Lament," or "The Generations Visiting his Family," to mention a few. These poems are stories Kruk narrates with a touch of nostalgia, both sadness and joy present in them.

The poet, a Professor of English Studies too, handles the language skillfully with surprising turns, syntactical "pranks" and overlapping meanings to enter and reemerge from the quicksands of feelings and experiences of all sorts. Karl Jirgens tells us her book "navigates the dangerous and shifting waters of mixed emotions." *(Taken from the book's back-cover comments by Jirgens)*

This is noticeable in "Pangaea" where the poet plays with the concepts of intimacy and unity beyond the context of land. She uses as an excuse the definition of Pangaea in both quotation and first stanza to introduce sustained, erotic imagery describing foreplay,

"This is where we begin, again / to melt edges / in night's rejoining," mapping out the scene: "My Northern thigh / mountained over your southern pelvis, / burnt savannah meeting snow." Kruk goes to the inexhaustible sources of wild life to craft fresh and versatile images I referred to in my introduction: "… in dreams of nakedness, one skin; / polar bears and white tigers / meeting / on the endless plains."

How she complains, "… when morning pries us apart," reminded me of another fine Canadian poet, Merle Amodeo, in her poem "Let Morning Never Come" *("I'd seal your lids / to hide the garish sun / that will divide us." Taken from Amodeo's book After Love, 2014, XLibris, Library of Congress).* Kruk blends land-couple allusions: "shifting continents / claim their hemispheres / wrapping themselves / in icy waves, warning shores, / invisible rocks / I wrap myself in morning kimono / you put on your coffee…"

Then the poet complements with routines and conversation, which focuses on a delicate Canadian issue: "… we debate Quebec's separation." Kruk has been able to combine geological, physical/emotional and local political themes in one poem. An author who gets involved and turns her poem into a thought-provoking piece that defends, travelling through space-time-personal references, what we were once: "One sea, one word / for land, for country / for family." Commitment to family and values I mentioned at the beginning.

Nostalgia in a woman, creatively exposed in her poetry, comes to us with "The Sound of You, Forgetting Me." I sense a poet's mind drifting ("mind restless as a cat"), memories floating and sitting on things and sounds: "something hums / above the refrigerator, making ice."

The first three stanzas have a suggestion of coldness ("chill" in the first one; "ice" in the second one and "the dusty sentence of winter" in the last one). In the third stanza, the poet proposes an apparently detached note about spring and winter to jump "Five thousand kilometers away" into "… days rushing to meet you." Now she places an adverb, "Carefully," at the beginning of the next sentence, as if to annul the previous "rushing," and enumerates objects – mementoes – on a different tempo, slowing down time perhaps.

The next two-line stanza ruptures the atmosphere just created ("clear the desk, clean out / the drawer") but the word "Still" in the following stanza restores memories, gives me a splendid metaphor, "… a quietness haunting / my breathing," and tells me of how concentrated – how "haunted" – the poet is, how time has decelerated – in the poet's wistful mind – that she can hear "the sound of leaves unfolding, / one by one..." Throughout the poem I could not help feeling the speaker/writer's eyes are closed while outer stimuli kindle bubbling sensations in her, recollections waft in and out, life and nature unfold and move on. The line "the sound of leaves unfolding" is particularly evocative of such an impression, as she does not *see* the leaves unfolding; she *hears* the sound.

The closing lines show victory of cleansing movement and warmth over coldness and "dark worries," and a contemplative poet who embraces what is to come: "… before ice / succumbs / to river's dance."

Canadian poets´ remarkable connection with the land and their identification with nature and wild life, features I mentioned at the beginning, peculiarly stand in Kruk's poem "lingering bird." Dedicated to Ian (to who the whole book is heartedly dedicated at the beginning: "For Ian, whose love always brings me (gratefully) back to earth"), the poem interacts in simple words with natural-human textures, weaving interplays of appealing, many-layered import. I instantly handpicked this poem for the next issue (094) of The Envoy, the CCLA digital newsletter, and volume 016 of The Ambassador, the CCLA flagship English-Spanish magazine, whose theme centers on nature, the elements and wild life.

The poet "pans her camera" with a description of outdoor life in a creative, imaging observation: "Clouds drop / and forests thin. A skin of ice slows the stream / as the land dreams of snow." Her eyes are alert, encompassing vistas and events: "The flight / is on, and wings are tested." They are set on a singular scene, "Still he lingers, the great blue / standing at the new edge / of the pool…," redolent of personal glimpses and intimate experiences that overlap in the lines: "… as we flash past, on track, / shaking the trees to the ground."

Is the poet likening the bird's lingering status to her personal background and history? Who is the bird? Is she addressing the bird *or Ian* – or both? This is tentatively suggested in the lines that follow: "… and still you linger / migratory companion," and evidenced to a perhaps more explicit degree next: "… appointments and errands fallen / like feathers / on the bedroom floor." The fact that Kruk shifts from "he" to "we" then to "you" and "your" is also potential evidence to support this notion.

A simile, an expressive means in the language used to "give rise to a new understanding of the object… establishing straightforwardly the analogy between… two objects in question" *(Taken from Stylistics, 1981, Moscow Vyssaja Skola, by I. R. Galperin)*, assists in the completion/intensification of the imagery the poet skillfully uses: "… like feathers / on the bedroom floor," which sparks, pivoting on the verb "fallen," a resemblance between human/social elements ("appointments and errands") and wild life elements ("feathers").

The last five lines bring closure to the poet, the "you" referred to in the poem and readers themselves, as the physical aspect is finally released – "warm wings lift, / open" – yet the spiritual one remains anchored by those wings that are "locking down / your heart." The heart, essentially decisive, stays – *lingers.*

This is Laurie Kruk in three poems. I invite readers to come to the journey the poet proposes in the forty-three poems of *Loving the Alien.* It is promising and immersed in the "odyssey of the heart" Jirgens says we will find. Thank you, Laurie.

Surrendering to the Seasons
Four Poems by Henry Beissel in
Tamaracks. Canadian Poetry for the 21st Century

(Poetry) (2018) Lummox Press. Canada

Canada's grandeur has come to me through many of its poets. They have sung to its vastness and exuberance, to its weather and landscape extremes, to its unique beauty. By only mentioning Al Purdy, I think I make my point clearly. However, one figure stands out too. He has produced a decades-long oeuvre, singly prominent his *Cantos North*, deemed by F. R. Scott as the first to see Canada and the North "… in its entirety, as a matrix which binds the whole together in a national mythology." *(Taken from Tamaracks. Canadian Poetry for the 21st Century. Lummox Press, 2018).* The poet who impressively treads on the provinces of mythology, and does not lose his bearings, is Henry Beissel.

As much as *Cantos North* is a formidable epic, he has also produced other significant pieces of length and short poems. *Tamaracks. Canadian Poetry for the 21st Century*, an anthology edited by James Deahl and conceived to offer readers home and abroad a panorama of contemporary Canadian poetry, included a wonderful host of 113 poets, among them Beissel.

He chose to send for publication four brief poems that captivated me as accurately as those poems captured the reality of changing seasons and how the events each poem narrates intertwine with human life – my hypothesis being we can say those seasons *who* come, the *who* justified in this analysis, define and shape our lives: Beissel has given them a superior order through personification, understood as "the attributing to abstract or inanimate objects qualities characteristic of persons." *(Taken from New Horizons, McClelland and Stewart Limited, Revised edition, Canada, 1965)* The poems are entitled "fall," "winter," "spring," and "summer." They were taken by the author from his book *Stones to Harvest (Alexandria: Ayorama Editions, 1987)* and submitted, with other two poems, for the anthology. All six were published.

There is an underlying connection between *Cantos North* and the four pieces under consideration here. On one side parades an epic *Cantos North* as a hymn to the North, to nature, to its being prevalent and dictating. On the other side, these four poems also address nature as it unfolds before us and delineates our existence.

"fall" limns a season that feels good in the poet's heart. He gently describes the setting, "… my shadow leans / across wet matted leaves / tall against the glistening / black trunks of maples…" and introduces a metaphorical expression, "… maples /

stretching naked into the dawn." Beissel joins in a scene that has kept him awake, as the dawn is coming. He enjoyed the "pizzicato rains" and contemplates his shadow.

Music being a substantial part of his life, the poet pauses to "… listen to the cool / blues in the sky" – blues-creating skies – and immediately relates thoughts: "You're the woods / and the wind whistling… for a solitary dance." Once more, nature and human blend in his next stanza: "… the frost will rob the birds / of their song / leaving us / to our loving." Notice that "the frost will rob the birds…" Indicative mood, empowering sentence: the frost is capable of robbing. Sequentially structured, this poem gives way to the next, "winter," as is anticipated in the last stanza: ""You're the melancholy / beneath the trees / mellowing into winter." Again, a human characteristic granted to inanimate/non-human objects: melancholy.

Personification continues in the poem "winter." The first lines read: "Stamping its feet on the roof / and howling down the chimney / a furious east wind pulls the clouds…," as well as epithets to enhance the power of the poem: "… a white / frenzy of whirling dances…," down below, a combination of epithet and personification: "winter's wild and murderous hordes. // … their ice-cold fury." The poet describes the scene in meticulous detail: His own identification with nature is transferred to the reader through keen observation. I loved the closing line for its implicit meaningfulness: "Our bodies are not / fortress enough / though we plug / every crack / with a passion." Humans endure but nature prevails?

Perhaps this notion may be best illustrated by Beissel's words in his lecture "A Threshold in the Mind. A Poet's View of the North," *(Taken from Beissel's Expanded lecture/reading delivered at "North and Nordicity" Conference at the University of Toronto, May 17, 2007, which he kindly sent to me)* where he clarifies that nature – the North – is the hero in his *Cantos North*; as much as coldness leads his poem "winter": "The true hero in these cantos is the North itself. It is the North that triumphs over the land and its inhabitants. If on the southern rim of Canada summer indulges our illusion that we can master this land, winter quickly comes marching down with inexorable regularity. It tramples down everything in its path and enforces a merciless occupation on us for at least half the year. Spring becomes a celebration of survivors."

This is a concept many forefront poets, I mentioned Purdy, have recreated in their works. Margaret Atwood, for example, acknowledges the land as a living entity. Her poem "The Moment" is illuminating: "We never belonged to you. You never found us." The egocentric human train of thought of the first stanza drowns in the logics of the third. The second stanza shows a rebel nature: "the trees unloose their soft arms from around you, the birds take back their language, the cliffs fissure and collapse, the air moves back from you like a wave… and you can't breathe." *(Fragment quoted from her poem taken from my essay on Margaret Atwood in my book In a Fragile Moment. A Landscape of Canadian Poetry. Reviews and Essays. Hidden Brook Press, 2020, Canada).*

My personification hypothesis holds up in "spring." The first stanza is a good example: "The young sun raises flowers / from dead leaves and greens / the fallow fields panting / with moist aromatic breath." The poet displays fields that pant – may I say *who* again – and have breath. The human component is hinted as an addition to the natural setting; nevertheless, the poet does not include people but objects driven by them: "A tractor stutters down the pasture / Steel hands rip the earth..."

Onomatopoeic echoes resound in the word "stutter." Onomatopoeia is a powerful device in the language to imitate "... sounds produced by nature... by things (machines or tools)..." *(Taken from Stylistics, 1981, Moscow Vyssaja Skola, by I. R. Galperin)* where "the sound of a word echoes its sense." *(Taken from New Horizons, McClelland and Stewart Limited, Revised edition, Canada, 1965)* Thus "stutter" represents sound-sense relations to a machine which, in my very personal view – probably intentionally played by the poet – disrupts the spring scene. The word "Tractor" rounds off my supposition, as the sound /r/ imposes ear-drilling loudness.

The poet returns to the birds ("Birds breed camouflaged..."). Nature's leading role is evident, as is noticeable that the poet does not fail to see *her* and produces two class-one metaphors with the verb *bend*, "The wind bends shadows," and the verb *blow*: "... (the wind) blows your hair / into torrents of desire. This latter metaphor reminded me, humbly, of a poem I wrote, "Pilots." I ended it: "... all she has on / are wings of desire // we fly."

A gentle passion flutters wings in Beissel's "torrents of desire," one that confers intimacy and sensuousness to the poem – emphasizing love's almighty fortitude – and has been present in the previous two ("You're the woods / and the wind whistling" in "fall;" "Our bodies... / we plug / every crack / with a passion" in "winter"). Why would the short phrase "with a passion" make me think of Elizabeth Barrett Browning and her classic piece "How Do I Love Thee"? Her line was: "... I love thee with the passion put to use..." The last stanza proves my assumptions about personification being at the center of these four poems: "Our moments of happiness / are in the hands of clocks / with nerves of steel."

Beissel's fourth poem in *Tamaracks* is "summer." It reverberates with majesty in portraying the higher, unstoppable forces of nature: "The force that pulls / trees and grasses... / pushes their roots / through silt and stone / down to the dark / pole of all beginnings." Beissel returns to music, "... ground bass figure in a major key," and grants human traits to flowers: "... every flower / sings hosanna to the sun..." It should be said that in some cultures the sun is revered as a god.

Repetition is used in the third stanza, a device to reflect the state of mind of a speaker/writer under marked emotion. Stylistically speaking, it aims at "logical emphasis, an emphasis necessary to fix the attention of the reader on the key word of the utterance." *(Taken from Stylistics, 1981, Moscow Vyssaja Skola, by I. R. Galperin).* The poet repeats "Green green green... and greener still..." Here Beissel directs the readers´ eyes and mind to the "footprints" of summer, displayed in colour, sound (music) and movement. The last three lines, which I will quote fully, revisit the intimacy and sensuousness of his companion I referred to before, metaphorically blended with music

– a must in the poet's life: "You dance through my heart / like a fantasy / for violin and piano."

Patrick White said "Henry Beissel is undoubtedly a Canadian poet of the first rank." *(Taken from Tamaracks. Canadian Poetry for the 21st Century. Lummox Press, 2018).* I agree after becoming acquainted with his magnificent poetry. He has made an extensive contribution to Canadian poetdom, which is enormously rich. Thank you, Henry.

Mission Accomplished
A Peek at Hugh Hazelton's Poetry in Bridges Series Book II, *Concave Mirrors*

(Poetry) (2013) SandCrab Books. Canada

In his introductory words to the Bridges Series Book II, *Concave Mirrors*, its Editor, Manuel Velázquez, noted the book as a whole was "fitted together in the lab of poetical physics." He added, "... a polyphonic harmony, at times delightful, at some moments painful, but always inviting to be read once again." Later, in Hugh's bio, he referred to the poet's own elucidation of poetry: (Hazelton) ... "believes that poetry should bite, caress, laugh at, confront, lament, name, envision, remember, invoke, oppose, and reflect."

The Hazelton collection included in Bridges II does live up to both the Editor's and the poet's comments: a harmonic physics is at play, unrestrained, apparently chaotic in its semiotics yet ultimately decanting into a formidable, sweeping logic, inasmuch as it voices, loud and clear, all of the "duties" of poetry, by extension, of a poet which, in a nutshell, must aim at leaving a multifarious, productively shaking and mind-blowing imprint.

The specific pieces I chose for my analyses accurately mirror these too. He is a committed, bold and incisive carver of words and images, packed with a critical poise, engaged yet, as Velázquez points out, also tender and aesthetically precise. Pablo Neruda penned it in these illuminating words: "Mis deberes caminan con mi canto: / soy y no soy: es ése mi destino... / mi poesía es cántico y castigo..." ("My duties walk side by side with my song: / I am and I am not: that is my destiny... my poetry is canticle and punishment." *(Taken from Neruda, 2004, pp. 34-35)* This is Hugh's poetry too.

The first poem under consideration is thought-provoking and intentionally web-like, "shipwrecked." Reading it made me remember my essay about Michael Mirolla's *Light and Time* ("Entering the book is entering a grid of images, those that may well hand you a key to a post-realm of words and syntax..."). That is how I felt with "shipwrecked."

As a complement, Hazelton uses no punctuation at all, on purpose, to create a fast-paced, staggering sensation – one bubbling in his own mind – in an unleashed succession of sentences, either short or longer ones.

While the poem might suggest post-realm contexts, we can visualize an inner (mental)/outer (dreamlike surroundings) one where the poet dapples the setting with bucketfuls of temporal vastness and movement, of fateful cycles, "tumbled and hurled by years of waves or waves of years / till I lost track of how many times or wheeling days or seasons / turned over and over and thrown across the depths / against the sandy ocean floor."

Amidst the misty maelstrom he is in, the character in the poem manages to infect with his predicament, transferring some – most – of his anguish to us: "… sandy ocean floor scraping off my skin / lungs begging for air rising bursting for oxygen / caught by a breaker when I hit the surface… / cast up here luckily not on the rocks…" Here we are "bit," one of poetry's roles, according to the poet.

Consequently, he is penetrating *and* aesthetically precise, as I said before, in rendering magnificent metaphors: "… lifted on twisted water's last collapsing arm…" and direct mythological allusions, "… an unsung Odysseus flung bleeding upon the beach of his home / island," or a veiled one (Prometheus punished and chained to a rock) I pick in "… gulls or crows… first they peck your body…" We are in the presence of Hazelton's "caress" function of poetry.

The absence of punctuation marks I mentioned earlier is skillfully handled integrated with an alliterative proposal: "Alliteration builds a melodic effect into the utterance and creates an emotional atmosphere, very much in line with the poet's rationale; it is a stylistically treated expressive means that sets more rhythm into a poem." *(Taken from In a Fragile Moment: A Landscape of Canadian Poetry, by Miguel Ángel Olivé Iglesias, Hidden Brook Press, Canada, 2020)* This alliterative input is in turn accentuated by an emphatic repetition of a negative prefix, un-: "… toward utterly unknown undreamt unimagined returning…" This combinatory acrobatics grants the poem more vertigo, in consonance with the author's intent.

The end lines manifest other uses of poetry in the poet's conceptions: confront, envision, invoke, oppose, and reflect. He tells us, "… and something must be done sometime about someone / somewhere here…"

Superfluous and unsubstantial jargon – and its baneful social influence – is exposed in "communiqué." Word-avalanches landslide against the reader in a syntactical freefall where absence of punctuation props the true nature of the message:

"from television circuitry
war bombards radio senses
walking billboards moving point this yes this
woods fields suddenly stop blocked
endless imperative…"

It is acceleration, a staggering rhythm dictated by long/short line chunks to re-create the gibberish, logic-threatening nothingness of publicity and propaganda, implicitly carved through stanza arrangements. Lines five and six in the fragment below were brilliantly split, "dis / in / formation," for special effect. Besides, readers today might add, as I did, a play-on-words in "dis." The word has grammatical meaning as a prefix, but semantically speaking – as it is presented (an alternate spelling is *diss)* – it took on a new meaning since the 1980s: in informal, colloquial or slangy English it means "disrespect toward another person; insult someone, belittle another person." *(Taken from Digital Babylon English-English Dictionary)* It comes as no surprise to me that these meanings may "contextwisely" mingle and coexist in the text. The "extra" meaning feels quite at home with the poet's motifs and the poem's circumstances.

"… flashing horizon

word bombs implode mediocrity

eat best drive love buy chrome new box now

battles

of dis in

formation

news propaganda publicity propaganda news

authority lies open

subtle image bludgeoning unreels

blasts

truth jabber…"

After giving us the "bite" and the "lament" roles, the closing lines, fortunately, elbow in with a cry for salvation: "human voicehands / fight back." Here, Hazelton's "invoke" and "oppose" battlefield poetic weapons – and a "bite" back.

To all appearances atypical if compared to the previous pieces, the poem "dancer" seems a more laid back rendering of beauty and movement. I had already stated Hazelton is capable of knitting fresh, tender images – some of which are evident in this poem – away from the metaphysical and inordinate suffocation felt in the two poems analyzed before. Strings of line-sentences fondle the eyes: "… the dancer / spread her arms music body / forward into space / beyond the light." This is achieved in the first lines.

Nonetheless, the latent onrush of violence, harshly criticized by Hazelton, surfaces in the following lines – a crude parallel reality – pushes through slitting the peaceful, nourishing sight. It dashes the spirituality of the moment, "… robot armies / push through gutted streets / fire into straw villages / empires / of death's heads…," affecting the reader in the process.

Then again "the dancer / arms clasped with her companion / rolls herself slowly across his back / slender shoulders…" The spectator struggles to return to the solace he finds in the image but "… there is no / Official Violence / lies in / a conspiracy to kill…" upsurges one more time. Blissfully, the last lines prevail as an omen of goodness and the triumph of beauty and peace over death, uncertainty, violence and pain, even when we have the unsettling sensation she has been targeted, " a conspiracy to kill / the dancer": "the dancer / slowly raising her head / beautiful throat / held curved / taut / against / air." Unaware and devoted to her art, she dances on. The situation can be sorrowfully likened to a butterfly's lifespan: so much beauty displayed to last but fleeting instants in the middle of so much promising life.

The structured contrast of realities proposed by the poet in this poem may as well reflect the very fabrics of life as it happens, either at mind level or actual social occurrences worldwide. Let's keep in mind the author is a well-known Hispanist, a connoisseur of Latin American culture, thus his texts are a repository of his knowledge and experience.

Humanity grapples with opposing circumstances, bereaving, denigrating ones vs. enriching, edifying ones. Our duty is to – as Neruda and Don Gutteridge said, a monumentally bright coincidence – respectively, "… walk towards the light," "towards the light."

The three pieces expose hard realities but end with a cry of optimism and spirituality establishing their own codes to express it. Hazelton has put his poems to the service of a "bite, caress, laugh at, confront, lament, name, envision, remember, invoke, oppose, and reflect" mission. He has accomplished it. Thank you, Hugh.

Three Poets, One Big Canadian Heart
A Look at K. V. Skene, Stella Mazur Preda
and Donna Allard in *The Dream The Glory and The Strife*

(Poetry Anthology) (2018) Hidden Brook Press. Canada

In his excellent essay "Archibald Lampman: Poet on the Cusp of Modernism," poet and profound connoisseur of Canadian poetry, James Deahl, stated that "... almost every Confederation Poet wrote a body of nature poetry." His well-grounded, qualified assertion was supported by his explanation about the manifold differences between the British Isles and the nation emerging as Canada: "The most obvious differences were landscape and climate..." *(Taken from Canadian Stories magazine, Volume 22, Number 129, Year 2019)*

His statement validates previous analyses I have made regarding the close bond Canadian poets have developed with nature, wildlife and weather conditions. In my studies of more than forty poets and their work, I cannot recall one who has not praised, described or been involved with nature. It is inherent in Canadians to view, implicate and depict in outstanding, imagery-rich pieces what Canada has to offer. Poets have been inspired by its beauty, by the clear-cut seasonal cycles, and in the process of eternalizing nature they have seen themselves as either a part of it or a resulting/co-existing entity.

My opinion in this respect continues to be complemented and corroborated by poets whose work comes to me every day. Three such cases are K. V. Skene, Stella Mazur Preda and Donna Allard. They were published in the 2018 edition of the Canada Cuba Literary Alliance (CCLA) members´ anthology issued by Hidden Brook Press, but their work has appeared systematically on other CCLA formats, like The Ambassador and The Envoy, and many publications beyond CCLA borders.

K. V. Skene

Skene submitted "Accidental Purpose," "Cold Comfort," "Climate Change" and "All the walls close in and the day...," which make reference to nature in association with human events. The first poem's title, an oxymoronic combination, tells us of the poet's contemplation of – and intentions about – the outside world. Her musing renders eloquent lines suggesting she takes time to ponder: "I take long walks..." Seasons come in already in the second stanza, "... buried beneath October leaf-litter," and splendid universe/nature in the fourth, "A hunter's moon bleeds through thin branches...," a moon singularly signed by a significant epithet, "hunter's," and made mortal – human? – with "bleeds." This convergence the poet aims at is reinforced in the line "… night shadows shiver."

In a happy and lofty coincidence of individual poetic wordings, Skene reminds us first and foremost of Bliss Carman's poem "A Vagabond Song": "There is something in the autumn that is native to my blood… // … There is something in October..." A French singer of renown also echoes for the present writer, Francis Cabrel, in her allusions to October. Cabrel´s "Octobre" (October) says: « Y´aura des feuilles partout / Couchées sur les cailloux / Octobre tiendra sa revanche » *("There will be leaves everywhere / lying on pebbles / October will have its revenge" Taken from Cabrel's 1994 Audio CD « Samedi soir sur la terre,» recorded at Studios Polygone, France)* Nature plays a significant role in their art, literary or musical.

Skene's delineation of life is intertwined with very personal glimpses overlapping throughout the poem, reflective of remembrances and insights of what is going on: "… (I) listen to ghosts – how little they say, // how soon I forget, will be forgotten…" The poet's concern focuses too on people she sees in her long walks: "Lovers huddle on park benches, plot- / tomorrows and more tomorrows." The fifth stanza harmonizes an apparently heterogeneous set, "leap trash bins, dodge lampposts / and glacier-blue memories solidify," as balanced as things show up on extended strolls. "Glacier-blue memories" colours the scene, adding once more a natural touch to the poem yet linking it to a human mental operation, storing experiences.

At the end, the poet is able to condense her understanding of what surrounds her, "… assertive adolescences – blasphemous / in their callousness, their credulity, their overt // curiosity…" and is led/tempted to "… lose myself." Hence, the title, now more expanded when she says that "… I lose myself. Not quite / deliberately. Not quite willfully." The end lines are revelatory, exposing what the poet was really "up to": "More like a mistake I've been wanting / to make."

Another nature poem we welcome is "Cold Comfort." Again, seasons, accompanied by lively menagerie, take a leading role in this poet-nature dance of words: "the first winter starts with our shoes… // and snow // will fall and paper leaves and pine needles / rise over whitened rooftops // frost-rimed foxes scavenge / in bins and tender wrens hungrily // berrying…"

Amidst these depictions, the poet places her personal notes: "… we have known children // not unlike ourselves / who fail to follow their footprints // all the way back home / but we are quietly confident…" The poet envelops these reminiscences with season references: "a sensible sliver of January sun / pins everything in place," and blends in more experiences through "a kiss / trapped between two mouths // can ripen / in fresh fallen snow." The closing lines evoke death, euphemistically laid out: "one of us falls backwards / grows the wings of an angel // one of us has never been this way before or since."

The following two poems, "Climate Change" and "All the walls close in and the day…," honor the themes Skene recreates in the previous ones. Nature and everyday scenes vibrate in both; the former a feat of "play-on-*syntax*" with nature as a protagonist, the latter a return of the "glacier-blue memories" we read in "Accidental Purpose," now rephrased: "… and those memories that drift underneath the duvet…" If "Cold Comfort" points the finger at "children… // … who fail to follow their footprints // all the way back home," in "All the walls close in and the day…" the poet hints departure and absence, endowing objects (suitcases) with a human trait: "The suitcases, / ready and waiting, will commence the countdown / and the taxi will come." This is K. V. Skene in a brief look at her poems, enough to praise her artistry. Thank you, K. V.

Stella Mazur Preda

The second poet to honor our essay is Stella Mazur Preda. She submitted four poems for the members´ anthology, two of which will be commented here: "The Garden" and "The Little Store on St. John's Road." In the first poem, Mazur reveals herself as a painter. The scenes she dabs on her paper canvas carry sights, colour, *movement and sound*; they come alive as we read: "white daisies sprinkled among tall grasses… // the setting sun splashes the darkening sky / hues of red, pink, yellow, mauve… / over the unravelling spectacle… // a soft murmur ripples through the grasses… // a supernatural world slowly unveils … / elves and gnomes dance…"

The poet is totally taken by the sunset moment and she wishes to share it. One of Canadian poets´ signature, nature, is beautifully displayed in Mazur's words: (white daisies) "… dot the meadow like snowflakes / on the first winter's day." Vivid metaphors and similes join in the concert of words: "… black-eyed Susans / hide their secret from the world," "… naked boulders protrude like / gently rounded bellies of pregnant women / soon to give birth / to the mysteries of the untended garden," "… the ebony night has unmasked its magic."

The view is enhanced by sound – even if not directly represented – evoked by sound-producing agents: "a celebration of life… / accompanied by a musical / incantation of fairy wings, crickets and cicadas." Prompted by that "musical incantation," I *almost hear* the wings´ flutter, the crickets´ and cicadas´ chirping.

What Mazur proposes to the reader goes beyond a plain textual composition limning outdoor life. She has managed to bring into her poem a rainbow of many-coloured, soundful, motionful events bursting "on the first winter's day." James Deahl, in reference to Lampman's style, said: "… when he wrote a poem he was speaking to his heart." *(Taken from Canadian Stories magazine, Volume 22, Number 129, Year 2019)* I truly believe Mazur is also speaking to her heart.

Charmed by the wondrous instant, she absorbed the sunset and outpoured it in words thus succeeding in translating her feelings to us speaking ***from*** her heart as well. She was, to put it in John B. Lee's thought-frame, the vessel: "I am grateful to have had the opportunity to write the poems that visit my desk and flow through my pen. I am simply a vessel, and I am thankful when the muses visit." *(Taken from a comment John B. Lee made* *in an email he sent me, which I quoted in my book In a Fragile Moment: A Landscape of Canadian Poetry, Hidden Brook Press, 2020)*

Mazur's second poem, "The Little Store on St. John's Road," is a powerful, glowing time-voyage down Memory Lane. I have a section in The Envoy, the CCLA newsletter, called "A Word About." It is devoted to introduce Canadian poets I have read lately. In The Envoy 093, November 2019, I summarized some of the most outstanding characteristics of Canadian poets: "Among the many generalizations I can make out of reading… Canadian poets who have entered my life (deep connection to the land; identification with nature and wild life; a rooted sense of belonging to Canadian geography…; a feeling of proud nationality/nationhood; freshness and versatility in the use of expressive means and images; etc.), some are particularly salient and heart-warming to me: their commitment to family and values… and transcend in terms of … what is loftier and spiritual. In addition are the poets´ reminiscences of childhood and their recollection of friends and friendship."

This is what the poem is about. Those undying remembrances we build as we grow, which accompany us the rest of our lives; those places The Beatles made eternal in their lyrics, "There are places I remember…," and many poets have tenderly treated in their work.

A kaleidoscope of feelings is activated in the poet's mind at the sight of the little store but we know it is happening "thirty years later" only at the end stanza. Memories come flooding in at the beginning: the "labyrinth of aisles awaited discovery / the exploration of childhood fantasies… / … it wrapped us / in good times and laughter." The experience that never faded was both a night and day one: "In the dark of night two huge storefront windows / eyed passers-by surreptitiously. / Reflections winked in the glow of moonlight… // In the bliss of daylight gleaming windows winked… / … beckoned neighborhood children / through the yawning door." We cannot help noticing the recurring use of personification as a strong expressive means in the language, one that allows us to cross the borderlines between humans and place.

It was interesting to see a meeting point where Skene and Mazur concur. The former said "(I) listen to ghosts" in her "Accidental Purpose," the latter speaks of "memories steered me / to the ghosts left behind…" Both travel back and remember. The end lines put a touch of sadness, perhaps, to the poem: "The little store had found a new life as a house. / The echoing laughter of childhood ghosts / retreated to the past as I pulled away." However, the phrase "… found a new life" soothes the loss and brings in a new angle through the notion that, as a house, new memories will be built and treasured by people inhabiting it.

Like Skene, Mazur is a proud representative of Canadian poetry. Her detailed and cordial descriptions have left for us the pulse of a million perceptions. These have come from her gifted pen and reached out to marvel us. Thank you, Stella.

Donna Allard

The third poet is Donna Allard. She submitted five poems to the anthology, two of which I will address here: "in my wild place" and "in defence of heron." Reality, all within it, is decoded by poets in words and meanings they regale us. They surprise us with "freshness and versatility in the use of expressive means and images." *(Taken from my section "A Word About" in CCLA The Envoy 093, November 2019)* So does the poet I am presenting now.

Her first poem, "in my wild place," abounds in expressions that capture *and provoke* the reader. She starts by sharing what she is enjoying: "I see fields of wild flowers." The poet swerves down the lines in a cascade of blending realities: "… dunes where shifting sands / unveil skeletal memories of dry kelp… / and summer dreams made of clouds // "in stained glass pools of memory I peer through / Alice's mirror…" We find metaphors as we go, as unpredictable and luring as the world Alice – a direct allusion to the character in Lewis Carroll's books *Alice's Adventures in Wonderland* and *Through the Looking Glass* – will open for us. And we read about memories that transport us to the past, to another dimension; memories that decorate the poet's mind.

From this moment on, Allard pulls us into the seemingly illogical unfolding of events and experiences, based on nature details: "I become a sun illusion / a daisy in a tall grass something you'd pick / and wear in your hair…" The last stanza is still dizzy, "this wild place tingles between its tides," an ebb-and-flow sensation to accentuate dizziness.

The last two lines bear a particular sensuousness I took great pleasure in. In the middle of Alice's world, the poet shifts from figurative allusions to a more concrete, "real" instance: "… you place the daisy there, as you once / placed your lips."

When I read "in defence of heron," I was reminded of Marvin Orbach's poetry book *Redwing*, Hidden Brook Press, 2018. In my introduction, titled "Flying High and Low beside Marvin Orbach's *Redwing*," I praised his book, which took us to "Orbach's beloved nature where cormorants seem to "hold the answer to the great beyond."" He centered on the redwing; Allard centers on the heron. His book came to me because I saw a connection between them, as both poets "… speak of the power of observation, of sitting still and connecting with the life that flows around us… of the simple beauty of… birds." *(Taken from Orbach's daughter's Foreword in Redwing, Hidden Brook Press, 2018)*

Allard finds shelter and forge in nature to give us this piece: "I just noticed… / the silhouette of a great blue heron / near a small lagoon…" The line that follows is metaphorical, "… desolate surface of white moon," and a preamble to more images: "… take refuge in the winds / shattering the mirror underfoot: / the shards of glass gut the fish below / the great red reflection is undeniable / against the pure snow."

Intensely observant and bonding with the reality before her eyes, the poet is true to the banner held high by Canadian poets: nature is a standard, a sacred leitmotif. Like her ancestors, the Confederations Poets, Allard has also written original nature poems. Thank you, Donna.

Emotions in Dorothy Cox Rothwell, Heide Brown and James Cockcroft Comments on their Poetry in *The Dream The Glory and The Strife*

(Poetry Anthology) (2018) Hidden Brook Press. Canada

Captivated by the authors featured in the 2018 edition of the Canada Cuba Literary Alliance (CCLA) members´ anthology issued by Hidden Brook Press (HBP), I had written an essay on three poets included in that anthology *(Read here too Three Poets, One Big Canadian Heart. A Look at K. V. Skene, Stella Mazur Preda and Donna Allard in The Dream The Glory and The Strife (Poetry Anthology) (2018) Hidden Brook Press. Canada)* The three new poets I write about today have appeared systematically on other CCLA formats, like The Ambassador and The Envoy, and publications beyond CCLA borders.

Dorothy Cox Rothwell

Nature-poet connection in Canadian poetry dates back to founding poets and remains magically present in contemporary ones. This is what I thought when I read Dorothy Cox Rothwell´s poem "The Woods on a Winter Night." I was instantly reminded of Robert Frost´s "Stopping by Woods on a Snowy Evening" for the theme linking both poems and the enthrallment shared by the two poets.

Such is Rothwell´s admiration of the sights before her that she starts telling us in her first line, "Motionless i stand at the edge of the woods," yet cannot resist the attraction and in line two confesses: "alone i enter deep into you / unafraid, plunging into your whiteness." The poet is engulfed by the whiteness. She does not just step in – she *plunges.*

From that moment on she embraces and is embraced by what surrounds her: "your tranquility / broken only by the snapping of a branch / or my footsteps breaking the crust of snow." Cox opens eyes, spirit, arms; every bit of her, to the scenes revealing in front of her – as Frost nostalgically did in his immortal poem – and pauses to eternalize it: "The winter moon lays solemn / in the frost-black winter sky / pearl-white, luminous; silvery moonbeams filtering / over the winter scene / making it unreal, mystical haunting…"

In the process she time-travels: "Suddenly i am a child again…" accompanying her mood with language vividly expressing her unleashed emotions: "light headed with joy and wonder / at the beauty…" Epithets fly to describe as only a poet can how influential place and instant are: "sparkling enchanting moment; / the woods on a moonlit winter night / unforgettable."

As Galperin states, epithets are a "forceful means… subtle and delicate in character… conveys the subjective attitude of the writer… based on the interplay of emotive and logical meaning in an attributive word, phrase or even sentence… The epithet is markedly subjective…" *(Taken from Stylistics, 1981, Moscow Vyssaja Skola, by I. R. Galperin)* Let´s recall Frost´s use of epithets in "Stopping by Woods…" for a second: "… easy winds and downy flakes… // … the woods are lovely, dark and deep…" *(Taken from The Literature of the U.S.A., Editorial Pueblo y Educación, Ciudad de La Habana, 1983)*

Amidst her dreamy recollections, Cox does not fail to acknowledge how inspiring nature is as opposed to "The World is Square/Round / the world man makes is square; / we live in square houses / that look like salt boxes…" The shift from winter ecstasy is expertly attained giving the reader a sense of flatness contrary to the roundness she describes at the beginning, the wintery setting: "But God has made the natural things round / the sun and moon, / the earth itself / round heads, breasts, mouths…"

How alert the poet is! She depicts winter and contrasts God´s creation to man´s "flat" product: "… all this / hard edged, square linear / world created by man." This poem is unforgettable and wisdom-filled, as Frost´s, like the winter scenes that stirred both writers.

Rothwell´s second poem is "Letting Go." It is based on an essential stylistic device, simile. It lets the reader see through the intense, mixed emotions aroused by sad understanding of what is to come, bound unequivocally to the past: "My memories / are like torn sheets…" The formal element, connective word, in this case is *like*, thus the simile, as Galperin correctly notes, "… gives rise to a new understanding of the object characterizing as well as the object characterized." *(Idem previous quotation by I. R. Galperin)*

Cox dexterously manages to limn exactly what and how she feels, knowing time is a thief, unstoppable, relentless: "torn sheets / threadbare, ragged / beyond repair / discoloured by time…"

This is a poem that evokes sadness; however, it also speaks loudly of a *conscious* sadness and the poet´s capacity to discern through what I have termed elsewhere "tomorrow's framework" and "fabric of the future." *(Read Bridges Series IV / Serie Puentes IV, Where the Heart Lies / Donde late el corazón (SandCrab Books, 2018))*

One poem of illumination and bliss and another of meditated construal and acceptance tell us of Rothwell´s broad poetic spectrum when she is visited by spirituality and emotions that turn her experiencc into poetry. Thank you, Dorothy.

Heide Brown

The second poet under my poemscope is Heide Brown. Her poet-painter duality is everywhere in her poem "Spring colours." It is an ode to colours, tones: "My world / is constantly re-born / dressed in more colours / than I can find / in my fabrics. // Winter subtleties / explode into / an infinite number / of Spring's extravagant shades."

Alongside, an actively pensive artist caught in the "glorious garden / in all its spring-full glory…," engaged and creative both wit pen and brush, bathing in and honoring the legacy bequeathed to her by classic, full colour movements, committed to produce worthy art: "The Impressionists / and the Expressionists / bring me comfort. // Their creations / inspire me / to practice my artistic license / with my art."

Finally, the ultimate "muse": "The love of my world / as it dresses for Spring / is all I need to express." Brown finds heart-core motivation in her surroundings, especially that spring that has touched her innermost fibers exposing fireworks of feelings, so now she tries – successfully – to bequeath to us.

One particularly heart-warming poem is "Lessons from Buddy (A Eulogy for my Beloved)." It sweetly displays human-pet bonds I would call love, as I have taken well in the significance the animal had for the poet. It is truly emotional, eulogistic, and stands as a wonderful story whose final stanzas are categorically educational pieces of tribute and indelible memories interwoven with affection and teachings.

The first two stanzas bring back those mementos Brown treasures in her mind, which present to us common yet still much precious scenes in many, many homes: "beside me, here on the couch, / thumping your tail and cooing / for more cuddles and more sweet-talk…" Her words grow metaphorical and lyrical as I am allowed to visualize what she accurately describes with tenderness overflowing the poem´s lines, and the nostalgia fondling our own brains: "but you've crossed Rainbow Bridge dear Buddy / and my couch will now remain empty and cold."

Beyond that, we notice – and must take note of – the numberless learning experiences she got from Buddy. These experiences are substantially elevated by the poet as qualities humans ought to observe and try to build into their values systems and every-day conducts: "But I've learned so much from you: always be curious… enjoy each scent… take daily walks… follow enjoyable habits… always be loyal to those I love… be happy… smile… trust my heart… trust my senses… remember being good to others…"

The poem rises from being just an ordinary farewell one to a pet up to a heartfelt, much instructive, finger-pointing piece of advice in the name of a special kind of love: "and I'll never stop loving you … until we meet again …" Thank you, Heide.

James Cockcroft

Our third poet today is a well-known writer who has been publishing with Hidden Brook Press. First time I "met" him was via his *Why? Por qué? Pour quoi?*, published in 2009. The poem I want to comment here is "Lying in bed I reached over."

As I went through the poems of the three poets I decided to feature in a single essay, I felt a constant in their production, emotions. Deep, varied, in-hues emotions where nature, society and humans interact and converge in a multiplicity of events and involvements.

The dictionary defines *emotion* as: "... a state of feeling c: a conscious mental reaction... subjectively experienced as strong feeling usually directed toward a specific object..." *(Taken from Merriam-Webster Collegiate Dictionary, Digital Babylon)* Readers will immediately realize that the previous two poets "qualify" as being overwhelmed by true emotions that prompted them to write their fine poems, and they will also see that Cockcroft is no exception to this commonality of feeling.

Cockcroft´s "Lying in bed I reached over" is a powerfully gentle poem where he reaches over to his wife – we are lucky witnesses and recipients of the act – in an attempt to explain sensations crisscrossing his (ours) spirit beyond and above mere physicality; nevertheless, he does not forsake it at all: "Lying in bed, / I reached over, / not taking you in my arms / as I sometimes do, / nor you me. // Not cuddling, / though often / we do."

Philosophical perhaps; truly mystical, revelatory and enlightening, the poem tenderly and mysteriously walks us into a discovery of love´s unseen dimensions translated poetically as "A kind of current / coursed from those / points of contact." The wording embraces the two confluent souls converging in that current I just quoted, in an all-inclusive instance of communion: "... all through me. // Back to you, / back to me, / with not one / of us left alone, / joined by the / arc ..."

The poet shares his intimate findings with his wife, those invisible emotions, those pins and needles pricking his body and mind, convinced it all comes "from somewhere inside / each of us..." He wants her to see and feel what is being revealed to him, he wants to share: "I told you of it and, / dull with sleep, / you replied: / *Uh-huh*."

Cockcroft ultimately gives in to *it* in a juncture of emotion and creation urging him to "*I will write a poem*." He invites us, readers, to ask questions too, to pursue feelings-dimensions unlocked and kindled "lying in bed" by the vibrant peek he has permitted us to have, which in my case leaves me expecting even more after the last line. Thank you, James.

Resonating Shifts in Laurence Hutchman's House A Review on Four of his Poems in *The House of Shifting Time*

(Poetry) (2019) Black Moss Press. Canada

Sunday mornings are becoming "postman day" here in my home. The last months have been noticeably fertile in bringing me news of poetry. It never occurred to me just four years ago I would spend glorious nights reading so many Canadian authors. I blame it all on Richard Grove (Tai), Canada Cuba Literary Alliance (CCLA) Founding President, and James Deahl, an invaluable CCLA asset. A few days ago I looked at the universe – the part we know and can see and the part we don't know and cannot see – and asked myself the questions humankind – great poets included – has been asking for millennia. Eva Kolacz's book, *Whatever We Are*, motivated me to do so.

Today it was Kolacz's husband, Professor Laurence Hutchman, who surprised me. The package he sent me had three books: a copy of Eva's book, and two books by Hutchman, *Personal Encounters* and *The House of Shifting Time.* I skimmed both books as I always do with poetry to breathe in their aura before I plunge into the enlightening act of writing about them. When I started reading poems from the latter, I could not hold back my sudden impulse to jot down ideas overflowing my mind, impressed by what I was discovering and experiencing in the process. What follows is my brief, yet fascinating, encounter with Hutchman's poetry.

Out of the forty-eight poems in the book, distributed in four sections, I was instantly drawn to four I am commenting here. My curiosity began with the front cover image. Eva, a dazzling painter, might agree that this 1923 Kandinsky reminds us of the classics. I was immediately visited by Salvador Dali and René Magritte, two giant surrealists. To round up this sensation, Hutchman decided to title his book *The House of Shifting Time*!

Interestingly, the first poem had a previous title ("Timeless Night"), which the poet changed to "Travel" for re-publication. The concepts of time and travel are, anyway, related in his work, as they have been in so many other fine poets, like Michael Mirolla with his book *Light and Time.* "Travel" is a preamble poem acting as a key that opens for us what Hutchman has to say. He chisels appealing epithets, "timeless night," "mauve air" and grants his flashlight a metaphorical decisive role in the poem: "... my flashlight became / a beacon to scan the stars..."

His path illuminates "… above the garden… up to the trees… and farther… beyond the clouds." Magically, the space travel he starts becomes time travel: "The child in me still shines in the cavern's moment." Hutchman revels in a moment that he recreates, a moment that stirs full motivation in him to render more poems. Consequently, a proper identification with "Travel" may lead us into our own "flashlight" adventure in his next poems.

Nature is a catalyst for admirable poetry. I have repeatedly posited this. A source of inspiration *par excellence*, what surrounds us is decoded by poets who write tender pieces, like "Autumn Afternoon." Here we have a poem of consideration where the poet finds peace. Nature is a central theme Hutchman honors: "… the poet is true to the banner held high by Canadian poets: nature is a standard, a sacred leitmotif." *(Taken from my words about Donna Allard in my essay "Three Poets, One Big Canadian Heart. A Look at K. V. Skene, Stella Mazur Preda and Donna Allard in The Dream The Glory and The Strife" (Poetry) (2018) Hidden Brook Press. Canada)*

The poem starts with a gentle request to "Look…," what means *to enjoy* the colours displayed before human eyes: "… the most recent violet / and the ultimate pink rose." The poet has learned to embrace what is beautiful and edifying in his surroundings, however fleeting they are: "… there is a recognition, / an acceptance of season's end." The last three lines epitomize the poet's feelings, his merging in the act of breathing, understood as being implicated, *living*: "Breathe, look at the pale warm sun."

A bright metaphor closes the poem, "Thought is a bird / poised in branches." It is clear evidence of the bond between mind and the world outside, between human and bird (nature) in a harmony that crystallizes with the season, with the colourful atmosphere he has been able to paint out of his easel. His choice of the word "poised" suggests to me that in bonding there is balance; the harmony of apparently different worlds lies in that balance.

Daniel Lockhart *(See the book's back-cover comments)* says that Hutchman writes "focusing upon the particular moments of life," – "Autumn Afternoon" is one of them – "but acknowledging the world, and its moving parts beyond." The statement applies to this poem and to the previously analyzed one: Hutchman masterfully combines in his writing all of the motion, spirit and multi-dimensional layers we take notice of in his work.

Russell Thornton says that "Here is a poet you can trust to be true to emotion and experience…" *(See the book's back-cover comments)* The poem "Resonance" is evidence of that. Hutchman will forgive (or thank) me for remembering Leo Sawyer's popular song "When I need you" ("When I need you I just close my eyes and I'm with you"). Through the power of mind, intensified by closing his eyes, the poet can conjure the past.

His first travel (Part 1) goes to "the sound of the sea" then "the sky turning dark," "the curlews calling out," "… the distant white caps," "the moon shining over the North Sea." Sweeping emotions roll side by side with equally moving experiences in the poem. The poet is mesmerized by what surrounded him in the past, what happened to him and still lingers on into the present. He also reminisces about a dear memory: "I can see my father standing in the turret with me..." and ends with an expression that more than just close the second stanza, may define the poem and the book: "That's magic."

Part 2 explodes in full recall: "I only have to close my eyes / to hear the power of my thoughts." Sundry sensations caress his mind: "... and feeling a warm mist streaming / through the woody smell of ties," "the oil glowing in blue and purple...," "... the sea's scent." In the end, an image in perspective, creating an effect of distancing or fading, "The railway tracks curve toward the horizon, / following the shape of hills," as graphic as the eye can discern them.

The last poem to comment is as relevant and opportunely placed in the book as the first one ("Travel"). Elizabeth Greene tells us that Hutchman "draws together many landscapes and times... His ´search for a special place´ takes him to... places rich with story and his ancestral history." *(See the book's back-cover comments)* We are quite aware of that after reading "We Are Always Searching for a Place."

This is a philosophically-grounded poem whose message connected me to a book I read and wrote about, *Whatever We Are*, by Eva Kolacz. Evidently, Canadian poets are more than qualified and profoundly involved to pose the attractively eerie and inquisitive questions Who-are-we? What-are-we-doing-here? I sense a biblical allusion in the phrase "love in the voice of many-tongued words, / in the mist of chaos."

In my notes about Eva Kolacz's book, I said: "The seeds of motivation go a long way back to the existence of humankind... Deeply rooted in the platform of human need, interest and stimulation, human beings have evolved... Why does history record such progress...? Why was humanity compelled to transform reality...? What invisible strings pulled at brain and hands to urge them to sow, build, create, write, love and reach beyond the stars? What "*furnaces of Heaven*" pushed into the adventure of Life?" *(Taken from my essay on Eva Kolacz´s Whatever We Are: "How We Wonder Who We Are. A Review of Five Poems by Eva Kolacz in Whatever We Are" (Poetry) (2019) Hidden Brook Press. Canada)*

In his *The House of Shifting Time*, Laurence Hutchman also questions, explores, proposes, travels back and forth in time and space, defines and dreams. He addresses in highly poetic lines the puzzling riddles of life, around him and his own: the universe and "the place where we grew up." In a wonder-world exploit of poetics, Hutchman *decodes now – and grasps*, as he ends "We Are Always Searching for a Place." Thank you, Laurence.

Social Concern and Nature: Two Themes, One Alert Poet Reading Bernice Lever in *Tenfold*

(Poetry) (2019) Beret Days Press. Canada

The year 2018 brought to light through Lummox Press an unquestionably essential anthology of poetry, *Tamaracks: Canadian Poetry for the 21st Century*, edited by James Deahl. It was meant for Canadians but also, especially, for their neighbors to the south and a broader public interested in an update with "... an indication of where Canadian poetry finds itself in 2018 and ... a hint of its possible future directions." *(Taken from Tamaracks: Canadian Poetry for the 21st Century, Lummox Press, 2018, Introduction by the Editor)*

One-hundred and thirteen poets were finally included – much more were invited to submit their poems. Out of this statistically and poetically praise-worthy representation of Canadian poets and their poems, I am privileged to have reviewed in my books, *In a Fragile Moment: A Landscape of Canadian Poetry* (Hidden Brook Press, 2020) and this present volume, which is a second edition of the previous title, *This Shower of Warm Light: Reviews and Essays on Canadian Poetry*, twenty-eight of them.

I add to these authors three I am currently working on: A. F. Moritz, Andreas Gripp and April Bulmer, plus our poet in this essay, Bernice Lever, totaling thirty-two "Tamarackers" – so far. Lever's two poems I modestly write about were taken from *Tenfold* (Beret Days Press, 2019), a special Ontario Poetry Society project, a volume the poet generously sent to me, which included ten (I take pride in saying I have reviewed seven of them!) outstanding contemporary authors. I will refer to Lever's "Young Eyes Ask Why" and "Fat Rain."

The first poem strikes me as a highly mature, critical one, as corresponds to a writer like Lever. Metonymical in its title and first line, the poem points at the puzzlement – and detachment – of the new generation regarding reality: "... behind / thick lenses / of gas masks / as they try to see / our reasons." The fact that in the first stanza the poet uses "reasons" in plural then in the second one she writes "reason," in singular, leads me to say that I pick a shift of meaning from "arguments," "statements" in the plural form to "conscience," "awareness," "mental stability" in the singular.

This is confirmed in line two of the second stanza: ("even our reason" /) "which *we lost* as we swam…" A metaphorical phrase props the full utterance: "… as we swam / neck-deep in our sewage…," that might hint an underlying euphemism within, an even stronger statement lurking behind "our own sewage." As well, the poet succeeds in creating an uncomfortable sensation in the reader with "… that last glorious fling / at world destruction." She couples "fling" with an epithet, "glorious," plus the prepositional phrase accompanying them in the line below, "at world destruction."

Their combination leaves an ironic flavor, for there is no actual glory in the act. Irony, a useful expressive means in the language, serves to achieve this by opposing word meanings: "The… word acquires a meaning quite the opposite to its primary dictionary meaning… It rather expresses a feeling of irritation, displeasure, pity or regret. A word used ironically may sometimes express very subtle, almost imperceptible nuances of meaning." *(Taken from Stylistics, 1981, Moscow Vyssaja Skola, by I. R. Galperin)* Richard Altick stated that "The effect of irony lies in the striking disparity between what is said and what is meant." *(Idem previous quotation)*

These assertions support my reference to ironical tones in the stanza. The impression holds up in the third one, worth quoting fully: "Don't question, children; / just erase any trace / of humanity, / just corrode and corrupt / all you touch." The request, from "erase…" to "… touch," obviously clashes logic, and makes irony work perfectly as an effective stylistic device. The closing line also contributes to the poem's whole ironical twist: "Do as we do." In the poet's conscience there is recognition that her generation is not on the right track either. This is clear enough in the final statement, and quite ironical in bittersweet degrees. Her poem is a forceful warning call.

Lever's focus on international peace affairs has motivated her insistent poetry to expose the dangerous course humanity has taken. This poem previously appeared in *Blessings* (Black Moss Press, 2000) and *Tamaracks: Canadian Poetry for the 21st Century* (Lummox Press, 2018).

The second poem, "Fat Rain," appeared as "1st Prize, Dr. Wm. Henry Drummond poetry contest, Cobalt, 2007 & Generation, (Black Moss Press, 2009)." *(Taken from the poem's footnote previously published reference)* It presents us a sensitive poet whose pen cannot resist the lure of nature. This is a grand constant in Canadian poets; Lever enriches the list. Wonderful imagery greets our eyes: "… the winter rain / slips straight down creating / plump orbs that cling / to bare bark until / our apple orchard / has diamonds adorning / every stiff branch." Eloquent opposition pops up between the optical-mental representations evoked by the metaphorical noun "diamonds" and direct dictionary meaning in the extended noun phrase "every *stiff* branch."

An interesting opposition flicks again in the second, and last, stanza from the line "silent water bombs," as silent is hardly a bomb's most appropriate description when it explodes. However, the poet softens, if you will, the actual significance of a bomb by attaching ("water bombs" /) "… that so delight us…" Personification rounds off the stanza in bestowing birds a human feature: ("nuthatches hide…" /) "… *amused* / by these gentle syllables on / our wooden eaves from fat rain." It activates a pleasing visualization of a songbird attentive to "rain language."

I have explored, humbly, metaphorical convergence of realities in my poems. In "Jargon," for example: "… rain clinks / on my windowpane, / an almost vertical message / of liquid and transparences… / becoming symbols on glass. / … cryptic sequences of fleeting / sounds and spellings / chatting cheerfully in a jargon of wetness…" *(Taken from my poetry book This Pulse of Life, These Words I Found, Hidden Brook Press, 2021)*

Lever expresses it at a higher level. She confers an implied power of sound-communication to rain: "… gentle *syllables* on / our wooden eaves from fat rain." Fully involved in the circumstance of rain, she proposes stimulating figurative connections of natural and socio-linguistic phenomena, delightfully molded in the creative vessel of poetry.

True to one of the key roles of poetry – wisely set forth by Sainte-Marie, "The job of a poet is to get information across in a way that's effective in making change." *(Taken from Tamaracks: Canadian Poetry for the 21st Century, Lummox Press, 2018. Introduction by the Editor. The Editor refers the reader to Reader's Digest Volume 191 Number 1,144 (November 2017). Page 38. Print)* – Lever is a socially-committed, nature-implicated poet who has justly earned her niche in the Canadian poetic mosaic. Thank you, Bernice.

Axiom-Inspiration in Andreas Gripp A Journey into Two of his Poems in *Tamaracks: Canadian Poetry for the 21st Century*

(Poetry) (2018) Lummox Press. USA

My readings of *Tamaracks: Canadian Poetry for the 21st Century* (Lummox Press, 2018) – a must read towards a comprehensive appreciation of contemporary Canadian poetry – have brought to my attention poets I was not familiar with or had had little access to samples of their poetry. One of these poets is Andreas Gripp, whom I had briefly "met" in *Window Fishing: The night we caught Beatlemania* (Hidden Brook Press, 2014).

I revisit Gripp through two of his poems, "The West Coast of Somewhere" and "Marooning the Muse." I dare consider the first one a kind of "bio-poem" in which the poet travels – and takes us along with him – from childhood ("As a boy") though youth ("As a single young man") to adulthood (middle age: "Now middle-aged in wedlock"), wearing his heart out on his sleeve.

From such emotions Gripp sculpts line after line and as we read, we are fortunate to detect evident nostalgia, "As a boy, I saw only sand and sea / and stones…," where the Canadian bond with nature I have discussed so many times surfaces: "… stones I pitched with a splash / beneath the shifting animal clouds / that I envisioned."

I notice that Gripp uses an expressive means helping to link eye perception in the act of reading with a suggestion at hearing too, onomatopoeia. This resource is based on "… sounds produced by nature… by things (machines or tools)…" *(Taken from Stylistics, 1981, Moscow Vyssaja Skola, by I. R. Galperin)* where "the sound of a word echoes its sense." *(Taken from New Horizons, McClelland and Stewart Limited, Revised edition, Canada, 1965)*

The poet handles both direct, "splash," (a word that echoes a sound) and indirect onomatopoeia, "…a splash / beneath the shifting animal clouds / that I envisioned," (a repeated combination of a sound – here /ʃ/ – occurring in more than one word – here "splash," "shifting" and "envisioned" represented by the graphemes *sh* and *s.*

He crosses and writes about time but also spaces (ocean, land and air) he refers to: "… sand and sea," "clouds / that I envisioned," "… a day of sun and cirrus… / "… and waves colliding with the shore…," "… the beach… / … this cumulus of savannah cats…" "Savannah cats" stands as a suggestive metonymical expression to refer to clouds and their shape-shifting properties "kneaded" at will by the wind push-sculpting them. He used cats but it may as well have been other shapes, animals or objects, as I describe in a poem I wrote to my daughter, "Shapes." Allow me to quote parts of my poem, as I was thrilled to see my humble writing coincide with a poet of renown: "proud ships of clouds / adrift in the skymap… // mystic horned fish preying on the city / fluffed streaks / like sitting lions / tents, gliding birds, butterflies / – infinite shapes… // fish become snakes, lions are balls now / floats are dinosaurs, ships are grey-silvery lines…" *(Taken from my poetry book Forge of Words, Hidden Brook Press. 2019)* "Savannah cats" is an expression that, for reasons I don't really know, reminded me of the hilarious Cheshire cat in *Alice´s Adventures in Wonderland*, by Lewis Carroll.

The first stanza, boyhood, mentions him alone in a relation with nature. The second one, youth, still includes nature but, acting his age, he is caught too in the lure of youthful interests: "… only the flash of skin and curves / exposed by browning." Again, a metonymical resource that aids in hinting attractive female bodies sunbathing covered only by their swimsuits.

Finally, the third stanza, adulthood, affirms the typical routine of human life as he sees himself committed to a singular woman, "Now middle-aged in wedlock, / ambling along the beach / beside my wife." Yet the fresh view of "… the crew of college girls, / jumping for *frisbees* in the surf…" still stirs him. He wisely chooses to "dissipate" them like "… a blur below / this cumulus… / overseeing their great, / ephemeral kingdom."

The last phrase, "ephemeral kingdom," alludes to the "cats" (the clouds) watching over the earth, where living things and people are fleeting beings but I identify between-the-lines semantic shades the poet colours these lines with a reference to his own transient lifespan, which ignited his musings and his "bio-poem" in the first place.

It is my contention that the second poem, "Marooning the Muse," is an ode to nature, the act of creative writing and a communion of love. Sources of inspiration are delicately illustrated and exhibited with a highly lyrical style and choice of wording, without losing its natural-personal foundation. These sources are inspiring views the poet and his companion see and share: "I looked at the horizon / and its meeting of sky and sea / and the cerulean they both shared."

In his attempt to justify he could not "… write a thing," the poet displays a gamut of uplifting every-day phenomena and events unfurling before their eyes: "You wrote of sandpipers / on the strand and the seagulls / encircling the trawler…" The last stanza carries an axiomatic message in my opinion. While the poet tells his companion "I left you the metaphors" and seems to get lost in "a reverie," he gives in to the conclusion that the most genuine, most intense sources of enlightenment and lofty poetry lie in what surrounds them: "… it's all an illusion, / this vortex of birds and their fish, / this looping of ships and our poems."

Gripp shows his lyrical prowess in both poems. Reading him was, as I commented at the beginning, travelling through his life; but it also made me look at my own life with nostalgia and willingness to learn how to craft sparking pieces, ones that help us discern with our feet firmly on the ground but in poetic, comforting words that "the world is round indeed." Thank you, Andreas.

A Communion of Spirituality in April Bulmer An Appraisal of Two of her Poems in *Beyond the Seventh Morning*

(Poetry) (2013) SandCrab Books. Canada

In my studies of Canadian poetry I have been enlightened by so many books and authors. Each one has stayed with me after I finished my essay on their work and moved on to the next poet. A recurring name in Canada Cuba Literary Alliance (CCLA) issues by Hidden Brook Press and SandCrab Books – and several other publishers outside CCLA – is April Bulmer. I will comment her poems "Medicine Bowls" and "The Grand," from *Beyond the Seventh Morning.*

To understand Bulmer's poetry I went first to the author's bio then read the Intro words by one of the book's editors, Manuel de J. Velázquez León, former CCLA VP (the other is John B. Lee). He said that "Another view is that what we call reality is nothing more than an illusion… We see with our eyes only that which our brains allow us to see." The assertion prepares readers for the wonderlands we will cross both in a physical but mostly a spiritual journey.

And I was reminded of Canadian poet Andreas Gripp, whose poetry I enjoyed and analyzed, and his piece, "Marooning the Muse": "it's all an illusion, / this vortex of birds and their fish, / this looping of ships and our poems." *(Taken from my essay "Axiom-Inspiration in Andreas Gripp. A Journey into Two of his Poems in Tamaracks: Canadian Poetry for the 21st Century (Poetry) (2018) Lummox Press. Canada," in this review book)*

Velázquez also invites readers to "… partake in a spiritual transfiguration" so this is what I did while reading Bulmer. "Medicine Bowls" vibrates with imagery – appreciated too in "The Grand" – complementing the vivid descriptions the poet regales us: "I did not die like a clock," "For my heart is a bulb… / rooted in light and ground," "virgin winters," "Then I rushed upward / in new-born wings," among others. As Velázquez notes, reality is transformed in the eyes of the poet.

Based on my readings of Canadian poet Elana Wolff, I pay particular attention in my analyses to what she explains: "… I moved from what I observed and heard in the text into what I felt to be dwelling between the lines, and behind and beyond the white." *(Taken from Author's Afterword in her book Implicate me. Guernica Editions, 2010)* Bulmer's line "For my heart is a bulb… / rooted in light and ground" allows interpretations centered on the fact that light is viewed as a natural phenomenon in motion, generally coming, or giving such impression, from an *above*. The ground on the other hand, implies an opposition, a *down*.

Given these elements, I venture in saying that her heart, "rooted in light and ground," moves, reaches out, elevates – as Bulmer confesses in the second stanza: "Then I rushed upward / on new-born wings." Why does the poet choose to say "I rushed"? Is she escaping dirtiness? Is she urged by circumstances?

In a context of dreamy exposures and atmosphere, I see the expression "new-born wings" as a metaphor for renewed hopes – or, more daringly, a sudden incursion into new dimensions, so in line with the poem's theme. Canadian poet Malca Litovitz comes to second me: "… I try to let the students discover the poetry for themselves and come up with their own interpretations. I only correct them if they're way off base, if it's an obvious language failure on their part. But otherwise, for example, when I teach "The Sick Rose" by William Blake they can have dozens of different interpretations of it, and that excites me." *(Taken from an interview made by Elana Wolff to her friend and poet Malca Litovitz, included in their book Slow Dancing (section Duologue). Guernica Editions, 2008)*

The range of interpretations is as varied as there are readers implicated in the act of reading, in exploring, as Wolff states, "… ideas and feelings, to go for the soul." *(Idem Wolff's quotation)* I am volunteering my own.

The third stanza depicts meditations-experiences shuffling around the poet. An encounter with God that the poet handles with humbleness and composure: "I offered the Lord a corn doll / and a book about birds." The indefinite "Someone" adds to the mood of the poem and the poet's intentions to create a special ambience that she shares with the reader: "Someone brought me turtledoves / and sang pretty words." There is no specific person, just *someone*. A metonymical expression closes the stanza, bringing the occurrences down to earth, possibly hinting the origin of all the experiences felt so far: "An Indian stirred milk and fish / in the moons of medicine bowls."

A distinct expressive means of the language, zeugma, is stylistically handled in the last stanza: "… the old snake / sheds her red skin, / her woman cloth." Zeugma is "… the use of a word in the same grammatical but different semantic relations to two adjacent words in the context, the semantic relations being, on the one hand, literal, and, on the other, transferred." *(Taken from Stylistics, 1981, Moscow Vyssaja Skola, by I. R. Galperin)* In the stanza, the verb *shed* operates with actual primary dictionary meaning in respect to "red skin" and with derivative, transferred meaning of figurative value in relation to "her woman cloth."

Metaphorical visions complete the poem in the last stanza: "… the weight of blossom / and of fruit. / Black plum nipples, teats and roots." The poet offers a picture of images-imaginations blending magically in that "spiritual transfiguration" Velázquez announced.

Digital Dictionary Babylon, English-English, registers the following meanings for *grand* as an adjective: "large, impressive; dignified; fancy, magnificent, splendid, wonderful; chief, main." I contend that the second poem's title, "The Grand," a river's name, takes on all of these "qualities" thanks to the poet's intended interplay with connotative implications and ramifications beyond textual appearance: primary reference to The Grand and its natural notability, broadens into an extended metaphorical reflection of humankind's primordial and necessary bond with the elements, with nature.

Early civilizations settled and flourished near water sources. The First Nations have never let go of this bond. Bulmer recognizes these tenets of development, this crucial awareness that humanity is part of a larger ecosystem that demands harmony and synergy of behavior and depends on nature. Many Canadian poets I have reviewed have approached this issue from their perspectives, Margaret Atwood, Katherine L. Gordon, Bernice Lever, etc.

John B. Lee, in his Intro words to *Beyond the Seventh Morning*, tells us: "When we pray, when we create, when we love and are loved… the soul in us shines, and we feel the covenant with God, the universe and all." April Bulmer reveals that covenant in "The Grand."

Filled with imagery, reverence, awe and soul-deep rendition, the poem is a showcase of interesting use of capitalization: "River is sensitive. / I have come to Her / in prayer // … I am many Women / … I live with Spirits. River knows this / … as though Horse. // God built many things… / His great Arms." Biblical readings show the use of capitalization in reference to God. Bulmer takes a step forward in capitalizing other words: possessive adjectives (determiners) and common nouns, which we do not see often in English, except in titles.

Again, the connection – existing unbeknownst to us or not – between God and nature, is emphasized with capitalization, a stylistic detail. Among the three basic uses of capitalization, we find one that is exploited in Bulmer's poem: "… the first letter of nouns that are personified." *(Taken from English Composition. Editorial de Libros para la Educación, 1981)* Also, capitalization heightens the connection between humans and nature, defined in the relevance it has for them. Capitalization acquires that status in the poem; it calls our attention to the essentials.

"The Grand" acknowledges the fundamental elements of life, found in natural resources, like water: its spirituality, its vital properties. Observe that the poet uses personification here, another expressive means: "the attributing to abstract or inanimate objects qualities characteristic of persons." *(Taken from New Horizons, McClelland and Stewart Limited, Revised edition, Canada, 1965)* propped by capitalization.

That is why Bulmer comes "… to Her / in prayer." That is why Bulmer pads "… Her ground / in soft shoes." The poet fully identifies with those around her: "I am many Women…" and with a spirituality embracing her: "I live with Spirits. / River knows this." Already aware of the river's healing, edifying powers, Bulmer had opened her poem with "River is sensitive."

Let's notice there is no definite article preceding the noun *river*. It tells me it stands more as *a name*: personification of the common noun. I tend to say *the river has been given…*

but in the core-meanings, style and message of the poem, I would have to say the river *is sentient*, the river *is a cognizant entity*, "River knows this;" therefore, the river has been given nothing; it has in its own right living-being characteristics, the river *feels*.

The last stanza corroborates my previous assertions about the intimate, inseparable convergence of God and nature – of God and the poet: "God built many things / and delivered them / in His great Arms." Besides, its contextual significance, semantic connotation, syntactical arrangement, enunciative import and creative re-presentation, struck me as a noteworthy allusion to the *Holy Bible*'s First Book, Genesis, Chapter 1, verses from 1 through 31, and Chapter 2, verses 2 and 3.

I find it pertinent to mention cross-examples that came to my mind in reading this poem. The first one is the film *Avatar*, its crystal-clear message of Earth (in our case) being a living organism, a theory that is not new. In this sense the film is didactical – as is "The Grand" – calling for self-admonishment and reflection on our role within the universe.

The second example is a video downloaded from the Web that I have used in my lessons, *Create a Different World (Taken from #CreateADifferentWorld)*, where a girl of aboriginal descent warns in poignant words of our indolence towards nature: "… and now we hear of animals and plants going extinct every day, vanishing forever… If you don't know how to fix it, please stop breaking it..."

The gravitas of the girl's lucid, thought-provoking speech articulates with what the Bible reads: "God said: Let the waters teem with living creatures, and let birds fly… and God saw that it was good. God blessed them." *(God's words in Genesis 1:20-21-22)*, "God made the wild animals… and God saw that it was good." *(God's words in Genesis 1:25)* and "God saw all that he had made, and it was very good" *(God's words in Genesis 1:31)*

Finally, Genesis 2:3 reads: "And God blessed the seventh day…" *(All biblical quotations taken from the Holy Bible, 1984, Zondervan Publishing House)* So have been blessed these poems by Bulmer in *Beyond the Seventh Morning* – a suitable title, as the collection takes thoughts and religiousness to realms she and the other poets have proffered in a communion of "spiritual transfiguration." Thank you, April.

Tangled in Becky D. Alexander's Forceful Style
An Analysis of Two of her Poems in
Beyond the Seventh Morning

(Poetry) (2013) SandCrab Books. Canada

Becky D. Alexander was published in *Tamaracks. Canadian Poetry for the 21st Century* (Lummox Press, 2018) with the poem "Buried Deep." She submitted a moving piece about Canadian soldiers thus deploying her broad poetic bandwidth, which I had already noticed in *Beyond the Seventh Morning* (2013) (Poetry) SandCrab Books, the book from where I took the two poems she included, "Myth-Morphosis" and "Seeking the Windigo," for analysis.

In his Intro words to *Beyond the Seventh Morning*, one of the book's editors, Manuel de J. Velázquez León, former CCLA VP (the other editor is John B. Lee), warns that "We see with our eyes only that which our brains allow us to see," and invites readers to "… partake in a spiritual transfiguration." With a degree in Visual Arts, Alexander wields visual tools to access our minds and make us *see-feel*, to the point of eerie sensations of *being there*, what she describes.

Both "Myth-Morphosis" and "Seeking the Windigo" made me recall a book I recently reviewed, *Night Echoes*, by Ronnie R. Brown *(See in this review book "To Sleep or Not to Sleep. An Essay on Four of Ronnie R. Brown's poems in Night Echoes" (Poetry) (2006) Black Moss Press. Canada)*. Brown's book's back-cover comment by Gary Geddes reads that one of her poems is "very evocative, it ought to serve as the basic script for a film about ghostly visitations, nocturnal emanations…" This is what I felt in reading Alexander's poems.

As a reader you are transported into the atmosphere of the poem, thanks to the poet's skills in handling word-images. The first poem is a fantasy where she visits different myths. Each stanza enters one envisioned myth-realm. Alexander touches upon one of man's oldest aspirations, flying. But, not using contrivances, engineered devices and crafts: rather propelled by wings: "… and it would be great to finally be able to fly."

The second stanza brings us freedom mixed with hinted eroticism, "… and I know lots of folks–some men / for sure whom I'd like to lure onto rocks…" besides a show of talents/pranks the poet wants to display: "I love singing… / … and lord knows I have the voice for it, / and for once could be as loud as ever I wanted."

Stanza three swiftly moves – as the poet's illusion-filled mind – into another mythological creature. The poet revels in the experiences and power flooding her: "A gorgon would be fine, too, / for I do not fear snakes, but like the cool warmth / of their crimpling bellies on my skin, and boy–oh, / to scare the crap out of anyone who hates snakes…"

An aspect of special interest to me was the use of a classic stylistic device, onomatopoeia. It is a useful device in the language to imitate "… sounds produced by nature… by things (machines or tools)…" *(Taken from Stylistics, 1981, Moscow Vyssaja Skola, by I. R. Galperin)* where "the sound of a word echoes its sense." *(Taken from New Horizons, McClelland and Stewart Limited, Revised edition, Canada, 1965)*

Alexander handles indirect onomatopoeia, "I can see me now...ssslithering my sssilent tressesss / into the sssanctity of their dreamsss" (a repeated combination of a sound – here /s/ – occurring in more than one word – here "ssslithering," "sssilent," "tressesss," "sssanctity" and "dreamsss," represented by the grapheme *s*. Two extra *s*'s are graphically added to each of these words to stress the phonetic (sound) element, where onomatopoeia crystallizes in the suggestion of the sibilance produced by hissing snakes.

The other stanzas lead the poet and us across more fantasies. She mentions the Windigo – next poem's theme – and the powers she might acquire should she become one: "… the Windigo, an aboriginal ghost, / a ragged deep-forest giant who lures the unwary / into dark woods... for dinner…/ I can see me sucking souls out through ears, / trapping trespassers into frozen lakes..."

Later it is a troll, when the poet exhibits a nature-loving side: "And ahh, to be a troll, how truly jolly / to live the space and realm of forest life, / with the spirits of trees and ferns, / no trucks, no cars, no motor choke…" Finally, she chooses to be a selkie for "background reasons": "But no, one can't escape the grip of ancestors, / even when cloaked in the veils of myth, / so most likely I'd become a selkie…" Her decision honors her ancestry.

If the first poem reminded me of my own fantasies and scary mental worlds, "Seeking the Windigo" certainly impresses. It starts creating a mystery context, a feeling of solitude in the middle of an uncanny place, "I walk these northern woods alone…," granting ordinarily beautiful views a chilling side, "Blue jays stare their ice blue glares / watching me from twisted limbs," reinforced by the combination of "stare," "ice," "glare" and "twisted."

More than reading a poem, readers begin to feel they are trapped in a story or movie: "The great trees thrum, the pulse / of their roots a drumming throb, / loudness increasing with each heartbeat." The place looms like a threatening entity. Then enters a character, *she* – who is *she*? – "The scent of death precedes her / –she strides closer and closer." As in the previous poem, the author employs an expressive means, repetition ("closer and closer"), to emphasize fast movement.

I welcome the presence of dialogue as a versatile resource. It increases the lifelike touch in making the situation more real. Poet and *she* engage in ominous conversation, stylistically coloured by other equally frightening references: "… her wizened lips don't move" (the poet hears what *she* "says," *she* enters her mind!), "The trees heave, a black wind rises: / *He will find you first*" (creepy moment enhanced by the "reaction" of the trees and the wind).

In the closing lines the poet succeeds in building up an impressive, overwhelming discomfort in the reader. Anticipation marked by suspense in the "supposed" climax/dénouement: "I step back against the tearing wind, / shiver to the marrow, / *Is he real*, I ask, *all I want to know... / is he real?* / A deep chuckle echoes, / her mouth curls into a toothless grin, / *Look behind you*, she laughs..."

These are Alexander's poems. Tall in the solemn poetry of "Buried Deep," she explodes too in a feat of artistic puissance, with a wide poetic register gripping the reader, tightening the grip to such lengths that we lapse into the mental labyrinth of desperately wanting to escape from the lurking darkness of the "northern woods." Thank you, Becky.

Content, Form and Transcendence in A. F. Moritz
A Memorable Encounter with Three of his Poems in *The Sparrow*

(Poetry) (2018) House of Anansi Press Inc. Canada

The significance of poetry and poets has been defined by many authors and scholars. Shakespeare told us in his Sonnet XVIII that what we pour down on a sheet of paper remains eternal: "When in eternal lines to time thou grow'st, / So long as men can breathe, or eyes can see, / So long lives this, and this gives life to thee." *(Taken from Complete Works of William Shakespeare, Volume XVIII, Philadelphia David McKay, Publisher, no year)*. Pablo Neruda, the great Latin American icon, saw the duties of poetry in the form of feeling for and with others: "Mis deberes caminan con mi canto: / soy y no soy: es ése mi destino. / No soy si no acompaño los dolores / de los que sufren: son dolores míos. / Porque no puedo ser sin ser de todos, / de todos los callados y oprimidos, / vengo del pueblo y canto para el pueblo: / mi poesía es cántico y castigo. *(Taken from Neruda, 2004) ("My duties tread side by side with my song: / I am and I am not: such is my destiny. / I am not if I don´t walk beside the pain / of the suffering: that is my pain too. / Because I cannot be if I do not belong to them all, / the silent and the downtrodden, / I come from the people and sing for the people: / my poetry is canticle and punishment.")*

Canadian poet Hugh Hazelton "believes that poetry should bite, caress, laugh at, confront, lament, name, envision, remember, invoke, oppose, and reflect." *(Taken from Bridges Series Book II, Concave Mirrors. SandCrab Books, 2013)* Sainte-Marie energetically states "The job of a poet is to get information across in a way that's effective in making change." *(Taken from Tamaracks: Canadian Poetry for the 21st Century, Lummox Press, 2018. Introduction by the Editor. The Editor refers the reader to Reader's Digest Volume 191 Number 1,144 (November 2017). Page 38. Print).*

Eva Kolacz in her poem Life, Part 1 *(Taken from What We Are. Hidden Brook Press, 2019)* tells us poets can define and change time, life: "Change becomes us—someone said. / The beginning leaves time behind. / This is what poet & mystic can define / effortlessly." Don Gutteridge in his poem "Letters" *(Taken from Point Taken. Hidden Brook Press, 2019)* speaks of transcendence through poetry, seconding Shakespeare in their approach: "I try again to catch / that fleeting face in the prism / of a poem / in the serendipity of a simile, // knowing that he will survive / as long as these letters / linger and thrive."

Malca Litovitz said: "… the human soul needs poetry and that it will always be around and that it serves a real function in our psyche." *(Taken from Slow Dancing, Guernica Editions, 2008).* Elana Wolff has said that "a poem is not only a form of self-expression, it is the writer's way of bearing witness to the world in which he or she lives…" *(Taken from Implicate me, Guernica Editions, 2010)*

John B. Lee has said: "I want the heart to feel true sentiment… the body to come alive… the soul to thrill… and the spirit to surround and be surrounded." *(Quoted from memory)*

James Deahl posits: "Poetry was something that could not only speak to the issues and concerns of one's own life but could operate as a tool to allow the poet to discover an organizing principle outside of day-to-day human life…" *(Taken from Under the Watchful Eye, Broken Jaw Press, 1995)*, Wilfred Owen, cited by Terry Barker, states: "All a poet can do today is warn… That is why the true poets must be truthful." *(Taken from After Acorn. Meditations on the Message of Canada's People's Poet. Mekler and Deahl Publishers, 1999)*, and Michael Ondaatje stated: "… most crucial duties of a poet: to map and to name" *(Taken from The Ambassador 015, 2018)*

I have traveled across all these names and quotations paving the way to write about Canadian poet A. F. Moritz. He referred to a poet's "job" in an interview as "To write well: creatively, authentically, powerfully, beautifully…poetry is partly self-development… is duty, belonging to a community…poetry's role is as the guardian and developer of language." *(Taken from an interview on the Web)*

In talks with Richard Grove (Tai) and James Deahl, they have always been emphatic on my approaching Moritz. Both have said he is a figure I cannot overlook in a review book. James has stressed on the fact that any poetry anthology must have his poems. Therefore, I chose to search in his latest book, *The Sparrow*, for some especially appealing poems to my humble reviewer eyes.

A. F. Moritz has been called "one of the best poets of his generation" by John Hollander and "a true poet" by Harold Bloom. He has received numerous awards and honors in North America: the Award in Literature of the American Academy of Arts and Letters, the Guggenheim Fellowship, Poetry magazine's Beth Hokin Prize, the Ingram Merrill Fellowship, and the Griffin Poetry Prize.

One of the book's back-cover comments refers to *The Sparrow: Selected Poems of A. F. Moritz* as a book that "surveys forty-five years of Moritz's published poems, from earlier, lesser-known pieces to the widely acclaimed works of the last twenty years. Here are poems of mystery and imagination; of identification with the other; of compassion, judgement, and rage; of love and eroticism; of mature philosophical, sociological, and political analysis; of history and current events; of contemplation of nature; of exaltation and ennui, fullness and emptiness, and the pure succession and splendour of earthly nights and days… *The Sparrow* is more than a selected poems; it is also a single vast poem, in which the individual pieces can be read as facets of an ever-moving whole. This is the world of A. F. Moritz — a unique combination of lyrical fire and meditative depth, and an imaginative renewal of style and never-ending discovery of form."

In this context of highly valued appreciation of the acclaimed author, I assumed a huge undertaking: selecting poems that would embody – from my perspective – Moritz's powerful style and make me vibrate. Reducing the analysis to a few poems seemed a futile challenge for a mentally-deranged reviewer; his work is vast and classic in many respects.

However, when I started reading, it fortunately dawned on me that *any* poem I picked would suffice to illustrate the poet's greatness. That is how I came to "Shade," "Morning Fragments" and "In the Dead of Night Only."

On the book's back cover, John Ashbury says that "we seem to hear shattered echoes from the Bible…" I was also privileged to hear other voices. I began my review by quoting Shakespeare. How serendipitous I was initially drawn to "Shade," our first piece. Moritz's technique flies, like a sparrow, in a polished range of multi-styles held in *his* concentrated style. The Toronto Star recognizes it as "polished turns of phrase and fluid cadences." *(Taken from the book's back cover)*; integrating an encompassing gamut of influences and flowing trajectories.

Here the poet introduces the reader into beauty and fantasy, hazy realms and visual-mental explorations: "Before you were born, summer's beauty died. / Now at times it brushes you / with its abstract wing." I pick a brave, ingenious variation from Shakespeare's Sonnet XVIII, "Shall I compare thee to a summer's day? / Thou art more lovely and more temperate… / And summer's lease hath all too short a date… / But thy eternal summer shall not fade…" *(Taken from Complete Works of William Shakespeare, Volume XVIII, Philadelphia David McKay, Publisher, no year)*

Moritz creatively eases from a second stanza describing metaphorical-concrete realities altogether: "The sounds of the beautiful ideas… / sit looking down through mist / at leaves... / and on both sides of the window the water / slowly condenses and rolls earthward" into the third one, where more figurative, imaginary proposals are unleashed: "… a thought of time dwelling in a timeless place / will fall, if a tree dares to dash across the sun. / A blow of shadow strikes your sleep in whitened light."

The next stanza is the meditative poet, caught up in the endless, fathomless well of time, asking the questions so many poets ask themselves *(Read, for example, my analyses on Eva Kolacz in this review book, or about Al Purdy's and Milton Acorn's musings on the same theme, in my previous review book In a Fragile Moment: A Landscape of Canadian Poetry, Hidden Brook Press, 2020. You can also read Henry Beissel's Fugitive Horizons, Guernica Editions, 2013)*, inquiring about existence, this enigma we were headlong-born to: "Again the image: days passing beneath oaks / to nothing but further days, further knowledge / of the sky held in fingered leaves: / it empties you into confusion." Is it a poet lanced by pessimism? Or should we rather discern an inquisitive man probing the entrails of living? His wise choice of language remains unaltered, metaphor-charged: "days passing beneath oaks," "sky held in fingered leaves."

The finale tends towards a possible calibration of events and states of mind, of attempts at charting one's cosmic bearings, physically and mentally – bodily and psychologically: "And that ancient being, you, sole citizen / of the shadow, waits, echoing with muted light; / alone, cannot pronounce itself alone / expecting someone, expecting pleasure…"

The last line reminds us of Shakespeare's Sonnet XVIII, "Nor shall death brag thou wander'st in his shade" again *(Taken from Complete Works of William Shakespeare, Volume XVIII, Philadelphia David McKay Publisher, no year)*, to give us a Moritz whose resourcefulness renders an imaginative deflection in his own poem: "nor shall you brag it wanders in death's shade." Two transcendental poets addressing similar issues.

Still focused on the marvel of life and time, Moritz displays more captivating images in his poem "Morning Fragments." This particularly philosophical poem brought to me the work of another iconic contemporary poet, John B. Lee, his poem "Morning Expectation": "hope's expectations of longer days / birds will soon return / insects waking / life's cycle renewed / in this morning of change…" *(Taken from Two Thousand Seventeen, Sanbun Publishers, 2018, New Delhi)*

In his poem, Moritz targets morning in *tropeful* insinuations of how it slowly glides in, the morning theme being an excuse to ponder over deeper questions: "And the morning fragments, / growing visible, seem to rebuild themselves / out of twilight, mildew, and melancholy / towards an edifice still darkened in you…" Somehow the poet invites to the search for answers, or provides them after posing firstly rhetorical questions: "And were you here yesterday already?... were you following / faint prints of a day before?"

Then the answers, cosmic, as I said before, delving into and out of doubt, a point made by the use of the conditional *if* (there is no *absolute* certainty): "You will know at last if the sun ages / or is created every dawn / out of nothing at the surface of the sea. / You will know if this dayspring is eternal / or lies on a heap of others, / a page just turned, reversing all."

Through his poetry, Moritz leads the reader to a fumbling limp towards an ultimate truth – if there is one. He places layer *after* layer, layer *beside* layer, layer *against* layer, of denotations and connotations of meanings that flit among syntactically engineered word-loops. Take this example: "And meanwhile night has sunk as a hedge / sinks into distance as you walk away. / Voices were making explanation behind it, / something you might have understood, some secret / of a former life…"

You stumble from your present into "a former life" and fall back into uncertainty: "… so that now you will never know what was being said, / if something is lost forever, / or if much, happily, / is put behind you and forgotten." As much as poetry is an act of solitude, the final product evolves into a dialogue in this poem. The use of "you" very much assists in this.

The third poem I chose is "In the Dead of Night Only." The poem is a substantial, sustained metaphor, overlapping with another expressive means, personification. The first stanza's last line is illustrative of this: "... night exhausted, dawn not yet." The poet puts together the idea of colour with the idea of feeling; he equates them with an accomplished symbolic treatment: "... a darkness blacker than the young night's / beautiful colour, known at last / now in nostalgia."

The last stanza is definitely surrealistic, a detail worthy of a Magritte or a Dali easel: "Then you recognize / the journey in which your bed is an evening's pause: / it's the house of this moment / in which the journey is a dream."

P. K. Page commented that "Some of [his] poems are... full of portent, with the gravity and power of myth." *(Read the book's back cover)* and the Toronto Star deemed them "... subtle, far-reaching... spiritually revitalizing." *(Idem previous reference).* I will finish by returning to Moritz's own criterion on how poems must be written: creatively, authentically, powerfully, beautifully." His forty-five-year fertility in poetic production has honored that principle and made the poet transcend in content and form, in time and space. Quite a contribution. Thank you, A. F.

Redirecting Thought and World-View with Brian T. W. Way A Comment on Seven Poems in his *redirection: the prime sonnets and other poems*

(Poetry) (2015) Hidden Brook Press. Canada

I have always been a follower of Shakespeare's sonnets. I even memorized some when I was in college majoring in English for teaching purposes, and used them later as a professor of English Stylistics to speak about transcending human traits explored by Shakespeare and to exemplify expressive means of the language. I was familiar, to a lesser degree, with the Italian sonnet. I have also written some very modest "free" Shakespearean versions of sonnets.

Then I "met" Brian T. Way and his idea about a Canadian sonnet! Brian and I exchanged quite a few emails – thanks to Richard Grove (Tai), Founding President of the Canada Cuba Literary Alliance (CCLA) – and he kindly forwarded me his *redirection: the prime sonnets and other poems* with his permission to use and translate his poems for publication in The Ambassador (CCLA official magazine), which I did in volumes 015 and 016.

The first thing that caught my eye was his decision to do away with what he deemed unnecessary elements in poetry, like capitalization and punctuation. His arguments are clearly reflected in these words: "… one of the first things I wanted to do was to distance poetry from prose and from the cadence of the sentimental ´rhyme.´ The simplest way to do that is to take away the punctuation and capitalization." *(Taken from Devour. Art and Lit Canada Magazine. Issue 003. Of Princes and Kings and Other Things – An Illustrated Interview with Brian T. W. Way)*

Curiosity led me to his style – propounded by classic and contemporary poets, one of which I reviewed in my first book, Bruce Kauffman *(Read In a Fragile Moment: A Landscape of Canadian Poetry. Hidden Brook Press, 2020)* – and to trying to see through the proposals he made. The book's title emerges form his conceptions of what *redirection* stands for: "… the unending search into things that you find the writing that you do, right? The journey leads to the journey. One redirection to another." Way defends the notion of poetry as constant testing, experimenting: "In some sense, a poem is like a scientific experiment – it's an attempt to come to some understanding of the universe as it unfolds." *(Idem previous quotations)*

His "theses" being valid, I entered both his "other poems" and his Canadian sonnets. In *redirection: the prime sonnets and other poems*, we will find high-quality poetry, sprinkled with humor, wit and solid evidence of Way's erudition "… to unearth the essence of what… he has to say, to find those divine nuggets that were somehow vital in… creation and extract as much as… he can from them." *(Idem previous quotations)*

The opening poem, "redirection," is therefore revolutionary and consistent with his radical "no-caps-no-puncts" position that so reminds me of email register that is fast, concrete without giving up understandability! The poem begins with a rhetorical question which is answered in-text anyway. Play on words shows in the "i"-"eye" combination ("is the transforming of i into eye"). In presenting his poem, Way regales us fine imagery he has not relinquished, and knows well how to handle with versatility and that innate Canadian nexus with nature. He finds and reveals true metaphors and personifications: "… the forensics of autumn every absence / and finding in the metaphor that remains a galaxy / autumn the honestest season / where the pure tree stands naked…" These are wonderful images strung together praising the "honesty" of the season, perceiving and helping us perceive too the significance of metaphor.

On a philosophical chord, this poem is about change, about the grand cycles of life set in space and time: "the precise willability to move back and forth / in space time form mood / to return to seed & emerge return & emerge / again & again…" Alongside, movement – Way's term is *redirection* – defining our lives, an allusion of reincarnation where autumn is the fulcrum: "soul becoming root tree zygote / autumn held in every pulse / a price a human price surely / but alive / in the only way to be scavenged in this mortal season…"

I see Purdy in this poem's perspective of life and the human aspect linked to universal occurrences. I am certain Way will approve of my venturing to compare him to Purdy, as he stated in his *Devour* interview that we must "… just read everything that's been written. And observe your world and write, write, write." *(Idem previous quotations)* Way has been doing that since he was a little child, reading, observing, learning, writing – and teaching! The last lines are prophetic in their own weight and right: "… engraving on a profane canvas / the invisible image of the visible thing" Way plays with words and meanings across his whole poem.

His skill to do that has rendered to this poem, and many others, special qualities that are worth-commenting. Let's take "the poppy," for example, where Way continues to be an insightful observant of nature – and solemn remembrance – as he elaborates on the significance a poppy has. There is an obvious allusion to the showy plant and its "role" within November, Remembrance Day, as its shape and colour led people to wear a pin resembling it in memory of all of those who died particularly in World Wars I and II: "the poppy fits november / where the cold winds play." The way the poet structures the poem and the noticeable rhymed patterns in the stanzas are highly suggestive of the word's second entry meaning, that of "tuneful and immediately appealing" *(Taken from Digital Babylon, Concise Oxford English Dictionary).*

This arrangement is in line with the very mood of the piece: Way opens and closes the poem with the same two lines, adding an extra musicality to it – its *tuneful* touch. There is gravitas in remembering yet also an added rhythm to the poem – and life – where the poem flows easily bringing colour to the forefront.

Way grants symbolism to each hue: "the red stands for blood / and the sacrifice made // the black is for sorrow / to remember and pray // once green was for hope…" Way is very insistent on the remembrance and religious side of his poem, as we must look back and never forget: "… the sacrifice made; remember and pray…" and that we must look into the future for "hope," sometimes fading as much as the custom… He is also concerned with historic facts in a critical attitude towards life in personal, ethical and commemorative terms.

A pleasant mixture of feelings arises as we read "to see the queen." The poem unfolds in rhyming patterns that are achieved by applying too an expressive means of the language called "stylistic inversion" where the poet changes the typical English syntactical format to assist rhythm and rhyme without compromising content. As I. R. Galperin says: (inversion) "… is one of the forms of what are known as emphatic constructions." *(Taken from Stylistics, 1981, Moscow Vyssaja Skola, by I. R. Galperin)* The last stanza's second line is a good example: "so please do not think too ill of me / **if ever aloof or distant i seem** / for once you know when i was young / i went to see the queen"

Way examines with tones of reverence, humor, bits of irony and a narrative style, the historic relevance of the Queen's visit and its impact on a young child, plus the ramifications stemming from such an experience: "it was her first visit to Canada / and i was so young and lean / but ive never forgot that merry day / when i went to see the queen // then two mounties clipped to attention / and a black limo from the gates careened / and all the people cheered and waved / as the car shot past with the queen / we rode the bus back into town / and had a lunch of biscuit and beans"

Finally, the last stanza, already mentioned in the paragraph before the previous one, where Way resorts to a pinch of humor in how "aloof" one might turn after having been a *quick* witness to the Queen's visit to Canada. Aloofness, how I see it, might have to do with ambivalent feelings of disappointment and excitement inside the child, who only caught a glimpse at the queen, an abrupt "car-shot-past-with-the-queen" impression.

As a follower of Shakespeare and many other great English poets, I welcomed an allusion to William Wordsworth's line in his poem "She Dwelt Among the Untrodden Ways": "… the difference to me!" Way presents a contemporary variation: "now many times throughout my life / ive wondered what it means / moments like this that we never forget / when we venture to see the queen // **and o the difference its made in me** / im sure it has it seems / in how ive come to see the world / having been to see the queen"

A piece that amuses for its simple, dialogic form is "prehistoric literary note." There is much irony, stylistically speaking, in this poem, starting with the contrasted language used in the very title ("literary note") and in the last line ("dinosaur shit"): a superb employment of both neutral, standard language and special colloquial language respectively to accentuate the concept of humor, irony and real message embedded in the second (last) stanza: the speaker regrets having eaten the plum not because he felt any qualms but because it was hard like "dinosaur shit"!

The use of such vulgar words, or vulgarisms, is avoided in formal, literary style. Nonetheless, authors have used them to attain certain degrees of informality and actual colouring of the situation depicted in their work. I. R. Galperin refers to their use today: "... in modern fiction these words have gained legitimacy." *(Taken from Stylistics, 1981, Moscow Vyssaja Skola, by I. R. Galperin)* So have they in poetry, skillfully and appropriately controlled by an expert poet like Way, of course.

I know of tall Cuban poets who have included them in their poems. Carilda Oliver Labra, for example, in her poem "Te borraré con una esponja de vinagre" uses a vulgar word, *whore*, to close her last stanza: "Te borraré con juegos inocentes, / con la vida o la muerte; / ¡aunque me vuelva monja o me haga *puta*!"[6] This is a strong ending the poet reaches in the end from an in crescendo exposition of arguments where that word is, contextually, most fitting. Way himself is aware of the pertinence of a word in the right context: "Always the key, the right word in the right places..." *(Idem previous quotations)*

Way's rich poetic texture leads us to other realistic, "sensually" meditative poems like "middle ages." The poet introduces attractive figurative speech into the interesting setting he proposes: "... in the shaft of moon through the flower stained curtains / like some articulated movement in the national ballet / the dark haired woman and i make love..."

He gives prominence to the act of making love and its remarkable power to reveal meanings for us in such ecstatic moments: "just knowing that we have solved / in the vacant smile of the pale moons light / the riddle of age and our dying" The phrase "...the vacant smile of the pale moons light" is evocative of peace, fulfillment and success. I reminded me of a poem I wrote also about lovemaking, "Awake," where I finish: "pause bodies sated smiles of fullness / souls now lighter than air. / And awake." *(Taken from This Pulse of Life, These Words I Found. Hidden Brook Press, 2021)*

Being a professor, I was touched by "a prayer for my students." Way speaks of "... teaching in five long decades, nearly forty years / forty years and ten thousand students" I have been teaching for thirty-two years and Way has made me recall the same things he expresses in his "prayer" The last lines feel so near my own reality, my own experience: "... but they are always fifteen / keeping us young and making us grow old / at the same time, i suppose"

The poem I chose to translate and include in The Ambassador 15 was "prologue." This is one of the prime sonnets Way contributes. Somehow, Purdy was also present in

---

[6] Carilda Oliver Labra is one of the highest representatives of Cuban poetry. She was featured as guest poet in The Ambassador 09. She was awarded the National Poetry Award in 1950. Her vast poetic production has been widely acclaimed. In 1997 she received the National Literary Award, the highest distinction bestowed by the Ministry of Culture of the Republic of Cuba. The poem's title is "I will erase you with a vinegar sponge." The lines read: "I will erase you with innocent games, / with life or death; / I don't care if I have to become a nun or a whore!"

my readings of this piece. Way gives us "rugged hawk that carves adamant across the big sky / and scatters the primal jack along its chiselled lakes / arcanum of diamond and nickel and atomic gold / provider of loam, lumber and homestead, of port and grave / chondrite in timeless mime" to present the land, formidable, ancient. Keen and in love, the poet is mesmerized by what he sees.

We notice the will to "seek some mental clearing and try to understand," evident in Purdy's poetry. Way talks about "... children at play wrap dark stones inside pressed snowballs / and cast them like coureurs errant across the stoic land / against the infinite finite of this absurd bush the still / loon calls / as we seek some mental clearing and try to understand"

This is Brian T. W. Way in a few poems I chose for commenting. In her review for the book, Hannah Renglich states: "Way's comfort and fluidity in many poetic styles, tones, and voices makes for a volume with variety enough to satisfy even the hungriest of poetic appetites." *(Taken from Press release and Onix information. Hidden Brook Press)*

I agree: Way´s style is varied, flexible, plentiful in texture and feeling, daring, piercing, critical and revelatory. Way knows his *way* around in writing, blending to the point of excellence academicism and colloquialism. In reading his book, I revisited my world-view, my way to look at things and my understanding of poetry. My reader's *poetic appetite* was sated. Thank you, Brian.

Keeping Life Alive with Stella Body Comments on Some of her Poems in *Keeping the Earth Alive*

(Poetry and Art) (2005) Hidden Brook Press. Canada

On Friday 17th, 2020, I had special visitors from Canada: a letter and three packages. Books traveled all the way to me from my dear friends James Deahl and Norma West Linder to enrich my fully-Canadian bookshelf. A newcomer, poet Stella Body, knocked at my door, my life and my spirit with a warm letter, a kind request I could not refuse and a poetry book.

I had read about Stella's *Keeping the Earth Alive* in the Canada Cuba Literary Alliance flagship magazine, The Ambassador 03, published in 2005, where Theresa E. Maguire-Garber, B. Comm., C.M.A CAO / Secretary Treasurer Conservation Halton, was quoted in saying the book was "… a wonderful collection of touching and thought provoking poems by Stella Body, this book has a strong and positive message about protecting the natural environment…"

It must be clarified that *Keeping the Earth Alive* is a book of poetry by Stella Body and art by well-known artist Robert Bateman. My review focuses on the poetry part; however, I can go as far as saying, from a layman's point of view, that Bateman impresses the eye with his spectacular work. Compelling images and fine poetry come together in sheer harmony and turn this book into a jewel of vision and imagery. The book's theme and the fact that Body was born in Africa, made me remember the classic film *Out of Africa.*

The poetry part contains seven sections. The opening poem, "Keepsakes," (Section 1) dedicated to Bateman, the contributing artist in the book, takes us down paths of reflection. Reading the first stanza, I thought it would be fantastic if we could keep the tradition of saving lockets, "Two hundred years ago, / a woman would save / a locket" instead of having to save our earth: "Now it's the earth / that's slipping away too soon…" The "too soon" echoed hard in my ears for its warning call, its ominous message: earth might die long before she is naturally due; and we are the guilty ones.

In an essay I wrote about April Bulmer *(Read here A Communion of Spirituality in April Bulmer. An Appraisal of Two of her Poems in Beyond the Seventh Morning (Poetry) (2013) SandCrab Books. Canada, in this same book)*, I commended her committed poetry and made reference to a video downloaded from the Web that I have used in my lessons, *Create a Different World (Taken from #CreateADifferentWorld)*, where a girl of aboriginal descent warns in poignant words of our indolence towards nature: "… and now we hear of animals and plants going extinct every day, vanishing forever… If you don't know how to fix it, please stop breaking it..." *(Taken from #CreateADifferentWorld)* Body's poetry, alongside Bateman's art, is a welcome expression of human efforts to overturn the situation, so vibrantly reflected in the girl's words.

Body is aware that "we all feel it" and makes a sad statement when she claims that "It's hard to know what to save, / what to try to keep…" The poet clings to hope when she says "Perhaps each of us will spend the last years / learning new ways to love her, / … so her song might live a short while longer."

It is reassuring to know that there are many poets – and artists – worried about these environmental problems. The Ambassador 15 published poems dedicated to earth by Cuban and Canadian poets. Adela González-Longoria Escalona, for example, wrote in her poem "The Land Weeps": "The land weeps, / Its entrails tremble… // The green fields miss their morning dew. / In spring time the landscape dies, / The blue sky is a shroud of black clouds…" and she closes her piece saying: "Where are we headed to? / A strong cry invades the earth, / It echoes over and over: / Humanity, wake up!!!!! / Save our planet!!!!!!!"

In evocative wording, Body also appeals to conscience. She gives prominence to little spiritual things, exemplified through Arabella who is "A woman I know." The poet says Arabella "loves the shape of a small glass ellipse. / She'll hold one in her palm – a blue orb / then share it with you, still warm." There is so much symbolism in these lines, warmth found "As you move through her house, you'll find them / in all the cherished places; they glow like small eggs / gentle as the earth / that still cradles them." This is a significant stanza in the poem, leading to the poet's acknowledgement of Robert Bateman.

The last four stanzas from "Late…" to "… and fell" speak of what the artist achieves as a saving mechanism, a necessary self-appointed guardian, his artistic horn being sounded loud and clear by him – and the poet – calling mankind to see the urgency of what is happening and the need to save our planet, its beauty, its life – our lives.

The lines "Slowly, he let the wind seize him, flay from him / each thought, each feeling" appear as a transformational moment in the man when he starts to blend with the earth as we move into the next stanza: "until the earth took up his being and whirled him… / deep into the blue love shimmer / she spins to keep us here…" Planet and man become one as he understands earth's "role," her spinning "to keep us here." Then, this maelstrom of feeling and emotion and fusion render offspring: "We have the brushstrokes / that scattered and fell." "Their book serves that earth, which is our world." These are words by Russell Brown taken from the book's back-cover comments. Brown points out the utility of the book and its import to awaken people.

Section 2 gave me a moving poem, "Light's story." She says that "In the room… ("I visit an art gallery") "… the colours mingle." As a reader, I feel her thoughts mingle too, as the painters´ work make her go back to her son: "… the gentle work / of the hand //

made me think / of my young son – / how he offers / what he's made, / *Look, this is a tree / Look, this is the sun.*"

As the poet describes the scenes in her innocent child's work, I saw hope everywhere in his tree and his sun: "… the happy accident / of being alive / among leaves, among sun-nourished, breathing things; / his shapes glow with it." Hope and more hope, light and more light surrounding Body's proposal of poems-notions-warnings.

Her references to Manet, Renoir, Cezanne, especially her constant allusions to light (in this poem and in many others in her book) reminded me of another fine Canadian poet and environmentalist, Katherine L. Gordon, whom I wrote about in a previous review book. About Gordon I said: "Light defines this poem and her poetry as a whole. Light explains her landscapes setting them on fire or lighting them up in mild shimmers. Light is ever present… The notion of light in Gordon transcends the boundary of her poems…" *(Read In a Fragile Moment: A Landscape of Canadian Poetry. Hidden Brook Press, 2020)*

I am taking my words about Gordon and rechanneling them in relation to Stella Body. She speaks of "light on water, light among leaves / chlorophyll light, light loving the body." Here the poet has masterfully turned an expressive means of the language, repetition *("An emphasis necessary to fix the attention of the reader on the key-word of the utterance" I. R. Galperin. Stylistics. Moscow Vyssaja Skola. 1981)*, into a versatile stylistic device.

This is also present in light-related words in the poem: "the colours mingle," "hues," "sun-nourished" and "shapes glow…" Thus, both colour and light are vital for the poet. She connects life and earth and their chromatic diversity, one that we must learn from and strive to keep alive, shining. Revelation arrives for the poet in first-class metaphorical lines: "I begin to see… // how we were cradled in the daily rhythms / of earth's love for the sun, / renewed by their passion…" The last lines warn us again: there will be no *us* at all if there is no earth in the future, our common home: "the lyric of how we are / as long as the earth still lives"

A lover of natural scenery and much aware of how well Canadian poets write about them, I enjoyed "Spring arrives along Sixteen-Mile Creek" in Section 3. Nature and spectacular sights are center stage in this piece. The poet starts with an aerial view: "Seen from above / the long, wide loop of the creek…"

The creek is starring figure and inspiration for Body, who incorporates human presence briefly, giving prominence to the beauty before her: "… and with each step we are lowered / into the heart of where water sings." She magnifies the grandeur of place and season: "Last week we stood here, numbed by silence / and the cold, a door of iron / closed over us."

The previous lines were reminiscent of another Canadian poet who has written about winter, Henry Beissel, and his lines "… winter's wild and murderous hordes. / Blizzards pack every niche and crevice / and stop at nothing short of walls…" *(Taken from Beissel's poem "winter" in Tamaracks: Canadian Poetry for the 21st Century. Edited by James Deahl. Lummox Press. San Pedro, California. 2018)*

Body closes her poem heralding the arrival of Spring and showing joy in human hearts: "Now, all around, small sounds melt the air, kindling / our ears, our skin, our blood. / the ice releases, stirs… this long winter / loosens, / might break away."

Section 4 presented me with one particularly heart-moving poem, "Sea of leaves." Imagery overflows this piece full of symbols and mysticism enveloping us as we read. The first stanza conquers me: "I wheel my smallest child / into the forest, watch his eyes / fill with a drench of green stars…"

The poem is enlightening in many ways and suggestive of an intimacy where nature and human find the perfect bond tenderly described by Body: "… and his feet lift, buoyed by light, bathed / as the leaves rush and turn // over and over he reaches / to catch the constellations…."

We learn of reverence to nature and joy in a mother who "offers" her son to it, sees her son accept it and nature accept him: "… rocking his infant body, small craft / adrift in the trees´ high sailing motion…" The poet mixes in fluent, carried away: "My thoughts move also, into a far-reaching cycle… / that takes me away / to where the rhythms begin: / tidal thinking, that wind or water finds…"

Body brings to scene metaphors activating not only eyes but also ears: letters and sounds are put to work to charm the reader/listener: "Each moving tree / is a bell / signalling the ellipse, telling and retelling / the form of what holds them." Somehow, the recurrent presence of "ll" in the combinatory vowel context ("e" in "bell," "i," "a" and "e" in "signalling," "ellipse," "telling" and "retelling) ignited by the initial metaphor, "Each moving tree / is a bell," reaches me in onomatopoeic rings.

Body closes this wonderful poem proposing/disclosing the cycle of motherhood (Body is a mother, nature is a mother too), the poet trusts nature as she sees that "my son never cries – / he knows he is loved / by the rhythms; / what we all know as mother: / the sway / of the earth's shape."

"Silent, she burns" (Section 5) is another striking poem. I see the burning reference as a symbol for life. Body tells us at the beginning: "Silent, she burns in her father's arms… this gentle air / not enough to dim / the inchoate fires of which she is made." In the second stanza, the poet uses a metaphorical expression, "Her head is a breathing coal / he can barely touch," adding strength to the lines, rounded off by "singed by its fervour, the dark contained energy / of her thought."

I *need* to quote the closing stanza of a poem I published in The Ambassador 15, "Boon," so readers can have an idea of Body's impact on me with her next stanza. I said: "A tiny thing, a thrill! / the joyful Heavens smile, / her presence here to fill / our lives for quite a while!" I wrote it when my child was born. The third stanza in Body's poem is hyperbolic and vividly descriptive of the contrast between the child's physical smallness and her meaningful presence in the parents´ lives: "Tiny, she consumes space: / all this room, all our light and thought / rush to her..." I thought too of Lord Byron's "… And all that's best of dark and bright / Meet in her aspect and her eyes" gently applied to a baby girl.

The last stanza embodies the feelings surging in parents at the miracle of birth: "… our random lives / that found their way, somehow / into her blood…" It is the one-time crossing labyrinths of fate and DNA crystallizing in a tiny new being.

I must comply with the tyrannical dictations of space and time and bring my comments to closure with Body's final piece, "Wild Light," in Section 7. Russell Brown said that the book "teaches us to see her (the earth) intensely–as with the fresh eyes of a new lover…" *(Idem, previous quotation by Brown).* This is what the poem is about, besides its adherence to the power of light, a feature I mentioned earlier in my review.

There is intensity in the lines, "This wild light / that leaps into Canada's leaves… / is energy – / it whoops like the tropics" We pick expectation and anticipation: "as though Africa found a crack in the earth / and came funneling through…" Africa is very present in Body, weighing on her thoughts, feelings, emotions, fears of losing her home-earth, as tumultuous as the very lines in the poem: "huge white clouds cannonading, / the blue pilot sky / grinning too wide, moving to fast – // the birds seem deranged, catapulting themselves; / the river swells to a green male monster…"

The whirlpool of images grows in crescendo to end swiftly in the last stanza. No matter what purposes Body poured onto her poem and this last stanza, I dare think the "passion" she refers to is in line with her (and Bateman's) attitude towards what may befall unless we take a stand, energetic one, before "it is too late," as Brown states. Body closes with: "this wild light / the leap of our blood / tells us / the darkness that will follow / is passion."

This is an excellent finish for both poem and book. Poet Tracy Lynn Repchuk said that *Keeping the Earth Alive* is "… a captivating voyage along landscapes and fragile environments… I have heard the words, and I encourage you to listen." *(Taken from the book's back-cover comments)* My full support to these words by Repchuk: We must listen, we must watch, we must stand and do something to keep life alive as Stella Body and Robert Bateman summon us to. Thank you, Stella (and Robert).

Hallmarks of a Poet´s Heart
A Review of Some Poems from Nancy M. Bell´s *Touchstone*

(Poetry) (2015) Nancy M. Bell. The United States of America

Fine poems continue to flow into my home these Cuban winter days. Welcome and warm, they capture my attention as Canadian poetry has always done. This time they come from an Albertan, Nancy M. Bell.

Her book is a reminder of how connected we are to the essences of life and points at our origins, our guiding principles, our salvation. It is a book about, with and for love. It exudes gratefulness and wholeheartedness from the very first proposal, "Touchstone," to its last poem, "Lost in the Choices."

There is an all-embracing, winning simplicity in the opening lines of the first poem, "We are linked by love / You and I," to present the readers the why of the poet´s writing, the depth achieved in the next lines and where she is leading us to. She skillfully and creatively resorts to a classic expressive means in the language, metaphors, to convey her message: "You have been… / My anchor in the stormy seas / My safe rock on which to stand… // The keeper of the wings of my spirit… / Touchstone of my soul…"

The poem closes with a hyperbole to accentuate the meaningfulness of her ideas she is sharing with us: "Transcending even the distance of death."

The second poem, "Tide," speaks of the poet´s direct, childlike involvement with nature: "Squatting on the rocks in the bay / I watch the tide come in." Patience surfaces through the lines, "Little trickle by little trickle / Filling the tiny spaces…," and reflection follows: ""'Each tiny wave a part of the whole…"

Bell connects nature with the human condition in the last stanza using a versatile expressive means, simile: The tide is coming in / Sliding up the shore / Sure and steady as mothers love." She is able to link sureness and steadiness of the ever-lapping sea with love, a leitmotif in her creation.

Song-like and merry, auspicious of gay colours and bustling life is "Spring," third poem in the book. Its musicality is achieved thanks to different language tools. The first one, parallel construction, understood as "… identical, or similar, syntactical structure in two or more sentences or parts of a sentence in close succession." *(Taken from Stylistics, 1981, Moscow Vyssaja Skola, by I. R. Galperin)* is seen in the repeated use of the -ing verbal ending in all three stanzas. As Galperin states, "Parallel constructions are often backed by repetition of words…" and "most frequently used in enumeration…" *(idem previous quotation)*, we encounter repetition in "Little people talking / Little people singing" and enumeration supported too by polysyndeton (use of the conjunction *and*) in "Trees and bulrush… / Grass and flowers… / Life and love… / Time and wars…"

All these devices in the language aid the poet to put poem, situation and season in context. In her enumeration, she moves from nature ("Trees and bulrush… / Grass and flowers…") to objective reality and/or abstractions ("Life and love… / Time…"). The phrase "… wars forgotten" reflects the poet´s hopeful claim for peace, away from human-provoked, devastating events like wars.

Finally, Bell closes her poem with a capital SPRING. Capitalization is also a strong mechanism to accentuate the season´s beauty and propitiousness. This aspect is constant in her production, as is masterfully revealed in another poem, "Miracle."

Nature-related poems abound in this book. Bell has the gift of being able to observe, decode and describe, in a synchronization of metaphorical lines, shapes, colours – hues – movement and sounds in, for example, "Musing on a June Afternoon": "On this blue and green day… / The swallows dive above the daisies / The butterflies play below / A soft breeze cuddles the lilacs… // … breathe the crystalline star music of the night… // And the finches sing… / And a hawk floats on the wind…"

The poet adds images and sounds in a succession of well-chosen words, an element that repeats in the next poem, "Autumn Foreshadow." Besides, from the very title of this poem, the writer invites us to the happy realization and full anticipation of autumn.

The Canada Cuba Literary Alliance´s flagship magazine, The Ambassador, issued its sixteenth volume, dedicated to the elements. Many poets from Canada and Cuba converged in a celebration of rain from their perspectives, as Bell does in her poem "Rain." Quite reflective – and reflecting the author´s innermost thoughts – it addresses in just ten calm, philosophical, assuming, propounding lines the notion of it all coming back to nature. Rain has been felt and sung by numberless poets and singers. She admits the inevitability of her death as an antithesis of the eternal character of nature: "The rain will always be / Always the same / And eons from now… / The rain will still fall." Nature is the "endurer" outliving the humankind: "The rain will still fall… / But I will no longer be… / … no one will care… / They will only know / That the rain still falls."

Mystique and evocations garland the next poem under analysis, "Dancing in the Moon." The alert readers will immediately pick a wafting sensuality in its lines: "On the beams that slant across the sill / My ancient lover comes riding // The tiny part of me who remembers still / Rises to dance in the moonlight." Nature – the moon – is an accomplice, an excuse, a catalyst of kindled memories, "Memories flood through me, wild and strong… / In a wild whirl of remembrance;" of a suggestive dance, "And the steps of the dance in the moonlight."

Bell says that "I search for the words / But they have no place in this time;" however, a stirring poem "Shining like motes of brighter light," filled with heartfelt words, has come to life.

I was impressed by a four-line poem entitled "Miracle." Haiku-like compact, concise and to-the-point, this piece soul-nourishes due to its power to move us, its sheer sense of renewal and unfailing, blooming expectation for what is splendorous and positive: "I have watched it every year…" The poet surrenders to the cycles of the seasons, welcomes spring and admits, tenderly and caught in the sensations of its ageless comeback, what it does to her spirit: "Yet each time I cannot / Help but wonder / At the miracle of Spring."

As I said at the beginning, this is a book of love. Being so, I finish my comments with one more fine piece, "Still in Love." This is a poem filled with warmth and a resolution reaching out to us in lines of pleasant reading. Memories, endurance, longing and LOVE come to us in simple wording, "I am in love still / With the happiness we shared / And the smiles we gave each other…," which is crafted with the heart.

Bell has a gift: she is able to pour out words with an emphatic and empathic tone that catches the reader as she turns concrete occurrences and a great love into an ever-lasting experience: "The memory of what we had / And what we were to each other… // With the summer days we lived together / And the love we shared."

When Nancy Bell sent me her books (*Touchstone* and *Through This Door*) encouraged by Canadian poet James Deahl, she did not ask me to write these comments. But her poetry is a hallmark for me, one that defines and rejoices in immersion, memories, life and love. How could I not feel the urge to write them? Thank you, Nancy.

Reading, Listening to and Writing about John Tyndall´s Poetry Comments on Some of his Poems in *Listen to People*

(Poetry) (2020) Hidden Brook Press. Canada

Canada Cuba Literary Alliance Founding President, Richard Marvin Grove (Tai), continues to forward and/or bring me books and books of Canadian poetry in his generous wish to help me with my writing. I wonder if I can already claim to own the largest private Canadian poetry collection in my country.

One of such treasured presents is *Listen to People*, by John Tyndall. The book is divided in three sections, inclusive of fifteen poems each. The first section opens with "White Oxfords," a tribute poem to his father dexterously combining monologue and retrospective dialogue in a piece that gets feedback from the poet´s memories. This integration of monologue and dialogue recurs in many of the poems.

Tyndall is a qualified heir of the best Canadian tradition of writing about remembrances and family, an aspect I explained in a section I have in The Envoy, the CCLA newsletter, called "A Word About." It is devoted to introduce Canadian poets I have read. In The Envoy 093, November 2019, I summarized some of the most outstanding characteristics of Canadian poets: "Among the many generalizations I can make out of reading… Canadian poets who have entered my life (deep connection to the land; identification with nature and wild life; a rooted sense of belonging to Canadian geography…), some are particularly salient and heart-warming to me: their commitment to family and values… In addition are the poets´ reminiscences of childhood and their recollection of friends and friendship."

"White Oxfords" shows us a sentient poet narrating his experiences linked to his father´s doings: "The last time I saw / my father alive / he was pilgrim / through his ninety years / sheltering under / Dover radar station / from German shelling / with women operators / and a bottle of whisky…"

Realistic and resonant, Tyndall starts to reveal right here why he entitled his book Listen to People. He is listening to his father´s voice: "he looked in my eyes / and warned You've got / to return home now / then he threw off / his hospital gown / and shouted Get me / my white oxfords…"

His father´s life, as it was, is depicted with direct and poetic (similes, for example) language: "Sometimes he'd / react that way / to sedatives / other nights he'd… / gaze at car-light / flowing upon the ceiling / like rainfall on glass / be mesmerized by red / smoke-detector flash / like an ambulance signal…"

Sharp in his descriptions, the poet gives us the sad final moments: "The last time I saw my father / his eyes had been / shut an hour already / although his mouth / gaped open / so I cupped his / still-warm chin / in my hand / trying to close it…"

Despite the sadness of the moment, Tyndall offers a less painful, tender coda to his poem: "… when his lips / parted they made / the minute sound / I'd heard countless / times just before / he'd begin to speak / saying perhaps his / signature Goodbye / Lots of love"

Other poems that pay tribute to family and family-related stories are "Falling Down: Father Tells Us": "Your great-great-uncle / Black Jack Tyndall / was an innkeeper / over in Lion's Head / and after serving customers / in his pub, serving them / and drinking himself / falling-down drunk…," "Miscreant," which approaches his mother´s side, wars and times brought into the poems´ plots to chronicle and place in context his ancestry: "On my mother's / side of the family / great-great-great-grandfather / Ludwig Wideman / fought with General Brock / during the War of 1812," "Ode to an Uncle": "then / everything is family / the man at the tiller / of his sailboat, my uncle / John Murray Allan Tyndall / takes us out of Midland / into Georgian Bay waters…" and many others.

"Keepers" is a poem of generational convergence where the poet time-travels from his early recollections of his father´s suggestions, "For years my father / urged me to discover / Jones Falls, boyhood / playground for him…," to his own life, "Now in Summer heat / my love and I hike / to the waterfall…," and to his offspring: "I must tell our son / to play here where / many bloodlines / have played / and become one / of the keepers / of flames and wind / and sand and falls"

I sense a proud nostalgia in the last lines. The poet is clear that he is handing not just memories down to his son but also a condition of belonging, of coming from a root, an origin, all of which once stood on the place where he plays now. As a nicely penned closer, the poet hopes – somehow yearns – his son symbolically becomes the keeper of the elements: "…flames and wind / and sand and falls"

The second section is a poet´s journey through pain and hope, seasoned with bits of irony and humor in the way he handles language. Especially salient is the poem that entitles the section as well, "Undetermined Significance." The poet is so intent on expressing his feelings that he resorts to the so-called obscene words. As I have commented in other essays, the use of such vulgar words, or vulgarisms, is avoided in formal, literary style. Nonetheless, authors have used them to attain certain degrees of informality and actual colouring of the situation depicted in their work. I. R. Galperin refers to their use today: "… in modern fiction these words have gained legitimacy." *(Taken from Stylistics, 1981, Moscow Vyssaja Skola, by I. R. Galperin).* Tyndall makes pertinent, intentional use of these words to mirror the oral variety of language in the poem.

Finally, in section three, poem "Tattered," Tyndall honors friendship, another theme treated by Canadian poets. I strongly believe his last words in the poem disclose his poetic stance and purpose in his writing: "I am ever sentimental / I am yet using, / washing / drying a towel my parents / received for their wedding / at the war's end and / as I cherish their memory / so I cherish Maureen's / my heart both tattered / and strong"

Another particularly appealing poem to me is "The First Time Alice Munro Asked Me a Question." Tyndall has managed to gather in this book family, friends, figures of renown, giving them a privileged treatment and a place in both his heart and his poetry.

A visit to the Canadian poetdom must include a stopover at John Tyndall´s work. We have to read, listen to and learn from this family/self/friends portrait. We will explore and find many of the landmarks of Canadian poetry and writing in general. Thank you, John.

Ars Longa, Poetry Eternal
Comments on John Di Leonardo´s
Conditions of Desire

(Poetry) (2018) Hidden Brook Press. Canada

In the weeks before the pandemic expansion of the virus scourging the world, the Canada Cuba Literary Alliance (CCLA) Founding President, Richard Grove, forwarded me a stock of first-rate books published by Hidden Brook Press (HBP), some of them under the John B. Lee Signature Series. To my honor and delight, many of the authors are poets I reviewed in my book *In a Fragile Moment: A Landscape of Canadian Poetry* (HBP, 2020) and in this second volume we are presenting now.

I wrote an essay about a poet who was not in my previous book, John Tyndall *(See here Reading, Listening to and Writing about John Tyndall´s Poetry. Comments on Some of his Poems in Listen to People (Poetry) (2020) Hidden Brook Press. Canada)*, and this essay on John Di Leonardo, who was not in my first book either. I was truly attracted to the profound meaningfulness of their poetry and what it made me feel and write.

The more I read Di Leonardo, the more I saw distinct elements in the poet in manners that motivated me to review his book. John B. Lee´s introductory words to it were helpful in many points I will try to reveal here. In a sad context of sickness and death, culture comes to us to soothe our bodies, bring a bit of comfort to our souls and necessary hope to our lives.

I remember now, amidst so much pain and so many deaths, what I wrote for The Envoy 84 (CCLA digital newsletter), a month after the tragic airplane crash in Havana where many Cubans and foreigners lost their lives, "… we seek peace and enlightenment reading… poetry and prose… The deep riddles of life and death must be decrypted by looking for and holding on to spiritual healing, and sheltering in human sympathies and love… let´s try to turn then to less rending realms." *(Taken from The Envoy 084, June 2018).* Spiritual healing, human sympathy, hope and love are what we need. Faith, fortitude and *love in times of virus* (paraphrasing García Márquez´s book title, *Amor en los tiempos del cólera (Love in Times of Cholera)*) – is what we must find today to overcome this dark hour.

Di Leonardo offers his spirituality and aesthetics by exploring and evoking, unveiling and *connecting* in that sentient human drive to build, either with words or with images – or with the overlapping produce that results from blending both, as we have enjoyed in the works of John B. Lee and Richard Grove *(A Small Payback, Ode to Victoria Lake (Poetry and*

Photography) (2016) Hidden Brook Press, Canada), James Deahl and Richard Grove *(North of Belleville (Haiku and Photography) (2011) Hidden Brook Press, Canada)*, Stella Body and Robert Bateman *(Keeping the Earth Alive (Poetry and Art) (2005) Hidden Brook Press, Canada)*, the Bridges Series Books I, II, III, IV (Poetry and Art) (2011, 2013, 2017, 2018) by SandCrab Books, an imprint of Hidden Brook Press, etc.

However, Di Leonardo takes a novel step up: many poets do include in their poetry pieces inspired by paintings or other works of art but I had never read an entire book of poems dedicated to – or stemming from – them. He writes inspired by images, he turns into poetics *what was already poetry*, as he lets us know opening his book with a quotation from Simonides of Ceos: "Painting is silent poetry; poetry is painting that speaks."

Well-known Canadian poet and professor, Antony Di Nardo, has wisely looked into and shed light on this notion too: "I often consider poetry as a form of visual art painted with words. As varied as that world of art can be with paintings ranging from the representational to the abstract, so too poetry encompasses such variety. The surreal and the absurd in poetry can be as intellectually effective as a Dali or painting by Frida Kahlo. In my mind, Picasso's *Guernica* is an epic poem like no other, and there are poems by Ashbery I consider echoes of the finest cubist paintings. Such parallels are endless. The image often dominates a poem's aesthetics." *(Taken from Di Nardo´s review on a work-in-progress poetry book of mine, This Pulse of Life, These Words I Found)*

Thus Di Leonardo repaints, in word form, the works of art he so admires. He engages in ingenious labor and materializes a second "reading" – that is, a re-construal of a reality that had been interpreted before by a visual artist – this time with words. While I read his poetry book, I was crossing readings of Joseph Gold´s *The Story Species*, where this author voices concerns clearly spelling for me that Di Leonardo grants an "extra salvation" to the paintings he writes about. Consider Gold´s question in his book: "Why is it that if a painting is burned, it is gone forever, but a poem… can be memorized intact, unaltered and transmittable as long as a human brain retains it?" *(Taken from Joseph Gold´s The Story Species, 2002, Fitzhenry and Whiteside. Canada)* I couldn't help thinking about K. V. Skene´s evocations of "all things beautiful and old / and otherworldly…" in her poem "Notre Dame de Paris Brûle" *(Published in The Envoy 088, June 2019 after the Notre Dame fire)*. I couldn't help thinking about the Alexandria Library fire…

Therefore, through highly emotional (the poet has been touched by the paintings) information transfer (visual/pictorial/graphic), Di Leonardo "saves" them via a re-perpetuation process. He is more than experienced to do so because he is a graduate of McMaster University, where he earned an Honorary BA in Fine Arts, taught Visual Arts for thirty years, and is an artist who divides his time between writing, painting, and travel. Being an artist *and* a poet, he becomes, fortunately for us, perfect vessel and "medium" enraptured by beauty/meaning/impact, aesthetic-cognitive-affective stimuli, absorbing a painting and returning it to us in another code.

His fascination is best measured when we read comments by Canadian poets Malca Litovitz and Elana Wolff: "You can only write from the depth of an emotion if you've been there." *(Taken from an interview made by Elana Wolff to her friend and poet Malca Litovitz, included in their book Slow Dancing (section Duologue). Guernica Editions, 2008)* and their competent decoding of what happens when we read/write poetry: "Malca Litovitz said: "… the human soul needs poetry and that it will always be around and that it serves a real function in our psyche." *(Taken from Slow Dancing, Guernica Editions, 2008).* Elana Wolff stated that "a poem is not only a form of self-expression, it is the writer's way of bearing witness to the world in which he or she lives…" *(Taken from Implicate me, Guernica Editions, 2010)*

Litovitz and Wolff stress on the role of emotions, of those emotions felt deeply by the individual, and how poetry is a necessary spiritual repository and "exhaust valve." Di Leonardo writes *after* the paintings with heartfelt surrender to their aesthetic and nurturing worth.

Ponder John B. Lee´s introductory words to Di Leonardo´s *Conditions of Desire*: "For what we experience, what we remember, what we dream, what we imagine, there is a language that reifies and makes real and true both original experience and the secondary experience of the poem as written," or Di Leonardo´s Preface to his own book citing Henry David Thoreau: "It is not what you look at, but what you see."

Yes, Di Leonardo saw word-stories streaming from the paintings he was looking at. He creatively re-transformed them into reified written text, not only letting us see through his own eyes the paintings we don´t have before ours but also unfolding the endless story-telling possibilities each art piece evokes and waxes as a new *dual* result.

At this point, let´s examine two poems by Di Leonardo for exemplification. "Conditions of Desire" (which entitles the book too), inspired by Alex Colville's "Refrigerator," acrylic, 1977, shows that duality of result I referred to earlier: we see the painting and the ensuing story Di Leonardo skillfully knits out of it. A fragment will suffice:

"When you are gone
I pace kitchen tiles, roam living room walls
hunger for the stars in your eyes
nibble self pity in the blue flicker of a fridge door.
Among cold things, I whisper your name
in the sweetness of morning jams, evening fruits
and the Atlantic that draws me towards you.
When you are away
I stalk the cell under cuticle moons
until its notes ring me a moonlight sonata.
I sleepwalk horizons, tip-toe a collage
of love's smallest details."

We also notice it in "Reproduction", inspired by Sandro Botticelli's "Birth of Venus," tempera, 1486:

"You linger –
like a milk-skin model
on the largest shell
my best lit wall… / /
… Your placid glaze will end
when the classical toes
step on shore
turn to good wife
The glow
below your torrent of hair
rose shower
makes us ashamed
for not making beds
clearing dishes
sipping morning coffee…"

John B. Lee asks in his introduction: "And how then might a poet hope to express something of the original in a parallel text when the medium of the original is paint and canvas and the medium of the poem is language written for contemplation on the page?" Of course Lee is not questioning the probability of attaining such feat (in fact, Di Leonardo did find the *expression fulcrum*); Lee is quite aware of that and is walking more on the wonder-thread he wishes to rhetorically make us see and walk on. I believe that the key word in Lee´s question is *contemplation.*

In both cases, painting and written poem, we pause for contemplation – defined in the dictionary in what is for me, more than just an enumeration of meanings, a sequence of brain processes, "looking at; thinking about; meditation, deep thought." *(Taken from Babylon, Digital Dictionary)* – where hedonic-intellectual nexuses are sparkled through the eyes.

Yet the key answer lies probably in Di Leonardo´s own explanation in his Preface: "… elaborate description of the artwork… interpret, confront, inhabit, mediate, or simply use the visual elements as a springboard for the poet's imagination to take flight." Let´s cry *Eureka!* for Di Leonardo, who has succeeded in finding the "tools" needed to make the transference, tools which are duly sharpened by factors such as the poet´s preparation and sensitivity, the painting´s – and the painter´s – unique significance to him, and, voilà, the "conditions of desire" ignited to prompt the poet to write all these jewels.

The poems in the book transcend beyond the poet´s urge to put in words what was so indelibly suggestive and substantial to him, logical trigger and outcome if we consider his formative years as a visual artist and his poetic flair as well. They are in their own right fine pieces of poetry, superbly signed with well-thought-out expressive means and stylistic carvings.

Let´s visit four of them, beginning with the end lines of the previous poem, "Reproduction," where Di Leonardo embraces his acknowledgement of life´s richness and sighs about the mixed sensations stirred sentimentally, olfactorily – and figuratively in the end phrase, "the scent of land."

"… our lives reflecting
living warmth, the scent
of land"

"Tangoing," inspired by Fernando Botero's "Dancing Couple," oil, 1982, where we are swept by the exquisite depiction of "tango mood" and the atmosphere, elegantly heightened by metaphorical phrases. Enjoy the last stanza:

"… Should you smile
with every breathy pause
I will inhale such pirouettes of scented hair
our shadows swirl of daily cares
to measure time in scattered blooms
your moonlit eyes entranced
as each rose in bud awaits an autumn rain."

"Breakup," inspired by Salvador Dali's "Girl at Window," oil, 1925, where more imagery engulfs us and invites, sensually, through between-the-lines insinuations; word-stories hinted and masterfully elaborated upon by the poet, impressively reminiscent, as we read the whole poem, of Dali´s surrealistic brush:

"Stillness
leaning on a sill.
Your tousled hair
vocal with love
learns to wait
across a muted sea
where stirrings
aloud with song
are not depicted… //

... muzzy eyes
the palest stars //
yearn the moan
of a tender kiss
if not to live, at least
to whiten your silence"

"Nude," inspired by A. Maillol's "Île -de France," sculpture/Bronze, 1925, in which the poet innovatively gives us a pre-existing time, a pre-condition – a pre-story!, something/somewhere *that step comes from*! – by simply starting with "Then."

Let´s keep in mind that this particular poem comes not from a painting but from a sculpture, which adds a more "realistic" sensation, being a sculpture tridimensional. He magically blends two seemingly different, distant realities: human ("the softness of her step") and natural ("autumn leaves"). To work this out, he resorts to a simile: "transient *as* autumn leaves" (Italics are mine). Distant realities perception is sensed in the closing lines: "autumn leaves on sullen passersby." Let´s read the full poem:

"Then the softness of her step
turned bronze
transient as
autumn leaves
on sullen passersby"

Imbued with Di Leonardo´s mesmeric, accomplished poems I go back to my initial tenet in these comments, the distinct elements marking his work. The poet is able to intensely explore and passionately evoke, imaginatively unveil and concretely connect; he becomes a *double mediator* (from painting to poem, from poem to reader/indirect "spectator"); he confirms Ceos´s adage; he responds Lee´s questions; and he stands as a *sui generis* convinced curator of art by re-framing it into a new format as a symbolically salvaging act that reinforces the old say, *Ars Longa*, for poetry *too* is art represented in a parallel code system.

Furthermore, Di Leonardo brings us relief for Joseph Gold´s unsettling worries about paintings and poems, and bequeaths to us his legacy/understanding of painting from a broader perspective, which will last – allow me to cite Shakespeare´s Sonnet XVIII, "When in eternal lines to time thou grow'st, / So long as men can breathe, or eyes can see, / So long lives this, and this gives life to thee." – as we have now two versions of one reality, a visual and a written one.

One last comment on the broad spectrum of paintings (and sculpture) Di Leonardo has included in his homage. Ranging from the 15th to our 21st century – notably outstanding 19th and 20th century works – the paintings mirrored in the poems "at our disposal" evidence the poet´s thorough voyage through the plastic arts´ world and his connoisseurship. We must thank him for "poetically collecting" the pieces in one book.

The eternalizing quality and value of what Di Leonardo has done in writing these poems inspired by paintings is, nonetheless, best worded lyrically by William Wordsworth: "Poetry is the first and last of all knowledge – it is as immortal as the heart of man." *(Taken from Joseph Gold´s The Story Species, 2002, Fitzhenry and Whiteside. Canada).*

That is why I quoted Margaret Atwood to begin this book: ""The arts"–as we've come to term them–are not a frill. They are the heart of the matter, because they are about our hearts… A society without poetry and other arts would have broken its mirror and cut out its heart."

This is Di Leonardo´s contribution. Poetry *is* "the heart of the matter," it *is* eternal; it immortalizes us and what it depicts. Thank you, John.

Nothing Gone, Nothing Missing in Antony Di Nardo's *Gone/Missng*

(Poetry) (2020) Hidden Brook Press. Canada

In early 2020, my review book *In a Fragile Moment: A Landscape of Canadian Poetry* was published by Hidden Brook Press. It was a compilation of thirty-five essays on thirty-one fine Canadian poets and prose writers. One of them was the well-known poet Antony Di Nardo and his book *Skylight* (Ronsdale Press, 2018).

I was fortunate to have feedback from the poet when I sent him what I had written. His response to my emails and our exchange for a period of time was heart-warming and edifying for me as an essay writer.

Perhaps because he was so overflowingly generous in his words I quote here what he said to me: "… it's my third or fourth time reading your review (I read it out loud to my wife and she thought it was marvelous)… your insights, your responses… I'm pleased… Thank you, for writing what you wrote… It's very well written, very precise, your words well conceived and very well connected to my text. You're so easy to read and how you clarify my own work. Incisive, penetrating, so easy to follow… You understand the alchemy of my poetry. Thank you for taking the time to think about how I try to get it done—the poetry and its aesthetics. You clearly considered what happens when I put certain words in order… Thanks, Miguel, for this review. Thanks for reading SKYLIGHT like you did." *(Published with Antony´s permission in my review book´s Afterword)*

His email obviously made my day and encouraged me to keep on writing. Now with a tickling sensation Di Nardo and I would eventually meet – we had to. It did happen in January 2020 when the poet and his wife, Ann Nadin Di Nardo, a professional photographer, came to Cuba with the Canada Cuba Literary Alliance (CCLA) wave of "CCLAers" who visit Holguín every year, invited by its Founding President, Richard Marvin Grove (Tai), and his wife, Kim Grove. That winter they were accompanied by Canadian painter and poet Eva Kolacz, poet and professor Laurence Hutchman, and writer Donna Wootton.

Meeting Antony Di Nardo is an act of pleasure and learning, a lesson of life. He has the ability to intoxicate you with his high spirits, his cultivation, his word and winning style in reading his poetry aloud. His friendliness and kindness, his jovial deportment were a blessing to me. Like me he had been a professor and it surfaces when he stands up, holds a poem in his hand – his or someone else´s – and rather than just read it he acts it out. Words sound magically different in his readings.

When he was about to return home he made it very clear that they would return to Gibara, a dreamy village to the north-eastern part of eastern Cuba in Holguín Province, in 2021. This announcement led to making plans for their return, further involvement into visits to my university, lectures, talks, high-quality poetry reading performed by this special man, sharing again with us Cubans.

He left me a manuscript with poems he was working on and was meaning to publish. He asked me if I would have some free time to go over them and give him my opinion. I was surprised and honoured. So many experts back in Canada would have been pleased to offer their qualified views about his work but Antony chose me! How could I say no?

That is how *Gone/Missng* fell on my hands. The first bait was the title itself, the *i* missing in *Missng*. Apart from the interesting conjugation of Gone and Missing, I instantly found it attention-grabbing, at least for me, that the letter he chose was *i*; not any other. Was it because the "I" (the poet) in the poems takes a step backwards and recedes into the darkness of the gone and missing? Was it because Di Nardo poured himself out entirely leaving no word unsaid, no stone unturned to pay tribute to Susan Briscoe, whom he calls "a formidable poet and friend," thus remaining – seemingly – in the background and shifting highlights towards her?

Gone/Missng is an impressive book, one of homage to friendship and poetry, from the multi-visionary world-view of a poet who knows his craft and opens up here with a varied yet well-structured bandwidth of styles I noticed as I moved across the sixty-eight poems therein grouped in three sections.

A poet who lives fully and action-immersed, whose feelings and sensations bubble in and around him, explodes in and explores sentiments we humans cannot avoid: loneliness, deference, social criticism. Above all, he embarks on a righteous journey of singing to life – even in the lines dedicated to death, as in writing to his friend he keeps her memory alive for posterity. We would have to remember Shakespeare´s Sonnet XVIII, "When in eternal lines to time thou grow'st, / So long as men can breathe, or eyes can see, / So long lives this, and this gives life to thee." This is what Di Nardo has done: memorialize through his poetry, for poetry will be read in years to come.

I remember one of his most intriguing phrases in his poem "I Write and Write" from *Skylight*, which I commented in my review book, *In A Fragile Moment.* I said: "I Write and Write" is a pause in Di Nardo's river of poems. I disagree with him saying that "I write and write and nothing happens." *(Taken from "Letting the Light In. A review of Antony Di Nardo´s Skylight" (Poetry) (2018) Ronsdale Press. Canada*) When we discussed these lines in Gibara, I discovered that I was in the presence of a committed poet. Di Nardo complains that he writes his poems yet nothing still changes the negative side of things, and that is why he continues his poetic crusade towards a change.

However, as he complains so he soldiers on to fight causes worth fighting for, noble duties he follows because it is in his nature to leave an imprint. In his transcending anthology *Tamaracks: Canadian Poetry for the 21st Century (Lummox Press, 2018)*, James Deahl cites: "Sainte-Marie has recently said, "The job of a poet is to get information across in a way that's effective in making change."" *(Quoted by Deahl from Reader's Digest Volume 191, Number 1,144 (November 2017). Page 38. Print).* Thus we see a Di Nardo imbued in effecting a change, the environmentalist, the engaged observer who clicks in and bleeds emotive words, the grieving friend who realizes some things are gone/missing and seeks out for them in his new book to secure them immortality.

Wide-ranging in tessitura and technique, we walk along poems like "Missng," for example, which speaks of absence, an absence suggesting this surreal impression in me both in time and space. The poem confirms my early assumptions about the lack of "i" as a letter and a first-person singular pronoun in the title, a skilled, purposeful maneouver by the poet. We encounter also "Bay of Quinte," with play on words, social criticism and a clear-cut ecological approach.

The poet observes. He unveils sights, describes them in both direct and figurative dabs, as happens in "Hiding Places," where personification is achieved. The poet is an explorer, as we mentioned before, of the physical world but also of a world an ordinary eye cannot see – Di Nardo does, using metaphorical keys.

The meditative poet is felt in "She Was By Herself." Like he does in the line "and flit between two thoughts," the poem skips from thought to thought, from mental swirling to a bustling outdoor life both flowing irreversibly towards a "beyond my sight." Further in the book we come across "Missing," now with the "i," that speaks sadly of emptiness, sense of loss yet does not fail to address social issues and be critical in doing so.

The environmentalist is also appreciated in "A Tree Is Missing." With his direct criticism, Di Nardo stands as a concerned poet and a nature lover. His preoccupation about writing and writing and nothing is happening vibrates in this poem, and many others. One deep source for writing is quite evocative in "one more poem." It is a piece on death and absence, central leitmotifs in Di Nardo´s *Missng.* The poem "Gone" reminded me of a Latin American classic, Pablo Neruda. Wording and syntax brought the Chilean giant to me.

The poem "graveside, exit" leaves for us the heavy gravitas of a distinctively heartrending moment. Particularly stylistic is the use of the Latin word *Exeunt.* A few pages ahead, we read "graveside, grim," with its message of an awareness of death, maybe fear or calmness before what is inevitable. Awe-inspiring phrases are "… a gaping hole stares back / ghosts and threads of past events re-appear // yet it´s the grimace of an afterlife that steals the show / in thrall that I can see myself in there"

A poet concerned with the premises of life amidst so much loss and pain arises in "Autumn Colours." We are told of how much we do and lose and wonder "When it´s in our nature to name a leaf and watch it fall."

"Dead Waste" is a highly ekphrastic kind of poem. It is naturalistic and direct, to get to the reader so the message strikes home. "Family Portraits" gives us one of Canadian poets´ most revered themes for writing, family remembrances. Di Nardo travels in time and reminisces to offer this tender piece we welcome. "First Draft" is a brilliant short piece, almost haiku-like, of a writer and his bond with a straight representation of things. The last words, "and copy the clouds / the way nature / intended," speak of a keen poet, connected with nature.

"It Takes an Owl to Make an Owl" is an example of the professor Di Nardo is, where he "teaches" jocosely and leaves for us this intensely "didactic" poem. Finally, we find a poem of reflection in "Moonlandings." Age comes as a realization to the poet. The idea has landed on him that he is old, that he can no longer conquer the moon – it rather "crushes" and urges him to write this poem.

I have hand-guided the readers through some examples of Di Nardo´s proposal in *Gone/Missng.* At the beginning of my comments I stated that the book shows how diverse Di Nardo can be in his writing. Nevertheless, there is a solid cohesion that unifies thought and pen in poetry forging, an individual input of mastery and passion, of creativity that is put to the service of mankind and, above all, of hope, because Antony Di Nardo writes, writes and many good things will happen. Thank you, Antony.

What Has and What Has not been Made Exploring an Indefatigable Explorer: Robert Sward´s *All That I Have Not Made*

(Poetry) (2020) Hidden Brook Press. Canada

It was a delight to read the poetic works by Robert Sward. His book entitled *All That I Have Not Made* is a gem of a book. Iconic Canadian poet A. F. Moritz referred to a poet's "job" in an interview as "To write well: creatively, authentically, powerfully, beautifully.... poetry is partly self-development... is duty, belonging to a community..." This description applies to many Canadian poets I have read during my years of reviewing Canadian poetry. Such is the exceptional case of Robert Sward, an American-Canadian who has been prolifically, systematically writing and publishing poetry since before I was born. In a Hidden Brook Press release a blurb reads: "Robert Sward´s life´s work has been and continues to be poetry." There are many ways to honour a man´s work but that statement caught my eye for its overwhelming, simple truth and that is how I took an interest in Sward´s poetry collection, *All That I Have Not Made* (Hidden Brook Press, 2020).

On the book´s back-cover you will find Earle Birney´s valuation: "Robert Sward proves himself to be one of this country's finest poets..." In a nation producing poets from coast to coast; where literature, including poetry, is deemed as a national treasure and its poets are deeply appreciated, the fact of being considered one of the finest among the fine, unquestionably speaks highly of the man and his talent. Poet Laureate (2016-2018) and recipient of many awards, Sward has published thirty books. He is, as Carolyn Kizer puts it, "still fresh, ingenuous, and funnier than ever..."

The title Sward chose for a collection that brings together his decades-long career of crafting poetry comes from his poem "All for a Day." It is noteworthy that Sward offers a formidable book proving he has indeed contributed so much to what I call "poetdom" yet still focuses on *what he has not made*. But, that is Sward, an endless seeker, an unstoppable human being on the go, a trespasser of the cobweb into what Foley refers to in the book´s Afterword: "Sward's poems are the result of a plunge into a never fully ironized, often hilarious sense of mysticism: they are the product of a restless, spiritually adventuresome sensibility...". This is the Sward we read and perceive in his poems. Foley describes him: "At once a Canadian *and* American poet, one with a foot in both worlds, Sward also inhabits an enormous in-between. It will come as no surprise to readers to find that his poems get at the moment of truth by being deeply unsettled, by refusing to rest in any particular other than the cosmic ambiguity of the wholly visionary and the wholly sensual. Past, present and future—and their tenses—assail him equally" (we will revisit this in our last poem under analysis).

Sward said of himself, "All I am really hungry for is everything". He opened his book with the breathtaking quotation, "I eat the words that remain, and am eaten. By nothing, by all that I have not made." In more than one manner, this is the poet I am revealing today from my perspective. His self-definition, his attitude before the world and his bearings in it will be with us through an understanding of his poems.

Robert Sward is, in my view, a chronicler of both his life and life around him. Canadian poet James Deahl postulated that "Poetry was something that could not only speak to the issues and concerns of one's own life but could operate as a tool to allow the poet to discover an organizing principle outside of day-to-day human life…" *(Quoted from Under the Watchful Eye, Broken Jaw Press, 1995).* Sward has done that too; he has attempted to look into the issues and concerns of his life to discover how the "outside" operates.

Foley quoted Sward saying that "many of his poems have to do with love, divorce, multiple marriage, aging, loss, and the challenge of bringing up children in a highly unstable world … What is sought in all this work is liberation, illumination—it. The joy of his writing is the joy of the quest." Such a quest has hand-guided Sward across his writing, where many poems reflect what he sees in a story-telling style, overlapping thoughts and experiences penciled with a conversational, oftentimes informal surrender in poems filled with polysyndeton, interjections, curse words, etc.

In reference to Sward´s work, Foley says it is "Outwardly "zany" and fanciful… inwardly serious, troubled and questioning. As well, the heaviness we might trek into in some of his poems is lightened by the funny component, a marked feature in his pieces. We are in the presence of live poetry that mirrors the poet´s states of mind and the extended anecdotes/urges he needs to burst out on his path to liberating his soul.

Thus, we begin our journey with "The Kite," a heartfelt piece opening the book. Superbly metaphorical, the poem deals with death coupled to flying a kite. Touching, premonitory lines like "I still heard Auntie Blue / after she did not want to come down / again," prepare us, if we are ever able to prepare ourselves for this, for the sadly wonderful integration of realities the poet achieves: "And the string fell down / slowly for a long time. I was afraid to pull it / down. Auntie Blue / was in the sky, / just like God. It was not my birthday / anymore." The poem ends with the insertion of an expressive means called detached construction (after the semicolon): "And it was too bad / it was so hard to pull her down; and flowers," which aims at connecting two lines of thought, the former being the way he assumed Auntie Blue´s demise and the latter the image of a burial place.

"A Walk in the Scenery" is very much the story-telling trait I mentioned earlier. The narrative takes the reader along the events being lived by the viewers. Descriptions, senses aroused, the sensation of entering and first-hand experience: "It is there. And we are there. In it. / Walking in it, talking, holding hands. / The nickel postcard—the glossy trees; / the waterfalls, the unsuspecting / deer." In addition, a Sward who honors the deeply-rooted Canadian tradition of contemplating and admiring nature: "The deer / we are watching, at the same time / (through cameras, binoculars, eyes…) / so perfectly wild, and concerned / —with the scene they are, their glossy fate / silence, Nature, their rotogravure pose— / that they remain, not watching; rather, / staring away from us, into the / earnest, green and inoffensive trees."

"Hello Poem" is a hilarious-serious piece where the poet, from an open, broad-view stance, looks at his life, the "feats" done, what was *not* done. Sward embraces everything trying to cover as much as he can using effective expressive means, enumeration ("Hello wife, hello world, hello God, / I love you. Hello certain monsters, / ghosts, office buildings, I love you. Dog, / dog-dogs, cat, cat-cats, I love you") and repetition ("I love you"). As readers we pick his satisfied attitude, his frankness and peace with all surrounding him, all happened – or not – to him.

I found "Chicago's Waldheim Cemetery" appealing. It reminded me of a poem I wrote, "So we can move on" ("The iron-gate looks gloomy / it knows well where it leads to / what it holds inside: / all those stolen from us / silence weighs heavily / suspended in time, / stagnant / shackled to tombstones…"), as the boy´s words hung over me: "We are at the stone beneath which lies / my father's mother. / There is embedded in it a pearl-shaped portrait. / I do not know this woman. / I never saw her…." The poem carries gravitas in silence only broken by the insistent weeping of the father.

A pinch of irony-humor engulfs the poem too, a resource to hint the divide between father and son; at least in feelings towards a person the boy does not know, but which might be a sign of future decision-making moments in his own life: "My father weeps. / He is Russian. He weeps with / conviction, sincerity, enthusiasm. / I am attentive. / I stand there listening beside him. / After a while, a little bored, / but moved, / I decide myself to make the effort. / I have paid strict attention. / I have listened carefully. / Now, I too will attempt tears. / They are like song. / They are like flight. / I fail."

Of the many themes Sward has written about, sex stands out. One of such poems is "Nightgown, Wife´s Gown" with a sensuousness that rolls on and overleaps the lines. A husband´s claim elegantly voiced, extremely evocative line, "There is no reply," and the end phrase, "I caress her wings": "I knock on their shoulder blades / ask to be let in. It is forbidden. / But you're my wife, I say. There is no reply. / Arms around her, I caress her wings." I saw points of coincidence between this poem and one of mine, "wings of desire" ("all she has on / are wings of desire / we fly…") in which I proudly quoted Sward´s "I caress her wings."

A poem I particularly liked, and also quoted a line from for one of my poems, is "All for a Day." This piece seems to follow Robert Sward everywhere. He quotes the poem often, and it is also quoted by others. Having baptized the book with a line from this poem as we mentioned before, I see a poet who holds it as a banner. The poem defines him from beginning to end: "All day I have written words… // A poem remains. / But in the words, in the words, / in the fire that / is now words. / I eat the words that remain, / and am eaten. By nothing, / by all that I have not / made."

The pleasure of being a poet and writing poetry has been expressed by many poets. I remember Glen Sorestad, for example: "I like the state I´m in when a poem takes hold / and won´t let go," Don Gutteridge: "The unstoppable urge to write" or Richard Grove: "Poetry and I found each other." This is what I felt with "Iowa." While still a chronicle of Sward´s "exploits," it turns out to be, from where I stand, an ode to poets and poetry writing. Its epigrammatic closing is self-explanatory: "What is the point in this? / Someone scrawls six lines and says them. / What a strange happiness." Slightly – apparently – oxymoronic, the words *strange* (adjective) and *happiness* (noun) harmonize in the cozy-itchy feel when we *have* to write. Well-accomplished piece.

I wish to end my comments on Sward talking about one more poem. Being a university professor myself (English as a foreign language), I do know how central grammar is in the learning of a language (I am part of "the vast chorus / of the lovers of English" Sward mentions in our next poem). I even shared the idea with Canadian poet friend, and professor, Antony Di Nardo, who generously offered me grammar books I will find precious use for in my English lessons. Now I have read Sward´s "Grammar as Hymnal" and his first-class "class" on grammar. I loved the poem. One particular stanza I enjoyed was "We sing of grammar which is our compass / providing, as it does, clues as to how / we might navigate the future, / at the same time it / illuminates the past." *Navigate* and *illuminate* strike me as key words not only in-context but also as a compass Sward has pursued his entire life.

Practically impossible to encompass all of Sward´s poems (or his poetics as a whole) in one humble review, I have briefly attempted to present my insight of his work both by making specific allusions to some of his pieces – those I felt more drawn to if you will – then making generalizations of his craftsmanship and the meaningfulness of his poetry. His input to literature is remarkable. I enjoyed many of his poems in *All That I Have Not Made*; however, the fact that Sward is published by Hidden Brook Press under the esteemed John B. Lee Signature Series is credit enough. Nevertheless, there is more. I will end with quotes from what authors and critics have said about Robert Sward:

"...fierce, new-minted and convincing... he has voice and a range..." The New York Times Book Review on *Kissing The Dancer.*

"I like the wide sweep of it. There are many mysteries between father and son that people don't talk about… There's much leaping, but each line, so to speak, steps firmly on something solid. The father figure comes through consistently, there's a lot of buoyancy, and the son is consistent and fine too." Robert Bly. Author of *Rosicrucian in the Basement.*

"Comic juxtapositions and startling wordplay heighten immediacy and expectation. [Sward's] larger-than-life [podiatrist] father dominates *Rosicrucian in the Basement*: 'Feet don't lie/don't cheat, don't kiss ass. Truth is/peoples' feet are too good for them.'" ["One-Stop Foot Shop"] Sylvia Adams, Canadian Bookseller.

And the most passionate of all: "Here is Robert Sward, still fresh, ingenuous, and funnier than ever. His life–and what a life–is an open book. You can read all about it here. What's more, you will want to call your friends and read poems to them over the phone. I know, I've done it." Carolyn Kizer, Pulitzer Prize Winner on *Four Incarnations.*

Anything else to say? Yes, Robert Sward has made *and done* so much in his long life. And there is much to make *and do*, much to explore to be "at the service of an essentially visionary impulse" as Foley says. Sward confessed he "saw two worlds interpenetrating… // World "A" and World "B"… // world like a skyful of blue suns…" *(Taken from his poem "The Biggest Party Animal of Them All").* Let´s trust he will go on seeing worlds, let´s toast to that! Thank you, Robert.

The Warmest Beat, the Brightest Light on Both Sides of Life´s Tunnel A Review on *Hearthbeat,* Edited by Don Gutteridge.

(Poetry) (2020) Hidden Brook Press. Canada

Fifty-nine poets, including the book´s editor, capture in heart-warming wording and fine style the sometimes time-diluted – or apparently passé-in-these-modern-hectic-days – idea of what family really means, in this anthological gem Don Gutteridge and the Hidden Brook Press publisher bring to us in 2020, *Hearthbeat.*

I have written about the subject in my reviews and essays (*In a Fragile Moment: A Landscape of Canadian Poetry*, HBP, 2020, and *A Shower of Warm Light: Reviews and Essays on Canadian Poetry,* work-in-progress) about many (twenty) of the authors invited to this family jubilee.

I have been motivated by the fortunate realization that Canadian poets do have an "umbilical" connection with their roots, understood as a national and family historic construction of an individual identity. It tells them where they come from and defines them, lighting up their paths: the hearth, aptly registered by Webster´s dictionary, digital version, as "*home and family life: the joys of hearth and home.*"

Take John B. Lee´s nostalgic poem, "After the Bath," where the poet´s reminiscences get to us and send us back in time. It is the great poet singing to the great small things marking his early life, outlining his formidable legacy of poems-to-come:

"*... as my mother*

came gripping a towel

a flag of love

she meant for the nation of me

and I newly cloaked like a terrycloth king

a hero of saltwater stripes

ran quickly away from my youth

in primordial mornings kept close to the heel

by the shade"

The following lines, taken from James Deahl´s "Hiorra Summer," speak not only of a poet recalling his boyhood and family attachments but also that poet laying foundation as well as original leitmotifs (landscapes) and motivations to write, which would become a lifetime career:

"Every boyhood summer

we'd visit the old home Ulysses built

on the high slopes of Chestnut Ridge.

When thunder invaded the night

I would listen to the mountains,

try to catch their words

when they thought no one could hear"

I have quoted Deahl explaining his devotion to poetry: "*I decided that I needed poetry in my life… If I could find a way to speak to people…*" Definitely, from boyhood mementoes to a tall poet is what we receive today.

In "Horses Against the Horizon" we read a transfigured Keith Inman: a poet turned into a painter who leaves pictorial, nearly expressionistic, impressions on me,

"and the children thin

and weak with summer soup spooned

into mouths leaned

over wide white bowls //

It came sharp

like light cracking the sky

as thunder bent her

into wind-whipped wheat"

As we move down the book, we glide with poetic proposals constantly inviting us back to the "family womb." Already pictorially provoked by Inman, now we read John Di Leonardo´s poems.

Di Leonardo offers his spirituality and aesthetics by exploring and evoking, unveiling and *connecting* in that sentient human drive to build, either with words or with images – or with the overlapping produce resulting from blending both. He writes inspired by images, he turns into poetics *what was already poetry*, as he lets us know opening his book, *Conditions of Desire*, with a quotation from Simonides of Ceos: "*Painting is silent poetry; poetry is painting that speaks.*"

Thus Di Leonardo repaints, in word form, the works of art he so admires. He engages in ingenious labor and materializes a second "reading" – that is, a re-construal of a reality that had been interpreted before by a visual artist – this time with words.

Enjoy these graphic lines from "Sweetheart" *(Inspired by E. Manet's, "A Bar at the Folies–Bergère" 1882.)*

"Between storms

your tears like rain,

all colours washed away. //

In our bones we all know

sweetheart, real genius

unfurls rainbows in others.

We are deeply moved by Ronnie R. Brown´s "Home Again." A delicately penned piece – the poet´s eye-heart-hand nexus crafting a highly responsive poem of remembrance and homesickness – that endears our recollections and evokes sweet reflection:

"You pull into that familiar drive

expecting everything to be

the same: crocheted afghan

on the couch, aroma of fresh-baked

cookies in the air, the flowers //

A perfect picture and then

they come into view.

Shrunken somehow, their skin

like ancient cellophane,

so slow you hold your breath

as they wrench themselves

from the cradle of easy chairs

to welcome you home again…"

Joyful anticipation from the title and expressiveness of memories are kindled in "Family Album," by Anna Yin. A poet and critic, Anna has all the ingredients to make us tremble with her poetics. Heiresses of a millenary culture of Chinese origin, her veins carry blood of family stock that she holds and moulds in her poetry:

"They state —

my father, a golden lion,

with a kingdom in mind; rolling and roaring –

the darkness descends, with sight lost,

my father, a silent lamb.

They swear —

my mother, a wooden house,

with windows peering through the foggy road.

When too tempted outside,

closing the door and learning to listen —

my mother, a hut for night."

Our road through so many impressive poetic memoirs I cannot, unfortunately, cover in full in this review, takes us to Richard Grove´s eloquent title, "Fragments of Memories." Because that is what they are, the memories: *fragments* flickering in our minds, which either fade or endure, oftentimes depending on our affective willpower.

The poet puts it vividly, transporting us back in time, telling exactly what it feels like. In between, a mixture of sadness and happiness in recollections melting in the web of time past:

"Mother is living with what is left

of memories, fragments of time

surfing on a milky pool of reality.

It was very cold when skating

with her father, her at twelve

walking when no one else dared

join them at the rink, scattered glimpses

of scarfed faces blurred into focus //

Now all these years later, knuckles white

gripping wheelchair, running to get warm.

Soft silver hair shadows the recollections

of tobogganing. Was it with her brother

or her children fifty or sixty years ago"

The sad-glad alternation of memory – linked to the notion of old events revisiting, or to irreparable loss – is masterly presented in Grove´s "The Sleep," a eulogy to his father. Here the poet blends first-class imagery and innermost feelings epitomized in lines like "*the timeless slumber,*" "*the threshold of the great sleep,*" "*the ocean of no horizons*" and "*where consciousness fades then vanishes into the eternal*":

"Sleep dear prince,

now at the leaf-fallen years

of swaying amber grass

you are in preparation

for the timeless slumber,

at the threshold of the great sleep,

the languid undulating endless seashore,

the ocean of no horizons

where sky and water blend

with the mist

where consciousness fades then

vanishes

into the eternal."

The editor, Don Gutteridge, whom I have written about before (he is one of the few authors who appear in my two books on Canadian poetry), understandably left his own poetry for the end. I have then left my comments about his poetry to close this review.

Don opened his book with a statement, "To the core called family." There is no better introduction to a collection of poetry that celebrates the institution of family in its varied manifestations and ramifications. When we read Don´s "Going," our hearts leap out to the grieving soul that writes these beautifully sad lines. However, we seek to find necessary, unavoidable comfort in the closing line…

"When I first saw you

in that incubator

taking baby breaths,

your wee fingers still

wizened from the womb, glancing

off any horizon,

I didn't think we'd see you

growing golden into your bones,

but we did, and you grew anew

each loving day

you gave us, and when Death

drew you into its darkness,

we mourned your lonely going,

knowing you would never be old."

As a compilation, one of the book´s virtues is in the group of poets summoned to make this book come true. Such choice granted from the beginning the literary-sentimental value of what we have in our hands today.

In my *A Shower of Warm Light: Reviews and Essays on Canadian Poetry* (work-in-progress) I quote from a poem by Don, "The Way Home" (from his book *Point Taken*, Hidden Brook Press, 2018): "The way home is thru / the heart, every blood-beat / hums with remembrance."

I stated in my review book that "Gutteridge´s *Point Taken* has brought happiness and homesickness to my mind." So has this new Hidden Brook Press release. *Hearthbeat* honors these quotations from cover to cover: family ties and memories beat in the mists of time never to fade because there are poets, editors and publishers who safeguard and remind us, readers, of the worth of family roots.

Where it comes to remembering about life and living, love and loving; we will always have the warmest beat and the brightest light shining on both sides of life´s tunnel, the one that leads us into, through and out of existence: family. Poetry certainly eases the passage.

Thank you, poets. Thank you, Don.

Classics

We cannot publish books like this without going back to the icons, the founding poets, to the roots, to remembering the greats. That is why I decided to include Leonard Cohen, Pauline Johnson, Bliss Carman and Raymond Souster. I must say that many and *any* poet from the endless Canadian poetdom – Confederation Poets, the Great Generation Poets and contemporary poets – could have been chosen. After much reading and hesitation, I finally decided on the four we present today.

Definitions of *classic* read: "judged over a period of time to be of the highest quality; a work of art of recognized and established value; a very good example of its kind; traditional, timeless, ageless." *(Taken from digital Babylon, English-English)* All these entries apply to the icons of Canadian literature, those I reviewed in my previous book, Margaret Atwood, Milton Acorn and Al Purdy *(In a Fragile Moment, A Landscape of Canadian Poetry, Hidden Brook Press, 2020)*, Cohen, Johnson, Carman and Souster now – and many others to come.

Thank you, Tai and James (and Merle Amodeo, who kindly gifted me with *Stranger Music*), for furnishing me with material and connecting me with authors to study and write about them and other poets, for encouraging me to do research, welcoming my humble writings and publishing them, and mostly for believing in me.

No Stranger in These Lines
Leonard Cohen's Sweeping Lyricism in
Stranger Music: Selected Poems and Songs

(Poetry and Songs) (1993) McClelland and Stewart Ltd. Canada

When I heard of Cohen's death a few years ago I wrote a few lines to honor him and his work. My lowly poem mentioned in the main his celebrated "A Thousand Kisses Deep." I ended it with: "… it feels so good to be a man / it feels so great to be loved / by the woman who opens / like a lily to the heat, / and to your legacy // somehow / somewhere / the thousand kisses burst and twinkle / and fall like blessing rain." *(The poem, titled "To Leonard Cohen," was published in the Canada Cuba Literary Alliance newsletter, The Envoy, issue 82, February 2018 and in Canadian Stories Magazine. Page 27, Volume 22, Number 126-April/May 2019)*

Cohen had already entered my life through the *History and Culture of the English Speaking Peoples* lessons taught in the Holguín University by one of the most revered doyens in our staff, Professor Manuel Velázquez. The Teacher Education English Major and the English Language Major include Canada in their curricula. Cohen is among the Canadian authors/artists studied.

During an international event held yearly in Guardalavaca Beach resort, in Holguín, conceived and promoted by the Holguín University Department of Canadian Studies and sponsored by many Canadian universities, I had the opportunity to exchange with Canadian professors from Montreal. Our conversation on Canadian poetry led to Al Purdy and Milton Acorn, among other poets. I felt motivated to ask about other top voices in the Canadian poetdom. They coincided Leonard Cohen was *absolutely* one of them.

In 2019 poet Merle Amodeo came to the event and brought me a copy of *Stranger Music: Selected Poems and Songs.* Reading the book was an enduring experience. My perception of the title was that it was simply and magically selected to mean exactly the opposite for the reader, even if in the original text ("Stranger Song") Cohen may have referred to an apparent stranger at the beginning, then gradually disclosing the gist of the message: "… I told you when I came I was a stranger."

By restating the *stranger* element in the title and inviting to read Cohen, readers who accept the invitation will soon realize he has been no stranger at all for the last sixty-five years since his artistic debut in 1956, as the Calgary Herald explains on the book's back cover: "... a Canadian artist who has been anything but a stranger to so many of us for so long."

Involved in my review writing, having published a first book on thirty-one Canadian poets and prose writers *(In a Fragile Moment: A Landscape of Canadian Poetry. Hidden Brook Press, 2020)*, I wanted to include such notable artist-poet-songwriter-singer in this second volume. I am glad I did, and proud Cohen sings in my book too.

However, I did not approach his best known songs, "Suzanne," for example. I let my eye-heart connection hand-guide me along pieces that would markedly reveal to me and open "like a lily to the heat" (from his well-known poem "A Thousand Kisses Deep") during my reading, those that would make me rush for paper and pen and jot down notes inspired by them.

That is how I was caught in the magnetism of "As the Mist Leaves no Scar," "Beneath my Hands," "Owning Everything," "For Anne," "I Tried to Leave You" and "Dance to Me to the End of Love." I have to confess that only out of strong self-imposed discipline I forced myself to commenting just these six pieces. I may have easily, happily and willingly commented another six or another more six... or all of them but that is not the scope of this modest review.

"As the Mist Leaves no Scar" strikes me as a nostalgic poem, yet very resolute in its message. End-of-line rhyme grants it an extra lyrical flow in a-b-a-b arrangements aiding in conferring musicality to it. For example, the first stanza goes "scar-hill-scar-will."

The poet fluently likens natural realities and phenomena to personal ones in a metaphorical concert. His poet heart allows him to see and decode those parallelisms we enjoy in his work: "As many nights endure / Without a moon or star, / So will we endure / When one is gone and far." This very stanza, third and last, shows us the resoluteness I mentioned. Its last line seems to have a euphemistic shade of meaning, "When one is gone and far," in a possible hint of not just a temporary but also definitive separation.

I read the second poem so many times. For some higher reason it reminded me of Pablo Neruda, the great Chilean poet. Probably the echo is in the cadency and sweetness attained masterfully by Cohen and the ways to refer to his lover, to talk to her, bearing a resemblance to Neruda's style. "Beneath my Hands" is that touching and that appealing to the senses.

Right from the first stanza we come across perfect images, "... your small breasts / are the upturned bellies / of breathing fallen sparrows." This metaphor denotes delicacy, trembling sensations and acute observation by the poet to forge it. The fourth stanza made me remember in a flash Linda Rogers´ poem "Love in the Rainforest" (which is also the book's title). Cohen's poem is too "... a sustained sensual metaphor from end to end." *(Taken from my review Passionate Wordforests in Linda Rogers. A review of some of Linda Rogers´ poems in Love in the Rainforest (Poetry) (1995) Exile Editions. Canada. It appears in my first review book, In a Fragile Moment: A Landscape of Canadian Poetry. Hidden Brook Press, 2020, Canada)*

The fifth stanza regales us forceful imagery resulting from the poet's turning to the power of nature, where the best tropes can be collected: the solidity of rocks, the clarity and transparency of light, the limpidness of water and its streaming-murmuring "qualities": "… I want to summon / the eyes and hidden mouths / of stone and light and water / to testify against you."

The man is so infatuated by his woman that he wants the elements to watch and taste her – and they will yield to her: "I want them to surrender before you." The line "… the trembling rhyme of your face" is a breathtaking metaphor. It speaks of a pleasing balance, rhythm, even melodiousness in that face. The last line, "… for your looking and laughing," suggests there is realization in the poet of how beautiful she is – in *his* eyes, in *his* body, in *his* hands. And he wants her to see that too in a mirror-like reflection, as "I want my body and my hands / to be pools / for your looking and laughing."

"Owning Everything" is spectacular. It is an epigrammatic poem, axiomatic in its essence. Its simplicity makes it a great poem. It operates with words and notions at a thoughtfulness level. It unfolds in three short sentences and a longer, two-line one, with the poet's closing argument to convince the woman. He sees her as "everything" and sees "everything" in her. They belong to each other: he is hers, she is his.

The poet achieves this with simple sentence structures, direct words and dialogical approach. Nevertheless, that straightforwardness embodies an elevated message he wants to convey: "I will not leave you… / Owning everything, / I have nowhere to go." Cohen will forgive me if I bring to my review the popular song by Air Supply, "Every Woman in the World": "You're every woman in the world to me… / You're everything I need…" An astonishingly coincidental emotion turned into music by both artists.

The next poem plays with the idea of one's realization of how important people are to us. "For Anne" places the lover in an unequaled position in the poet's sentimental demonstration. In his doing so, I could feel a Shakespearean reminiscence: "Shall I compare Thee to a Summer's Day" *(Sonnet XVIII, taken from Complete Works of William Shakespeare, Volume XVIII, Philadelphia David McKay, Publisher, no year)* There is no other woman for the inspired poet. An implied metaphor sweetly shines in the lines "Whose eyes to compare / With the morning sun?" Rhetorical by definition, the statement is anyway pre-answered in the poem's first line: only she compares to the sun, "With Anne gone…"

The poet's passion and handling of imagery are shown at the start in "I tried to Leave You." A hyperbolic connotation lingers in the metaphorical phrase "I closed the book on us at least a / hundred times." Tenderness envelops the poem, noticed in his way of addressing the woman, "Good night, my darling."

The poem reflects what was commented by the Toronto Star on the book's back cover: "The poet's imaginative journey… through the extremes of love and despair." We can feel these extremes tightly bound at their conflicting yet inseparable frontiers. Phrases in the poem hint at an opposition of what is narrow (physical object) and the man's open-wide arms (a physical allusion too but meaning a lover's call, a lover's "cooing" to receive her, embrace her – and their relationship. This is confirmed in the last line. He wants – longs for – her smile; at least, and does all he can to win it: "And here's a man still / working for your smile."

The last poem, "Dance Me to the End of Love," plays with rhyming in its stanzas to give it the musicality it deserves. There are fresh, spellbinding metaphors throughout the poem, which explore the conquered limits of imagery: "Dance me to your beauty / with a burning violin." We see similes too, ""Lift me like an olive branch," gentleness made metaphors in "… and be my homeward dove / Dance me to the end of love."

The ritornello ("Dance me to the end of love") is repeated in the stanzas as part of that songlike distinctive Cohen element, to facilitate rhythm in the poem and ear-caressing flow to move a woman. Across the poem we read chosen phrases leading gradually to the physical part. The poet knows well how to word them in stunning lines.

Periphrasis as an expressive means in the language is "the use of a longer phrasing in place of a possible shorter… form of expression" *(Taken from Stylistics, 1981, Moscow Vyssaja Skola, by I. R. Galperin)*, which is found in the lines, "Let me see your beauty / when the witnesses are gone." It helps us decode this intimation the poet is sharing with us, asking the woman to undress. The whole poem is a process towards *and* of lovemaking, sensuously and carefully delineated by the poet.

On the book's back cover we read the Ottawa Citizen call *Stranger Music* "… an invaluable record of a shining voice. It burns still." Oh, yes it burns with a soft, simmering flame that warms and lingers in a sweeping lyricism so at home with an iconic Canadian artist who is categorically no stranger to us. Thank you, Leonard.

Nature-won Poetry in Pauline Johnson
An Analysis of Two of her Poems

(Poetry) Taken from https://www.poemhunter.com/emily-pauline-johnson/biography

In his notable anthology, *Tamaracks: Canadian Poetry for the 21st Century*, Lummox Press, 2018, Editor James Deahl approaches the legitimate concept of a multicultural Canadian poetry. He stated: "… multiculturalism… is the reality of the 21st century Canada… Our present poetry is as fine as it was in prior generations…" He had previously said that "Our legacy…, dating from the Confederation Poets of the late 19th century, has survived into the new century…"

Based on these assertions, posited by a poet and scholar who has devoted his life to studying, writing and promoting poetry, the present essay aims at bringing to stage the figure and work of a woman poet, Pauline Johnson. She was born in 1861 and died in 1913 thus sharing contemporaneity with great Confederation Poets like Archibald Lampman, Bliss Carman and Duncan Campbell Scott, among many others.

Johnson was "a Canadian writer and performer popular in the late 19th century… her poems and performances… celebrated her First Nations heritage. Her father was a Mohawk chief of mixed ancestry, and her mother an English immigrant…" *(Taken from https://www.poemhunter.com/emily-pauline-johnson/biography. Downloaded December, Thursday 5, 2019. 10:09 am)*

Her origins, the contexts where and the period when she lived are reflected in her poetry. A woman poet who made a difference in her times, she left outstanding pieces still remembered and quoted today, one of them is "The Song my Paddle Sings." In an essay about Milton Acorn *(See In a Fragile Moment: A Landscape of Canadian Poetry, Hidden Brook Press, 2020)* the author of this essay mentioned another moving poem by Johnson, "A Cry from an Indian Wife."

Johnson was part, and not an insignificant one, of the writers who defined and developed an emerging Canadian poetry that was taking steps away from English – and American – literary influence and paving its own paths.

Her position within Canada's literary world is undoubtedly reflected in these words: "… since the late 20th century, Johnson's writings and performance career have been reevaluated by literary, feminist, and postcolonial critics. They have appreciated her importance as a New Woman and a figure of resistance to dominant ideas about race, gender, Native Rights, and Canada. The growth in literature written by First Nations people during the 1980s and 1990s has prompted writers and scholars to investigate Native oral and written literary history, to which Johnson made a significant contribution…" *(Taken from https://www.poemhunter.com/emily-pauline-johnson/biography. Downloaded December, Thursday 5, 2019. 10:07 am)*

Cuban universities include her poetry on the English Majors´ curricular map and studies of her poems are submitted and presented in international events celebrated in Cuba *(WEFLA-SECAN, a scientific event yearly held in Holguín, Cuba, sponsored by the Holguín University and many Canadian counterparts, focused chiefly on the teaching of English as a foreign language and Canadian studies. One example was the work "Journey to the Roots: First Nations Poetry in the Voices of Pauline Johnson and Louise Halfe," by Adonay Bárbara Pérez Luengo, Manuel de Jesús Velázquez León and Yanelis Aguilera Cruz. Access wefla.org for further information)*

In the spirit of Deahl's judicious statements and the fresh look taken at her work, this essay addresses her poetry. Imbued in the magnificence of Canadian scenery, Johnson left us impressive pieces marked by a high lyrical and romantic style. Her varied origins plus literary influences still lingering, endowed her with an expressiveness stirringly evidenced in her poems.

North American romanticism as a movement that grew out of its English root is deeply felt. Features like *feeling, love and heart*, understood as "… genuine, emotional vitality, feeling being more introverted and personal and an open show of joy, rapture, love, longing… fear, hope, faith, enthusiasm…" *(Taken from The Literature of the U.S.A., Editorial Pueblo y Educación, Ciudad de La Habana, 1983)* took hold of poets, prose writers – and artists in general, as was clear in the Group of Seven.

Other features of romanticism are noticeable, *interest in nature*: "… nature was a spiritual resource… a living being speaking to the soul in a language that feeling and imagination could understand." *(Idem previous source)* Authors displayed their artistry creatively bequeathing true, new Canadian art and literature. Pauline Johnson is an indisputable recipient and mirror of these characteristics, as will be discussed below.

One of the most salient traits of her poetry is rhyme. It made me joyfully *and* nostalgically remember the English and American classics I studied during my college years. The pieces included here follow specific patterns. Both stanzas of the first poem to comment, "Low Tide at St. Andrews," were arranged abbacc: "indistinct / dream / gleam / land-linked / breast / west." The poem is full of other expressive means and stylistic devices conferring it special cadence and rhythm, echoing tides.

Some examples are semantic means: similes, "The far-off shores swim blue and indistinct, / Like half-lost memories of some old dream." The poet likens the shores´ indistinct aspect with memories. Metaphorical expressions abound too: "Leaving a strange grey silence… / The silence of the sands." As well, phonetic devices assist in the general mood of the poem: alliteration, the repetition of the consonant "l": Light with young laughter… / Leaving a strange grey silence / Their loads, returning laden… / … low."

To complement the effects conveyed, there are syntactical means: polysyndeton, the recurrence of the conjunction *and*, "And naked-footed children / To gather dulse and sea clams and then heave…," which reinforces rhythm and rhyme. We are in the presence of a poem that describes nature in motion. Its imagery and passionate ways to craft it tell us how enraptured the poet is. An heiress – and pioneer in her own right – of the best of English and American romantic poets, Johnson eternalizes nature.

In reference to this, I quote the opening lines of my essay "Three Poets, One Big Canadian Heart. A Look at K. V. Skene, Stella Mazur Preda and Donna Allard in *The Dream The Glory and The Strife* (Poetry) (2018) Hidden Brook Press. Canada" *(Taken from A Shower of Warm Light: Reviews and Essays on Canadian Poetry)*:

"In his excellent essay "Archibald Lampman: Poet on the Cusp of Modernism," poet and profound connoisseur of Canadian poetry, James Deahl, stated that "… almost every Confederation Poet wrote a body of nature poetry."" *(Deahl's words taken from Canadian Stories magazine, Volume 22, Number 129, Year 2019)* Johnson stands as one of those poets who felt and produced nature poetry.

The second poem under consideration is titled "Wave-won." The stanzas are arranged in the pattern a-a-b-c-c-b: "so / know / dream / canoe / through / stream." Apart from rhyme, Johnson makes extensive and skilled utilization of expressive means in the language; interesting ones are interjections.

They are "… words we use when we express our feelings strongly and which may be said to exist in language as conventional symbols of human emotions… are direct signals that the utterance is emotionally charged and insufficient attention on the part of the literary critic… will deprive him of a truer understanding of the writer's aims." *(Taken from I. R. Galperin. Stylistics. Moscow Vyssaja Skola. 1981)*

This quotation throws light on Johnson's touching style, and validates the assumptions made earlier regarding the characteristics of romanticism in respect to the poet's profound implication in the process of creation, motivated by surrounding reality and her underlying, sweeping feelings.

Carried away by the excitement in her mind and heart, the poet pens metaphors, "… the dream that haunted our canoe, / And wove its witchcraft through / Our hearts…, … pools of pearls…;" similes, "My arm as strong as steel;" epithets-metaphors, "splendid eyes aflame…," "god-like head;" personification, "laughing rapids;" hyperboles, "Your splendid eyes aflame / Put heaven's stars to shame;" and a versatile syntactical device, stylistic inversion, enriched by a metaphor, "The shores in shadows clad."

This device enhances rhythm, which by extension helps in a proper and more aesthetical layout of the poetic result. Galperin explains: "There is a tendency to account for inversion in poetry by rhythmical considerations… in the majority of the cases inversion is called forth by considerations of content… one of the forms of what are known as emphatic constructions." *(Idem previous source)*

A full reading of the stanza allows us to realize that the change in word-order responds to both form and content strategies. Consequently, the rhyming pattern established in the poem is observed. The word "clad" rhymes with the next line-end, "sad."

The poem's last line might be suggestive of a euphemistic touch. A woman above her time, a "New Woman," Johnson could be expressing in arresting lyrical form that circumstances led them to the act of love: "Where, in *delirium reeled* / Our maddened hearts that kneeled / To idolize the perfect world, *to taste of love at last*." *(Italics by the author of this essay)*

Nature won the heart of the poet leaving no chamber vacant. It filled her eyes and flooded her soul. An ardently watchful Johnson is spellbound by sights she watches. She is captured by their splendidness, turned joyfully and voluntarily into an experiential witness and participant of the moments she minutely details.

Both poems brought to us natural descriptions which reveal "… the close bond Canadian poets have developed with nature, wildlife and weather conditions… It is inherent in Canadians to view, implicate and depict in outstanding, imagery-rich pieces what Canada has to offer. Poets have been inspired by its beauty, by the clear-cut seasonal cycles, and in the process of eternalizing nature they have seen themselves as either a part of it or a resulting/co-existing entity." *(Taken from A Shower of Warm Light: Reviews and Essays on Canadian Poetry)*

Content and form harmonize in Johnson, who renders unique pieces knit with perfect stitches. More than a century later, we read the finished product, and fortunately sense that "… the artisan stands back with me / to survey the masterpiece." *(Taken from the poem "Nature's Needlepoint", by Canadian poet Kimberley Grove, in The Bridges Series Book IV, Where the Heart Lies, Hidden Brook Press, 2018)* This is what we inherit from a Confederation Poet who earned her place in the Canadian poetdom. Thank you, Pauline.

Heaven Revealed in Bliss Carman's Poetry An Essay on Three of his Poems

(Poetry) Taken from https://mypoeticside.com › poets › william-bliss-carman-poems

My readings and studies of Canadian poetry began with contemporary authors whose works came to me through the Canada Cuba Literary Alliance (CCLA). The CCLA was founded in 2004 by Canadian poet Richard Marvin Grove, seconded by a group of writers and artists from Canada and Cuba. Its purpose was, and continues to be, the promotion of the two nations´ cultures. Reality and poet friends – especially Grove and James Deahl – guided me little by little towards further studies to enrich and complement my insights of Canadian poetry from its origins.

That is why in my book *In a Fragile Moment: A Landscape of Canadian Poetry* (Hidden Brook Press, 2020) I addressed three icons, Margaret Atwood, Milton Acorn and Al Purdy, alongside other outstanding contemporary writers totaling thirty-one. In this new book, *A Shower of Warm Light: Reviews and Essays on Canadian Poetry* (a second volume of the previous one), I travel a bit backwards in the search of deeper roots. Thus, in the "Classics" section you are reading Pauline Johnson and Bliss Carman, and more contemporary names I approach: Leonard Cohen and Raymond Souster.

The True North has been "discovered," rediscovered, revealed, defined and redefined by numerous scholars and poets like Terry Barker *(for example, his "Recalling the True North: A Context for People's Poetry" in After Acorn. Meditations on the Message of Canada's People's Poet, Mekkler and Deahl Publishers, 1999)*, James Deahl *(Read his "Archibald Lampman: Poet on the Cusp of Modernism" in Canadian Stories magazine, Volume 22, Number 129, Year 2019; and "William Dough Lighthall: Poet of the Songs" in Canadian Stories magazine, Volume 22, Number 127, Year 2019)* and Henry Beissel *(read Beissel's Expanded lecture/reading delivered at "North and Nordicity" Conference at the University of Toronto, May 17, 2007)*, to mention just a few authors and a few of their works that have reached me.

Deahl has stated that "… various True Norths were created. Indeed, Confederation Poets like Bliss Carman and Sir Charles G.D. Roberts helped develop these "new" True Norths." *(Taken from "Archibald Lampman: Poet on the Cusp of Modernism" in Canadian Stories magazine, Volume 22, Number 129, Year 2019)* Carman was a poet who "lived for years in the United States… He was never forgotten in Canada though and they made him their Poet Laureate. He was a lyrical poet who was numbered amongst the so-called Confederation Poets in Canada and shared this status with the likes of Duncan Campbell Scott and Archibald Lampman. Carman stood out from some of his contemporaries in that he dedicated himself to poetry, occasionally writing critical commentaries on philosophical or literary topics. Others often chose to diversify into journalism or writing novels." *(Taken from* https://mypoeticside.com › poets › william-bliss-carman-poems. *December, Thursday 5, 2019. 09:15 am)*

According to Bert Case Diltz and Ronald Joseph McMaster, Carman was "Greek in his love of the beautiful and in his search for perfection. He was Canadian in his love of nature. He was deft in his creation of imaginative and melodious lyrics." *(Taken from New Horizons, McClelland and Stewart Limited, Revised edition, Canada, 1965)* The three poems chosen for discussion here are fine examples of this quotation: "Daisies," "Spring's Saraband" and "Vestigia."

The poet sings the praises of nature and how it envelops him and lifts his spirit in the first poem. Like Pauline Johnson, he has been influenced by the high lyricism of English poets, showing his creativeness and skill in pieces which reflect his Canadian soul. He also made me gladly *and* wistfully go back to the English and American classics I studied during my college years.

"Daisies" follows the rhyming pattern a-b-a-b, as in the first stanza: "dune," "sea," "June," "free") thus achieving the melodious ring stated in the previous quotation. The poet also resorts to other expressive means in the language like metonymy, "… the shoulders… of the dune." His eyes behold the whole natural spectacle: from flora and ocean, "the white daisies go down to the sea" (where hyperbolic expressions are incorporated in the next line: "… A host in the sunshine, an army in June"), to wild life "the bobolinks… the orioles.")

The poet puts words in wildlife: "And all of their singing was, "Earth, it is well!" And all of their dancing was, "Life, thou art good!"" This technique prompts a dialogue between beholder and his surroundings. Let's keep in mind what I remarked in my essay about Pauline Johnson *("Nature-won Poetry in Pauline Johnson. An Analysis of Two of her Poems." Taken from https://www.poemhunter.com/emily-pauline-johnson/biography)*: "*… interest in nature*: "… nature was a spiritual resource… a living being speaking to the soul in a language that feeling and imagination could understand."" *(Taken from The Literature of the U.S.A., Editorial Pueblo y Educación, Ciudad de La Habana, 1983)* The last line is a cry of optimism, placed in the birds´ beaks, and proof of his love of nature and complete identification with it: "And all of their dancing was, "Life, thou art good!""

Rhyme and rhythm solidly contribute to add musicality to a poem. In the case of the second poem, "Spring's Saraband," the reader notices it right away. The rhyming pattern is arranged as abcbdefe; sustained semantic expressive means (personification) enter to recreate the mood and liveliness of spring, starting with the title, "… Saraband," an allusion to a Spanish dance which permeates the whole poem. It is Spring that (who?!) dances: "Over the hills of April / With soft winds hand in hand, / Impassionate and dreamy-eyed, / Spring leads her saraband. / Her garments float and gather / And swirl along the plain…"

Colour, sound, smell, lands, wildlife, streams, humans, movement are combined in the poem's stanzas, and musical instruments are mentioned too: "With colour and with music, / With perfumes and with pomp, // By meadowland and upland, / Through pasture, wood, and swamp // ... on the hill. // And children in the city / squares / Keep time, to tambourines. // ... The blue bird in the orchard." Carman proposes a concert where the "*prima ballerina*" is spring.

The poet is absolutely focused on and overwhelmed by nature. His spirit is thus lifted and hopeful, as in the poem analyzed before: "O hark, hear thou the summons, / Put every grief away // Alack, that any mortal / Should less than gladness bring / Into the choral joy that sounds / The saraband of spring!" He invites to the exultation found in the seasons, especially in the beauty and embrace of spring.

The third poem is "Vestigia." It was written with an established rhyming stanza pattern, aabba, and using enjambments: "Far off in the deep shadows, where / A solitary hermit thrush," "At last with evening as I turned / Homeward..." This resource within metrical patterns known as run-on line too, is seen as a "departure from the norms of classic verse... but there is a definite metrical scheme and pattern of rhyming... they add much variety and charm to the verse." *(Taken from Stylistics, 1981, Moscow Vyssaja Skola, by I. R. Galperin)* Superb epithets and metaphorical expressions accompany the poem: "... holy twilight hush," "Where the last fires of sunset burned."

I consider this piece bears a significant religiousness felt in the poet's realization of the presence of God across the natural sceneries he views. Notice that he "alarmingly" opens the poem saying "I took a day to search for God, / And found Him not." However, he begins to enumerate endless places, settings, experiences and winning sensations through which the reader becomes aware that the initial line is but an excellent poetic springboard into the full understanding of where God is and what He means to the poet.

Carman names all the sites where he encounters God thus proving His presence covers all that surrounds us in beauty and vastness. The poet discloses the parallel between God and what He gives us in nature: "... rocky ledge, through woods untamed, / Just where one scarlet lily flamed, / I saw His footprint in the sod," "... in the deep shadows, where / A solitary hermit thrush / Sang through the holy twilight hush— / I heard His voice upon the air," "In a stir of wind that hardly shook / The poplar leaves beside the brook— / His hand was light upon my brow," "At last with evening as I turned / Homeward, and thought what I had learned / And all that there was still to probe — / I caught the glory of His robe / Where the last fires of sunset burned." Carman explains in poetic language that God's glory lies right before our eyes. The poet finally perceives He dwells within us: "I knew God dwelt within my heart."

There are two meaningful lines in this compelling poem propounding that nature is God, He created it and reveals Himself in it. The third stanza's second line, despite being in mid-poem, is in my belief essentially enlightening in the poet's conception of God's ubiquitous presence and as evocative and humbling as the fourth line in the same stanza ("His hand was light upon my brow"): "God gives us Heaven here and now."

The poet's faith and fulfillment prevails then in the last stanza: "Back to the world with quickening start / I looked and longed for any part / In making saving Beauty be....

/ And from that kindling ecstasy / I knew God dwelt within my heart." Such revelation dawns magnificently on the blessed poet. The three poems in this essay show this revelation.

This is Bliss Carman. His legacy – along with the other major poets´ contribution – "… continued into the Great Generation Poets… And perhaps one can see that Bliss Carman's "In Apple Time" was the spark that ignited Al Purdy's "Selling Apples."" *(Taken from James Deahl's "William Dough Lighthall: Poet of the Songs" in Canadian Stories magazine, Volume 22, Number 127, Year 2019)* My previous book concentrated on Great Generation Poets; this one has brought to the reader two relevant Confederation Poets. In this essay we have discussed one of them and exposed his consummate style. Thank you, Bliss.

A Foundational Beacon
Reading Collected Poems of
Raymond Souster (Ten-volume Collection)

(Poetry) (2004) Ottawa: Oberon Press. Canada

Poet and friend, Richard Marvin Grove, Tai, Founding President of the Canada Cuba Literary Alliance (CCLA), forwarded me some poems from the *Collected Poems of Raymond Souster*, on the eve of the year 2020. He and James Deahl had praised my reviews on Margaret Atwood, Milton Acorn and Al Purdy *(In my first review book, In a Fragile Moment: A Landscape of Canadian Poetry. Hidden Brook Press, 2020)* and were encouraging me to write about other iconic figures of Canadian literature.

This second review book includes my modest analyses on Leonard Cohen, Pauline Johnson, Bliss Carman, and now Raymond Souster; a must read, an unavoidable name in the Canadian poetdom, deemed by James Deahl as one of the most important dozen poets in the Canadian 20th century.

Deahl's words I read about Souster might at first discourage anyone attempting at approaching this poet, "No anthology can come close to celebrating the life and work of such an important, indeed essential, figure in the history of Canadian literature; several large books would be required." *(Taken from Under the Mulberry Tree: Poems for & about Raymond Souster. Quattro Books Inc. 2014. Edited by James Deahl, his introductory words: "Simply Ray: An Introduction")*[7]

As I moved down his discourse I realized the intention was quite the opposite of my initial perception: "… But my publisher and I will do our best." What Deahl did was put sheer stress on the greatness of the poet. I join then publisher and editor in trying to condense in a few, always insufficient, pages my understanding of one of the seminal authors of Canada, a worthy representative of the Great Generation Poets.

It was a promising coincidence to learn of Grove's appreciation of Souster and his decision to send me the collection, and Deahl's admiration for him in his explicit allusion to *Collected Poems of Raymond Souster* as "… essential reading for anyone interested in fine poetry." *(See footnote 7)* Hence, I devoted my end-of-year days off from work to read and comment some of Souster's poems.

---

[7] Unless otherwise noted in-text by the essayist, all non-post-bracketed, non-referenced quotations of James Deahl were taken from his introduction to the book cited.

Souster's concerns about social affairs are reflected in "Four Girls at a Corner." (Volume 3) Deahl tells us that the poet pointed at "… social/political issues… Poverty, oppression, violence, racism, anti-Semitism, avarice, and human degeneration were all targets of his poetry." There are deeply critical lines in the poem, "four girls at the corner, / three about eighteen, / the fourth not more / than thirteen, I swear, / Not one day more…,"[8] which bring to the surface scenes like the one Souster presents in descriptive style, no embellishment for the crude reality he depicts.

The poet pokes deeper at the issue by saying: "… waiting for the Man / to come and take them / for a few short hours / out of misery…" It stands to sad reason that the misery he describes too hits the streets and is commonplace. Such plights do not escape the poet's committed pen. However, if the reader thought it was it, Souster becomes sarcastic and inquisitive in the last lines: "… God, the taxi-driver said, / but He hadn't come along yet either."

The seemingly strong descriptions read in the previous poem pale when you move to the next, "Girl at the Corner of Dundas & Elizabeth." (Volume 1) Straightforward and incisive, the poem lashes again at social scourges. Souster introduces slang and direct dialogue – no circumlocutions – to reinforce the realistic character of the situation: "You want it / or you don't / I'm twenty-one / I ain't / got any time / to waste…"

In terms of language use, Deahl states: "What appealed to Ray was the mixture of image-based poetry with realism. Such poems would utilize plain speech, and avoid Classical or academic references. This poetry could easily embrace both urban and rural themes, both social-political issues and nature."

"Mister / make up your mind" is the poem's last line. It brought to me scenes from the movie *Pretty Woman*, to mention a lightly-treated reference, where Roberts and her "partner" engage in similar exchanges with "potential customers."

One of Souster's themes is love. I cannot think of one poet – there are, perhaps – who has not written love poems, at least – not necessarily – during his/her early writing stages. "Night on the Uplands" (Volume 2) is a brief, intense, humorous one. Nature commingles with love, opens the poem as a fitting preamble: "A fire on such a warm night? / Crazy, wasn't it, but then / the mosquitoes wanted our flesh / as much as we wanted each other…"

The subordination of end-lines "… and as I remember / won out in the end!" to the previous line, "as much as we wanted each other," and the absence of "they" or "we" – I am positive there is intentionality in this – before "won out," really makes me pleasurably wonder whether Souster refers to the insects or themselves – or he *purposefully* made me feel that. It endows the short piece with a gentle sensuousness I value as a reader.

---

[8] Fragments from all the poems taken from *Collected Poems of Raymond Souster*. Ottawa: Oberon Press. 2004.

In his poem "Raymond Souster," Laurence Hutchman summarizes what "Night on the Uplands" stirs in me as a reader: "Your poems drawn subtlety / of the desire of lovers / uncovering their shy naked bodies." In the same poem, Hutchman also acknowledges Souter's mastery to "size up" his city, as I explained in the poems "Four Girls at a Corner" and "Girl at the Corner of Dundas & Elizabeth": "No one has painted this city as you have, / made its history our own." *(Taken from the contributors´ poems included in the anthology Under the Mulberry Tree: Poems for & about Raymond Souster. Quattro Books Inc. 2014)*

Another sweet piece is the indeed to-the-point four-line poem, "Short Short Song," (Volume 7) dedicated to Susi, his wife Rosalia. In my opinion, the fact that Souster uses rhyme here, final rhyme in lines two and four, no rhyme in one and three, enhances the message of the poem and its warmth, and assists in rhythm. By extension, these elements foster musicality, which is the poet's declared intention in his title. In simple but resolute words, Souster praises his relationship with his wife: "When Susi smiles I'm happy, / when Susi's sad I'm sad…" Deahl commented that "In fact, the romance of Ray and Rosalia is a love story for the ages."

"Night on the Uplands" is a fleeting hint at nature, deriving into a love composition. Nature poetry was very emotional in Souster, as Deahl tells: "… nature images appear in Ray's poetry from the very beginning… The natural world is used… to remind the reader of beauty in poems… and… poems directly about the joy… of… nature."

A breathtaking, tender example that blends the beauty and the joy elements and brings nature to the full forefront of the beholder is "Queen Anne's Lace." (Volume 3) In his substantial essay "Archibald Lampman: Poet on the Cusp of Modernism," James Deahl clarifies: "This emphasis on the natural landscape of Canada and on nature poetry, so visible in the work of Confederation Poets, continued into the Great Generation Poets like Milton Acorn… and Raymond Souster… became leading nature poets during the last half of the 20th century." *(Taken from Canadian Stories magazine, Volume 22, Number 129, Year 2019)*

As a "leading nature poet," Souster crafted this poem that sings to beauty and delicacy and makes human eyes turn to them: "It's a kind of flower / that if you didn't know it / you'd pass by the rest of your life. / But once it's been pointed out / you'll look for it always…" Souster's passion goes as far as letting the reader know that "You'll never tire / of bending over to examine, / of marvelling at this / shyest filigree of wonder / born among grasses…" Finally, he forecasts: "You'll imagine poems // so natural with themselves / as to take your breath away."

The book I have taken most of the quotations from in my essay (chiefly from James Deahl's introduction) was a tribute to Raymond Souster. Thirty-five contributors sent their material to produce the book. I will illustrate how profoundly impactful and transcendental Souster's poetry and life are with only three examples of phrases used in their poems. *(Taken from the contributors´ poems included in the anthology Under the Mulberry Tree: Poems for & about Raymond Souster. Quattro Books Inc. 2014)*

James Deahl, editor, friend of Souster's, impassioned reader and inveterate advocate of poetry, said in "Japanese Maple": "You, true master / of the backyard poem…" Terry Ann Carter showed her high regard with much similar direct, colloquial language Souster uses: "… for better, or worse, / Raymond — I'm hooked…" And in "The shy man was absent," Chis Faiers devotedly said: "But tonight the shy man's legacy connects / a tribal gathering of poets his tribute / **not one empty chair.**" Impressive.

When I read about Souster's blindness, I shivered with Henry Beissel's proclamation in his poem "Others Are Writing this Poem" *(Fugitive Horizons. Guernica Editions, 2013)*: "Sight / was never a necessary condition of existence," and re-read, moved, Deahl's words about Souster's resolute, brave attitude: "Ray went blind, and despite becoming blind, which he expected to happen, he kept on with his usual daily life as long as possible. He wrote hundreds of poems after he lost his sight. Every time I visited him, Ray was in a good mood. He accepted his condition, and did not allow it to depress or define him."

What a lesson of life and rock-solid determination! Deahl summarized it with his assertion: "He was a rare and true example of how to fully *live* a life." I do not have better words to finish this essay. All I can come up with is that I am grateful to Grove and Deahl for pointing me in the direction of Souster. I feel I have rounded off my second essay book with his name among so many other fine poets and prose writers. I'm hooked too, I'll follow the beacon. Thank you, Ray.

Including a Bit of Prose

Even when my "less-weak" suit is reviewing poets, I am some times tempted to write about prose writers too. As was done in my previous book, *In a Fragile Moment: A Landscape of Canadian Poetry*, we have included two authors, Donna Wootton and Don Gutteridge.

Flames of Endurance and Courage
A Review on Don Gutteridge's
Lily Fairchild

(Prose) (2019) Hidden Brook Press. Canada

An unquestionably outstanding and well-established poet, Don Gutteridge shows the rich tessiture of his writing in this superb, heart-touching piece of prose, Lily Fairchild. The novel is an ode to sacrifice and endurance, to determination and courage, to freedom of thought and act, to faith magnificently worded in one of the book's final meditations: "… belief is a hard flame to extinguish…"

As a reader I don't need a more suitable way to connect with a book than the one chosen by the author, as he starts by describing Lily's childhood settings, packed with family details: "Lily was glad to be in the comfort of the trees' canopy. It was cozy here, like the cabin with Papa's fire blazing… While outside, heard only by her, the snow sang to the wind and no one in the world was lonely… She would surprise Papa at his work, celebrate another tree felled, and laugh when he swept her up and twirled her around, saying ´Lady Fair Child, may I have the pleasure of this dance?´"

The opening line in the book, "Something stirred in the darkness ahead," can be considered premonitory of what would befall Lily - prefaced in her Mama being sick. I value the allusions to Old Samuels´ mumbled stories, a thoughtfully depicted character in both personality and language, an element that is appreciated in Gutteridge´s choice of all dialogues, idioms, turns, graphic representation of speech, etc., which speaks highly of his meticulous studies to write the novel.

Furthermore, at the threshold of Chapter 6 Gutteridge displays still another ominous act, "I'm...Lily… Papa sent me… Sensing the bewilderment in the woman's face, Lil's heart sank. She fought against the faintness and vertigo as best she could, but it felt as if her bones had melted outright in a treacherous sun."

Exploiting these factors, Gutteridge prepares the reader for the avalanche of events unfurling from his pen. In many ways those early chores and experiences Lily, seven years old, had to assume and learn from molded her charisma, and may have given her strength to face the hardships and setbacks she would encounter along the way.

Two especially tender-sad moments come to us with the mother's "Let's-have-tea,-little-one" instant when she tells Lily of her and Papa's previous life and how they came to a new country, and the scene with the cameo pendant with a silver chain that Lily's mother showed her: "With a start, Lily recognized her own eyes. "Your grandmother." Mama's eyes filled with tears. She reached into the box again. "I saved this, out of the storm." She held up a gold chain on the end of which dangled a slender cross no more than half an inch long. Instinctively Lily leaned forward and the crucifix settled on her throat as if it had always expected to be there." Auspiciously, this moving minute comes back to us at the end.

Lily Fairchild finely chronicles, in its status as historical fiction, a period – rather a succession of periods – in the Canadian past that approaches natives´ life – stylishly accompanied by the use of words coming from their languages, what brings the reader closer to the textual atmosphere – and sketches crisscrossing seeds that grew into the Canada we have today.

Alongside, Gutteridge remains loyal, and constantly refers to one of the central motifs in Canadian writers, nature. He is faithful as well to his excellent treatment of family themes – skillfully addressed too in his poetry – placed either in the 1850s or in more contemporary contexts.

Another welcome virtue in the book is place references constantly being made – a tribute to Al Purdy's devotion to Canadian geography? –, which play an important role throughout the novel, not just spatially but also from a historic-contextual perspective. More significantly, Gutteridge´s accounts are the result of deep research to recreate locations and situations accurately.

Despite Lily's misfortunes and hard times, Gutteridge does stimulate the reader with some high peaks in her life in the form of her Aunt Bridie – family – "Bridie wanted to be severe but couldn't manage it… (Her Aunt enrolled Lily in Common School, giving Lily up as help around the house), and "Don't you fret about it, child," Bridie soothed. "Not much learnin' goes on in schools anyway. Come September, we'll teach you to read proper." She was looking at Lily now. "Remember this: We're not gonna spend all our life chewin' dirt." (Bridie gave Lily consolation after humiliation in school). Once more, Gutteridge leans confidently on family ties to channel these two emotional instances in the novel.

A most delicate matter becomes the centerpiece in the story when Lily gets pregnant. Such occurrence in the late 19th century would certainly be critical for a woman, given the epoch, which I won't advance here, of course. From this incident up to the dénouement, readers will be taken on a carrousel ride, going up, going down with Lily's predicaments. Were it not enough, Gutteridge gives us a soul-rending scene in Chapter 12: ""I do love you, Tom." "Then you'll marry me?" Lily looked away, then back. "I can't," she said. "But why?" She felt the full weight of his hurt and her own. "I can't marry a soldier.""

This is *Lily Fairchild.* The book is masterfully filled with wise dialogue and monologue, with profound reflections, introspective and clear intentions to teach and leave an imprint on the reader. I have enjoyed Gutteridge´s way to deal with history in the making blended with memories and an intensely personal story. These ingredients will please the most demanding of readers. Thank you, Don.

What Readers should not Miss
A Review of Donna Wootton's Novel
What Shirley Missed

(Prose) (2019) Hidden Brook Press. Canada

"*A celebration of life involves stories.*" This is the first line of the book's last Chapter. This is what Donna Wootton's book is about. Family issues, secrets and stories are inevitable and ideal for authors to explore. There are delicate themes, but worth writing about. Everyone has a family, everyone weaves through the "slings and arrows" of family conflicts. *What Shirley Missed* gives us a taste of what we know well, of what many of us have experienced. The author does it in a fast-moving, snow-balling unfolding of events from the very beginning.

The characters are wonderfully credible. Wootton paints a picture of their behavior with a confident hand. She exploits their predicaments letting mini-plots in the conversations rise and shock me. These fuel the crescendo of the main plot when Pamela, Shirley's daughter, bursts into the room: "*How could you?" Pamela barged past her mother. "What were you thinking?" she said as she stomped into the hallway without hugging her mother.*" Once the conversation starts, it is one discovery after another. Wootton provides surprise turns that create suspense and interest.

To my delight, I detected nuances of humor as well, despite the tense situations, in Shirley's thoughts trailing off to her many precautions ("*Shirley kept her hands folded, thinking how clever she'd been wearing that hat. Not only did it hide her face from the dealers, it also hid her from any road cameras they passed.*") and arrangements for what she had done that upset her daughter and the family then to her comments about her pregnancy. Such feeling remained with me throughout the book. On page sixteen I was already determined to go all the way to the end.

Another example of the author's skills is her time interplay with scenes, the overlapping of events that shift from the family conversation to Shirley's thoughts, both to the far past and to the moment her husband and daughter are pressing her to talk. The author succeeds in charging the atmosphere with more and more questions, which give Chapter 1 material enough to fill the next 200 pages.

What follows turns into an excellent meditation about immigration, doubt, faith, human values, vanity, old age, etc. As if this were not enough, she covers the philosophical ideas of how life unfurls, people's lives, dreams and sacrifices, and of course finally, death. This confers Wootton's style a plasticity that I enjoyed as a reader.

There are social-psychological ramifications at play throughout the book. Wootton handles them chapter by chapter, through the characters´ reflections and aspirations.

The author moves on different themes, touches upon them or develops them, but they pivot on the main plot, as I argued before: the human sketches and circumstances described by Wootton are understandable and believable, a quality I appreciate as a reader.

The story, the plot, the characters and the message are valid for those like me who have accumulated anecdotes and memories with the years. It is helpful too for younger generations experiencing life. The book is a welcome voyage into people like us, no overdoing in its proposal, no superfluous lines or unnecessary characters.

Wootton writes with ease and insight, showing ins and outs, ups and downs in the scenes, the inner lacking and desires bubbling in Shirley, which affect those around her. Wootton also unveils society's multi-cultural fabric and traditions; objectivity, elegance and poise in her seasoned pen, and looks at the gentle threads of family interaction, chiefly the intergenerational one.

I could notice the fineness with which Wootton outlines people's hopes and subjects of conversation. Solidly based on family values and synergy, the author achieves in painting, beyond words, the cultural input brought in by a diverse inflow of immigrants, exceptionally harmonized alongside the existing one. Family is the core, the forge and springboard to venture into the world or come seeking warmth and love.

Wootton also does well in displaying for the reader a variety of events, customs, and musts in social attachments. She knits the chapters together not only on a temporal plane of space, place and concrete names but also blends with the ethereal construct of time.

I was pleased by the author's dedication to the prom. In Cuba, one important date in the life of a teenage girl is the "quince party." In Cuban culture this party is held for a girl when she turns fifteen. It is a celebratory day with joyful rituals and ceremonies. It includes a convertible car parade for the birthday girl, photo sessions, new clothes, party with friends, etc. The author's intention to give the reader all the details of the prom stroke home with me.

The prom, the bridge game, the market, the beach, home, the golf tournament, the demonstration, the police station, funerals, etc. are the author's socially-projected "alibi" to ripen the novel's plot. They are the contexts where human thoughts are ignited and acts performed and made visible by Wootton.

Enjoy this new book by Donna Wootton. Readers should not miss it, as they should not miss the author's graceful depiction of people and places, of circumstances and fate. Wootton has celebrated lives, starting with Shirley's, and in doing so has left us a story that deserves to be read and pondered. Thank you, Donna.

Twisted arms, second season
Essays on three key supporters of my literary work

After rounds of talks with my publisher, I persuaded him (again, he was against it) that I wanted to collect, revise and organize brief literary comments I was systematically voicing in "A Word About," my section in the CCLA The Envoy newsletter, about Canadian poets and poems they send to the Editor – focusing on Richard Marvin Grove (Tai), John B. Lee and James Deahl. Many other The Envoy contributing poets are included in this book already.

As a thank-you coda to Grove, Lee and Deahl for this book, my previous one and my poetry books – achievements I have attained especially thanks to them – I am including this resulting, enriched essay here, heartily smiling at my three friends´ You-don't-have-to-do-this modest stance, and much to my pleasure in letting the public know how vital and huge their support has been.

As a bonus, I have included four more essays on them. The first, about a book by Grove that reminisces his visits to Cuba years ago, *Cuba Poems. In Celebration of a Trip to the Caribbean*; the second is on *This is How We See the World*, by Lee; the third one about *Travelling The Lost Highway*, by Deahl; and the last one about *Tamaracks: Canadian Poetry for the 21st Century*, edited by Deahl.

The three poets embody, like all Canadian poets, the Canadian poetdom I have always talked about. Thank you, my friends.

Architects and Epitomes.
A Word about Three Canadian Poets:
Richard Marvin Grove (Tai),
John B. Lee
James Deahl.

Comments on poetry they have published in *The Envoy, the CCLA newsletter*

(Poetry) (2019) Hidden Brook Press. Canada

The year 2016 was a landmark – why not say a timemark – in my life: I was introduced to Canada Cuba Literary Alliance (CCLA) Founding President Richard Grove by CCLA Ambassador in Gibara, Jorge Pérez. From then on I was immersed in an extensive, intense and refreshing exchange with Canadian poets and their craft.

My college studies, Teacher Education English Major, had provided insight of Canada from a bird's-eye-view cultural-literary approach as part of my curricular pursuits but it fell short of really fanning out for me the wealth, depth, width and prominence of Canadian literature.

Richard Grove filled that void with a wonderful host of digital and conventional books coming in from 2016 until today, and also invited authors to send their works to me. It turned me into an avid recipient of poetry chiefly, but also prose, essays and research carried out by scholars (Terry Barker, for example) on outstanding Canadian authors and Canadian poetry in general.

His support, along with many other poet friends – like John B. Lee, who *actually read* my humble poems and took time to suggest, respectfully, changes for improvement! – was motivation enough to work on and soon publish my book *In a Fragile Moment: A Landscape of Canadian Poetry* (Hidden Brook Press, 2020), a tribute compilation of thirty-six reviews and essays I wrote about the CCLA and thirty-one Canadian writers. Such a project was immediately supported by Grove (who put love, faith, personal budget, publishing house, and unlimited efforts into seeing it come to fruition), Grove's wife (Kim, who gently gifted me with a line from her poetry to title my book), Lee and James Deahl.

Many other Canadian poets celebrated the idea too. During the past months, the inflow has gathered spectacular momentum. I have been receiving books from Canadian poets who, encouraged by dear poet friend James, have generously contributed to my bookshelf, my knowledge of their literary prowess and my further appreciation of Canadian poetdom.

Among the many generalizations I can make out of reading them and all Canadian poets who have entered my life (deep connection to the land; identification with nature and wild life; a rooted sense of belonging to Canadian geography plus social-thought ramifications therefrom; a feeling of proud nationality/nationhood; freshness and versatility in the use of expressive means and images; etc.), some are particularly salient and heart-warming to me: their commitment to family and values – values to champion, besides, what is true and what is moral beyond and above family contexts, and transcend in terms of aesthetics, cognition and axiology to what is loftier and spiritual. In addition are the poets´ reminiscences of childhood and their recollection of friends and friendship.

Both from the very opening dedication pages in their books, poems and in-memoriam poems, we are moved by this convergence of leitmotifs which stand the test of time, finely penned and felt by the poets. May this "warm light upon this land" *(Taken from the title of a poetry book by James Deahl, Even This Land Was Born Of Light, 1993, Moonstone Press. Canada)* continue to shine and bless Canadians, Cubans and lit-loving people of good will everywhere.

Richard Marvin Grove (Tai)

Grove is every inch a poet. He captures the world's everydayness, eternalizing it for us and for those to come. He exudes poetry, delicacy/passion and experience in every thing he writes and does. His poem "Spring" *(Published in The Envoy 88, June 2019)* is an ode to nature, a deep-rooted love affair Canadian poets have. Irony is handled as an expressive means of the language: "April is the cruelest month / with temperatures rising / finally into life, even at night."

The utility of the means works in the following terms: "A word used ironically may sometimes express very subtle, almost imperceptible nuances of meaning." *(Taken from Stylistics, 1981, Moscow Vyssaja Skola, by I. R. Galperin)* Richard Altick stated that "The effect of irony lies in the striking disparity between what is said and what is meant." *(Idem previous quotation)*

As readers, we sense this "disparity" immediately, as we are aware of the season's majesty, but the next lines in the poem also contribute to help us see the masterful use of irony: "Lilac buds are kissing / the warm air with swelling buds…" Grove meant precisely the opposite in the opening lines! Spring is presented too as opposed to winter, "… frost threatened landscape / that swirls memory with desire / only to be slammed / by her sister, winter's / punishing joke." The poet contrasts the two seasons: "The last of shadowed snow / the melancholy reminders / of hunkering down / are all but gone." And goes on in obvious joy: "Black budding branches bulge / with the promise of life / now full of winged music… / … it will not snow – again."

His poem "My Heart Grows Wings," *(Published in The Envoy 92, October 2019; previously in A Small Payback, Ode to Victoria Lake. Hidden Brook Press, 2016)* is rich in beauty and plasticity of image and metaphor: "Ebony branches part / to brilliant sundrenched view…" Repetition as a stylistic device is appreciated in "… down, down over the tree tip spires / to vast wilderness panorama…" emphasizing the notion of movement and expansion. Epithets enhance his interpretation of the natural scenario: "… vast wilderness panorama… unsullied, pristine. From the general view, the poet now zooms in on a spectacular sight he describes in unique tropes: "Wing tips deep, / loon lances / silver mirrored sky."

The universe leans softly onto his sheet of paper, gently star-guiding his pen in poems that echo "… a gentle whisper of harmony…," for example, in his piece "A silent echo heard" *(Published in The Envoy 93, November 2019)*: "a gentle whisper of harmony / ripples across / the mist covered lake / into the universe."

Tai's sensitive, artistic eye knows how to give a poetic touch to reality, granting it the colours of nature, in its role of gracing human presence: "From our hotel window / we can see a small group / gathered / in a willow-draped park…" There are key **word-images** in the poem to really construe how imbued the poet is in what he watches (we cannot forget he is also an artist) and how he is able to draw out cosmic connotations from a common sight and serve it to us, nature once more a blazoning element: "in slow motion / doing Tai Chi. / Fifteen or more / filling the early morning, / **swaying in unison**, / a gentle **whisper of harmony** / **ripples across** / the mist covered lake / **into the universe**."

We enjoy wonder-poetry reaching the readership through The Envoy. Grove and my next poets honor the newsletter with their submissions and publish edifying creations. Thank you, Tai, for your poetry flowing so freely, so intimately.

John B. Lee

John B. Lee's writing gift has made him a recipient of as many awards as is humanly possible. He has tirelessly crafted piece after piece in his long, prolific career. He has written nearly about everything with unique perspective and style. He has memorialized his travelling experiences in books about his own and other countries. As well, Lee's contribution and adherence to the long-standing tradition of celebrating nature – awesome, edifying, unavoidably present, whether we see it or not, whether we want to see it or not – is transcendental.

Canada's formidable scenery owes to poets as much as they owe to its being so glorious: an all embracing foundry of beauty and spiritual growth. Lee also celebrates life and turns his language and his style into forging tools leaving us with such poems. No better insight into Lee than my closing quotation: "… a true idiosyncrasy of style is the result of an author's success in compelling language to conform to his… experience." *(Taken from In a Fragile Moment: A Landscape of Canadian Poetry. Hidden Brook Press, 2020)*

Lee's elegance has notably achieved that. For example, his poem "My Love is Like an All-Day Rain," *(Published in The Envoy 93, November 2019)* one of the many he has sent to me during our e-mail exchanges along with his permission to publish them, invites the reader to the unique experience of love from an in-depth look at nature in a sustained orchestration of similes and metaphors.

Lee eases us into the natural world, the coupling of rain and soil and the chain of unfolding events, revealing the magic of what otherwise might seem like ordinary. The perspective he reveals for us is sweetly magnificent. Amidst this explosion of images capitalizing on the wonders of nature, Lee allows us to anticipate sensuousness that blossoms – to honor the poet's chord – in the end-lines: "but keep this rain in mind, my love / these ethers gauzed in grey / were / once the amorous continuum of weather / caught within the petals of your crimson rose." I have read the poem several times, each taking me nearer to a heaven-on-earth state, each uncovering a fresh path. Thank you, John, for this extraordinary gift you share with us.

James Deahl

James Deahl, another prolific poet friend, who regales us with artistry at its best. James writes with a style that envelops and snuggles warmly, even when winter is the subject. The poem "Sarnia By Starlight" *(Published in The Envoy 93, November 2019. Poem taken from Travelling the Lost Highway, Guernica Editions, 2019)* is a harmony of cityscape and natural scenery, superbly, sensually blended by James to sing to his beloved Sarnia: "Sarnia's adorned / by a skein of lights / strung between sky / and night's river."

The city is suspended in a symphony of blue pulses, evening falling, a girl's open blouse, a skein of lights, sky, night's river and starlight giving us a cozy feeling of home, sweet home: "Must every object / that summons desire / be beautiful? / An ashplant? / That girl's open blouse?" Nature is a diva in his poetry: "A slow, blue pulse / from cold water. / Call and response / of smoke and wind / as evening falls" and he magically bestows it with human traits in a first-class combination of simile, metaphor and personification: "Starlight enters / with ancient airs / like a bride, / the music dancing / on her shy lips."

The second poem, "Quince-bush In Winter," is the poet's sharp eye capturing beauty in winter and trees. Still connected to the human reference in the poem, James grants the leading role to the quinces´ warmth that "spreads through January's cold." He portrays the bright side of things with metaphorical expressions: "My neighbour's quinces have all put on white caps. / She never harvests her quinces / so they hang all winter, orange globes / lighting my mornings as the sun begins to rise."

James Deahl appeared in 2020 as our Guest Poet, together with Norma West Linder, on the 16th The Ambassador volume, the CCLA official magazine. Thank you, James, for your touching poetry.

I have tried to condense in a few words my modest insight of three exceptional poets´ writing. My first review book, *In a Fragile Moment: A Landscape of Canadian Poetry (Hidden Brook Press, 2020)* included longer analyses on specific books they published. Hence, their reluctance to appear here again.

I am lucky to have been able to read their poetry, understand and enjoy it. In the process they contributed to my personal growth, both though their poems and their advice, support and encouragement. I cannot think of a more fitting title for this essay than calling them poetry architects and poet epitomes. Thank you, Tai, John, James!

Travelling through Poetry with Richard Marvin Grove
A Journey of Pleasures in his
Cuba Poems. In Celebration of a Trip to the Caribbean

(Poetry) (2002) Hidden Brook Press. Canada

I have been blessed during my personal and professional life by demonstrations of acknowledgement that I have welcomed with obvious self-pride at having accomplished something, or brought joy and satisfaction to someone, an acquaintance, a total stranger, or as is the case now, to a friend I care about: Richard Marvin Grove (Tai), Founding President of the Canada Cuba Literary Alliance (CCLA). Yet I have also taken it with a mature awareness and objectivity that if I am acknowledged by an experienced, qualified friend, it is because I have earned his praise and what I do has some worth.

Recognition comes in many forms, one of them is being asked in my present status as CCLA member – promoted later by "conspiring" friends and members to CCLA Cuban President and Editor-in-chief of The Ambassador magazine – to edit books and anthologies, cooperate with other writers and editors, translate, revise and finally write reviews about poetry and prose.

Poets like John B. Lee, Bruce Meyer, Ronnie R. Brown, Elana Wolff, Laurence Hutchman, Eva Kolacz, Ed Woods, Michael Mirolla, Laurie Kruk, Henry Beissel, etc., have kindly asked me to write a few words about some of their works and include them in my review books. Actually, my second volume, the one I am presenting here, came to life thanks to Grove and CCLA key player, James Deahl, who put brain, brawn and heart into promoting my work and encouraging those fine authors to send me their books, which they did in a most generous gesture, filling my bookshelf with treasures.

It is my privilege today to talk about a book by a prolific writer and artist, Richard Grove. I cherish a personal collection of over twelve of his books, photography, poetry, prose or an integration of these, he has sent or brought to me these last four years, ranging from his early works to more recent publications. I chose a particularly interesting book to write about thus honoring in return his having honored me with his friendship, trust and help in many circumstances and ways.

Nevertheless, my review does not stem from a mechanical, biased reason based on his being my friend; it fully responds to his contribution to Cuba – through *his* CCLA, founded in 2004 and still floating above objective and subjective setbacks; vigorously, invaluably supported by many judicious patriots and friends – to Canadian and Cuban culture, and logically to poetry.

Cuba Poems. In Celebration of a Trip to the Caribbean is a book of fond memories, eagerness to visit, know, meet, mix; conceived in the very same "wide-eyed with anticipation" favorable atmosphere Grove refers to in his opening piece, "Cuba, Here We Come." The title reflects his joyful experience with a key phrase, "in celebration of."

We are invited to a trip across the book's proposal of poems and anecdotes, forged from a tourist's vision of a Cuba he faces. His first-world individuality enters a third-world reality with expectations and curiosity – and an open heart. I remember the first time I wrote about him, some four years ago: I reviewed the collaborative John B. Lee-Richard Grove *In This We Hear The Light* (Hidden Brook Press, 2013, photography-poems) and said the authors "… do not wish to veil their way of expressing themselves from a very personal and outsider who has been inside perspective, which is raw sometimes, but never irreverent, in my view." *(Taken from my review book In a Fragile Moment: A Landscape of Canadian Poetry, Hidden Brook Press, 2020, my essay Touched by the Light. A review of John B. Lee and Richard M. Grove's In This We Hear The Light (Poetry and Photography) (2013) Hidden Brook Press. Canada)* In the book I am commenting today, we will encounter this mood, and will understand it inasmuch as there is empathy and appreciation in his heart for the Cuba he knows now and loves.

Grove's initial "tourist excitement" is sensed in the end-lines: "Passports clutched in one hand / tickets and reservations / clenched in other with / dreams and hopes / of sun, sand and snoozes." The richness of the poet's style begins to shine right at this point: "Passports clutched in one hand / tickets and reservations / clenched in other…" is a direct primary dictionary meaning sentence; however, two elements jump at me as a reader.

The first one is the employment of two effective transitive verbs (they are in fact non-finite verb forms, *ed*-participles, acting as noun-modifiers, adjectives) to describe the state of elation or nervousness or impatience the poet is in, "clutched" and "clenched." He could have simply used *held* or *carried* but he chose, intentionally, to colour the poem with more semantically-charged words, stylistically enhancing the intended message. The second detail is that passports, tickets and reservations are clutched and clenched respectively, yet these verbs are added a metaphorical meaning-role when the poet pairs them with the next sentence unit, a prepositional phrase: "clenched in other with / dreams and hopes / of sun, sand and snoozes." Now the brand-new linguistic-stylistic hue is evident.

An extra element I *dare* refer to regarding the verbs *clutched* and *clenched* is that together with their metaphorical value, there is also a latent zeugma in their use. Zeugma is "… the use of a word in the same grammatical but different semantic relations to two adjacent words in the context, the semantic relations being, on the one hand, literal, and, on the other, transferred." *(Taken from Stylistics, 1981, Moscow Vyssaja Skola, by I. R. Galperin)* Both verbs function literally in "Passports clutched in one hand / tickets and reservations / clenched in other…" and transfer their meanings to figurative enclosed in the prepositional phrase "clenched in other with / dreams and hopes / of sun, sand and snoozes."

The setbacks I mentioned before are hinted in the second poem, "Never Leave Home Without it." The tour guide, "with wide eyed smile," reminds them and readers that American Express cards cannot be used in Cuba due to blockade issues imposed by the US government. Fortunately, "Visa and MasterCard are welcome."

A tempting blend of nature-loving body and heart, willingness to escape the hectic mazes of Toronto life and gratefulness for being at a Cuban beach resort, are the aspects finely recreated by Grove in his "Hard to Believe We are in Cuba." Thus we are pleased to read "… I woke from my sun-worshipping / dream state to the sudden salty / reminder that I was on a soft, / tan, sandy beach of Cuba," understand the radical – agreeable – change he has undergone as "I was no longer in my Toronto condo bed / being lured by computer, email, / time restraints and the bottom line" and swim in his "… cool, green ocean, / paces away, beckoning me."

The poet's fascination reaches a cusp in the next poem, "More." He broadly contrasts being in Toronto against being in Cuba: "In the middle of November, / everything is sweeter, / better in Cuba than in Toronto." To illustrate his sensations he engages in a sequence of allusions to nature, sun, breeze, evening; even the galaxy: "The blossom kissing afternoon sun / shines more brightly. // The palm shimmering breeze / of early evening is more alluring. // Orion's midnight belt / sparkles more clearly." Between the lines, an environmentalist vision is noticed. Orion is more discernible from a pollution-free geographical location.

The poem ends as it began, the first stanza is repeated. In a way, I see rhythm in the words chosen and in this structural arrangement, much in line with the musical context the poet is a part of.

In my words about Richard Grove's poem "My Heart Grows Wings," I said it is "… rich in beauty and plasticity of image and metaphor." *(Read the whole review in this book: Architects and Epitomes. A Word about Three Canadian Poets: Richard Marvin Grove (Tai), John B. Lee and James Deahl. Comments on poetry they have published in The Envoy, the CCLA newsletter (Poetry) (2019)* My opinion applies entirely to Grove's next poem, "A Cuban Sun Shower." On the course of my explanation, I will present the poem whole, as it is brief and worth-quoting.

The poet rejoices in the exuberance of the place, "Lush, outstretched palm branches, / sweep the Cuban sky, / gently fanning in salt air," deploying a sustained metaphor that lasts through the whole piece: "… the single cloud / that grins overhead / christening our morning…" Personification as an expressive means – "… the attributing to abstract or inanimate objects qualities characteristic of persons." *(Taken from New Horizons, McClelland and Stewart Limited, Revised edition, Canada, 1965)* – is attained through the verbs "grins" and "christening." This language means occurs as a result of interplay of realities fused by the poet, who reveals metaphorical nexuses-implications textually overlapping: "… the single cloud… christening our morning…"

The finish lines heighten this figurative conjuration conceived and achieved by Grove: "christening our morning / with a sun shower / of expectation."

To my pleasure, I want to revisit prior views I have written about Grove's style. As my conclusion to John B. Lee and Richard Grove's book, *Two Thousand Seventeen* (2018) Sanbun Publishers. New Delhi. India, I said "The fountain of imagery expressed by both writers and the freshness in their style do not cease to amaze me." *(Taken from Timeless Poetry in a Timeless Land. A brief review of Richard Marvin Grove and John B. Lee's Two Thousand Seventeen (Poetry) (2018) Sanbun Publishers. New Delhi, India, in my review book In a Fragile Moment: A Landscape of Canadian Poetry, Hidden Brook Press, 2020)* My assertion holds up to characterize "A Cuban Sun Shower."

I know Richard Grove personally, I call him my friend. I can say for a fact that Tai (that is how friends call him) is a man of many qualities. Apart from his artistry in photography and writing, his generosity (proven in many occasions), his profound faith, his way with words and his gift as a public speaker, we also enjoy his humor. Logically, it is present in his poetry. "I Only Have Eyes For You My Love" is a fine example of humor and use of expressive means, like suspense and repetition.

Suspense operates on the anticipatory mechanisms a poet triggers in the reader or listener (we cannot forget the original orality of poetry) therefore its "main purpose is to prepare the reader for the… logical conclusion of the utterance," *(Taken from I. R. Galperin. Stylistics. Moscow Vyssaja Skola. 1981)* That is what Grove does in the poem aided by repeating (another expedient expressive tool) the opening refrain "I only have eyes for you, my love, / though I must confess."

Grove does not leave out **metaphors**, "I only have eyes for you, my love, / though I must confess / the copper tone buxom senorita, / **licked by the Caribbean sun, / caressed by the Cuban breeze**, / beamed for me." In order to really display more realistically the nature of a poem, which recreates a true event, the poet incorporates a seemingly conversational twist. I say *seemingly* because we are not fully certain of how much his words materialize from his "confessional" attitude into the tangible act of confessing.

To build up a conversational style, the poet resorts to colloquial phrases and idiomatic turns: "… a pretty Cuban **head turner**." "the… senorita, / … **beamed** for me," "bronze **toy boy**, / blond, with tattooed **pecs**…" (this latter, a final clipping in lexicological terms) to which he incorporates one example of foreignism, "senorita," to put the situation in the Cuban context (Spanish language).

How the poem finishes, unexpected ending, is the expression of humor, assisted by the ways in which he depicts both the "senorita" and the boy. The last two lines, "I only have eyes for you, my love / though I must confess," are reminiscent of sincere love and the religiousness that is part of Grove's profound faith I mentioned earlier: notice that in all the previous stanzas the verb, "confess," is transitive (it has a direct object); on the other hand, in the last line it changes to its intransitive function (no direct object), so it transfigures into an allusion to a possible act of religious confession.

My last poem under analysis is "A View of Contrasts." Grove shows his expertise in depicting nature, be it Canadian or Cuban, with superb images. As he does, we distinguish as well the contrasts he made explicit in his poem, "Hard to Believe We are in Cuba." Highly descriptive to the minutest detail, "… the dirge of dry red clay earth / with palm rimmed horizons / capping jungle homogeny. / Lush banana plantations fill gently rolling valleys past / concrete, tin capped, peasant huts…," the poet talks about an everyday Cuban scene: "… modest, laboured gardens from / roving speckled pigs and / white bearded billygoats…"

The contrast is shown in his lines: "… adventures end, takes us back / to North American style opulence called / creature comforts of pressed linen…," strengthened in the closing ones, "Home, past roadside open wells where / post siesta / farmers water their / rib-clad burros, / sending us on our way with gentle / smiling waves…" Grove has portrayed an idyllic setting, his nostalgia seeping beneath the lines, metaphors alive and moving: "… gentle / smiling waves."

I have traveled with Richard Grove. I have embarked on a journey of pleasures in resemblances and contrasts, content and form, text and context, literality and tropes. And I have returned for a celebration, too, of my Cuba. Thank you, Tai.

John B. Lee: A Poetry Writer – Not a Poet
An Appraisal of Five of his Poems in
This is How We See the World

(Poetry) (2017) Hidden Brook Press. Canada

For someone who would "… far rather be referred to as someone who writes poetry than be called a poet" *(Taken from John B. Lee's book This is How We See the World, Hidden Brook Press, 2017. His introductory words)*, Canadian poet John B. Lee has an irresistibly mysterious way with words and images few ever acquire, much less develop in a lifetime. Bernice Lever says Lee is a "master craftsman… (his) … lines flow smoothly from one fresh new metaphor to the next." *(Taken from back-cover comments on This is How We See the World, Hidden Brook Press, 2017)*

I leapt in childlike pride – and naïve incredulity at my "feat" – when I read the first three lines from Lee's "… how to read this poem": "This poem / is a dance / a ritual…" I had scribbled a modest one, "Dance of Words," where I used the same analogies: "They follow their own rhythms / a ritual into the most fruitful of moments, / in a dance / of poet / and words." *(Taken from Bridges Series Book IV, Where the Heart Lies. Hidden Brook Press. 2018. Re-published in my second poetry book, This Pulse of Life, These Words I Found. Hidden Brook Press, 2021)*

If we assume poetry as a remarkably creative, lettered crystallization of outer and inner realities, we will discern the poet's identification with his lines: "Imagine yourself as one / or all of these lines." The poet is one with his creation; he is part of that reality he cups in his hand and magic-wand-touches in his mind. The poet indentifies with the reader, and sees himself as a reader too.

By using a simile, "Imagine the poem closing you in / like a cell…" Lee proposes a micro-instant of experiencing a physical-mental solitude in encasement; to then oppose the idea with a thesis of unbound freedom writing/reading provides: "read this poem / to set yourself free."

Implicated in the act of crafting poetry and extolling it, the poet never forgets the woman his books are consistently dedicated to, Cathy, his wife. Shakespeare would have blushed in his secret wish to have forged "I Wake to Breathe Your Beauty In." *(Shakespeare's Sonnet XLI reads: "Thy beauty, and thy years full well befits, / For still temptation follows where thou art. / Gentle thou art, and therefore to be won, / Beauteous thou art…" Taken from Complete Works of William Shakespeare, Volume XVIII, Philadelphia David McKay Publisher, no year)*

Neruda would applaud this poem and cite his Sonnet XXVII, "… tienes líneas de luna, caminos de manzana, // Desnuda eres azul como la noche en Cuba…" ("You have moonlines, apple roads // Nude you are blue like the night in Cuba") *(Taken from En el corazón de un poeta. Instituto Cubano del Libro. Editorial de Ediciones Especiales, 2006, Biblioteca Familiar)*

Lee sets this piece in the after-waking moment, a soft, dream-like atmosphere nudging his hand to pen "I wake to breathe your beauty in / your soft pink sex…" Bare sensuality, as the woman's, throbs in the lines. The phrase "… your shape procures / a note so faintly played / upon the felts / it leaves no mark…," suggests *not* that her shape is unsubstantial. It rather highlights in stunning poetic dissertation its delicacy, how it gently sits on the textile, probably kindling in the poet's eye a proud notion that her shape is worthy of posing for an artist.

Surmising she is asleep while he watches her, I could not refrain myself from recalling Margaret Atwood's loving ""Variation on the Word Sleep," a poem I commented in my first review book. *(In a Fragile Moment: A Landscape of Canadian Poetry. Hidden Brook Press, 2020)* I said then that poets – artists and singers as well[9] – "find a source of inspiration in watching their beloved ones sleep. Atwood has created a lyrically sweet poem, a peaceful contemplation of her lover."

So has Lee, singing to his wife, finding beauty in her, as much as Edgar Allan Poe expressed in his classic "To Helen" *("Helen, thy beauty is to me / Like those Nicean barks of yore, / That / gently, o'er a perfumed sea… // Thy hyacinth hair, thy classic face, / Thy Naiad airs…" Quoted from memory)*. We tremble in the physicality of Lee's poem, how it fuses with "… the interior journey, the progress of the soul…" Roger Bell refers to in his Foreword to John B. Lee's book *This is How We See the World. (Hidden Brook Press, 2017)*

The poet achieves a crest where an illumination of spirituality communes with the physical element. One complements the other, eroticism handled with artistry: "… and I with sad melodies unsung / with wordless names and voiceless calling / dream the mild narcotic / of your gently moving breast."

Please take the previous poem as a first season, and "Lovely Woman in the Lake, My Wife, My Love" as season two – and expect more. Aphrodisia unfolds slowly, as the letters the poet gracefully molds, one by one, in his inspired ode to Cathy.

This is a poem that sensually *drips* water – remember Songs of Solomon: "I arose to open for my beloved, and my hands dripped with myrrh, my fingers with flowing myrrh, on the handles of the bolt. I opened for my beloved…" *(Also known as "Song of Songs" (The Holy Bible) www.biblegateway.com/passage/?search=Song...Songs)* – where the poet skillfully exploits the element: "… a kind of liquid everywhereness / fluxed within contours / inner motion and the softened fulcrums of your sex"

---

[9] One of the most touching songs I've ever heard is "I don't want to miss a thing" by Aerosmith. The sleeping lover is admired; tender lyrics unfold like poetry for me: "I could stay awake just to hear you breathing, watch you smile as you are sleeping… I don't want to close my eyes, I don't want to fall asleep… and I don't want to miss a thing…"

The lake and the "Lovely Woman" unite: "Where you move / water *is* desire – desire *water.*" The poet is *caught up* in the sight he rejoices in and carves unstoppable imagery out of like magic: "all flag and wind / is man / caught up, / his architecture aping strength / until the instant of forgetting…" The last three lines are immortal, as much as the poet implies he wants to be: "… reside within the incredible dominion of your flesh / thinking about being alive / and nothing else."

What we expect to find in a poem, an explanation of beauty, life – death, a philosophy of the soul unfurling in tropes of genuine birth; what has been said and written so many times now re-worded and re-engraved in floating, streaming poetic lines, which finally perch upon our trembling realization – an enlightenment – and construal of veiled things and feelings, and sit upon our sentient, vulnerable hearts, is explored by the poet in "By the Shore's Collapsing Waters I am Bound."

Lee finds it all and exposes it resorting to an inspiring source, the sea, which he acknowledges in his closing simile, "… like the surface of the sea." He enters meditative, inquisitive realms only chosen ones tread on, leaving behind his revelatory penning: "Something you notice / in memory / some half-forgotten pain / some darkening flaw of love…" The line "The long shadow you cast / standing in your lifelight," invites to an inward reflection of our lives, to a revision of that shadow we cast, understood as influence, mark, legacy; that he puts in perspective for us to see and ponder.

I leapt again in reading this poem and remembering mine, "The First Day," a contemplative piece I sent to him and he generously praised and offered advice for improvement – that *other* gift he has of helping others, honoring James Deahl's words: "No poet learns the craft without help and sage advice from those who have already achieved a higher level of writing." *(Taken from Under the Mulberry Tree: Poems for & about Raymond Souster. Quattro Books Inc. 2014. Edited by James Deahl)* I have been helped by many poet friends of "a higher level of writing."

In my piece I say, humbly, "… awake at this hour in the sleepy waterside / I calibrate my existence as I surf / with the tide / weigh my crests and shallows / skin-deep essences retained / substantial unrepeated // this is where I stand, / before the primordial source. // my eyes receive awakening / this pulse of life refreshed / to embrace me / like the first day of all creation." *(Published In The Envoy 92, Newsletter of the Canada Cuba Literary Alliance. October, 2019, and re-published in my second poetry book, This Pulse of Life, These Words I Found. Hidden Brook Press, 2021)*

Lee confers dreams a special significance in his poem, as we lie down and rise every day from our transit phase of sleeping and dreaming. Such phase is biologically mandatory in human and natural cycles, and is lyrically drafted by Lee in his poem's final lines: "The Kama sutra of many sleeps / where you curl and change / like the surface of the sea." Dialectical in its underlying sinews, the poem claims for change – over sleep; change that must be channeled positively – in awakening, in our reflection of living, coloured by the manifold interpretations sparkled in the readers through this allusion to Kama sutra.

One of my reviews of Lee's oeuvre led me to say that "I had to force myself to commenting on only seven poems, tempted by scores of them!" *(Read Lucky Seven: Monumental Architecture. A review of seven poems from John B. Lee's Bread, Water, Love (Poetry), in These Are the Words, by George Elliott Clarke and John B. Lee. In a Fragile Moment: A Landscape of Canadian Poetry. Hidden Brook Press, 2020)* Therefore, I will have to stop my analyses here as well by briefly referring to the poem "Starless and Blue at Midnight."

Universe and nature are described and related in seven lines – a biblical-seven allusion? – where the poet uses attractive images like "the moon has lost her clock," poetically giving a personification symbolism to the satellite. The poet himself pauses to contemplate what he has been able to hold in his poet hand and *sigh* into a poem: "… the water colder for that hour / where the bunting flutters / and goes quiet."

He charmingly bonds in one scene the "Baffin skies," "midnight," "the moon," "the mountains," "the water," even "that hour" and the fluttering "bunting." It is an observant, all-inclusive apprehension by the poet of what surrounds him at midnight: scenarios, phenomena, nature (fauna and landscape), time, open spaces ("skies") and references to absent objects ("starless"). The poet pans around the vista, from upper-layer observation through more earthward, far sights, to closer land "companion": "the water colder…," and in-mid-air creature that complies to the hour and "flutters and goes quiet" – in the seventh line… Peace soars in place and time.

In his Foreword to Richard Grove's *A Small Payback, Ode to Victoria Lake (Hidden Brook Press, 2016)*, Lee said: "In this book… you have the spirit of the place… A glimpse of grace. Rare and precious." I dare state Lee's "Starless and Blue at Midnight" captures that essence too, that spirit of the place flitting about in the tranquility provided after the bird "goes quiet."

A further – and final – observation I do not want to obviate. Reading Lee's poems, especially "By the Shore's Collapsing Waters I am Bound" and "Starless and Blue at Midnight," I felt flashes of Al Purdy's poems "Pause," and "Red Leaves." *(For in-depth comparison you will have to read The Canadian Titan of Land and Time. A review of some of Al Purdy's poems in Beyond Remembering: The Collected Poems of Al Purdy (Poetry) (2000) Harbour Publishing. Canada; and of course these two poems in Beyond Remembering: The Collected Poems of Al Purdy)*

Purdy's "Pause" "presents a moment when poet and reader sit together and watch. Dimensional layers are peeled off and a conundrum floats up for Al and for the reader, one combination where frontiers are blurred…" *(Taken from the aforementioned review)* Admiringly, Lee journeys on this path of enigmas he poses to the reader (which he has posed to himself before), this earnest questioning and search for answers in "By the Shore's Collapsing Waters I am Bound."

On the other hand, the Purdy poem "Red Leaves" is, in Dennis Lee's statement, Purdy's "broad movement in space time." *(Taken from Al Purdy. Essays on his Works, Guernica Editions Inc., 2002, edited by Linda Rogers. Denis Lee's words in his essay "The Poetry of Al Purdy." He thoroughly analyzes this concept in Purdy's "Love at Roblin Lake")* Matters connected to the universe "... and higher questions... and finally back to Purdy's line "this tranquil season," *(Idem previous quotation)* reflect John B. Lee's own serious scrutiny of these subjects, as is skillfully evoked in "Starless and Blue at Midnight" and most of his poetry.

George Whipple calls John B. Lee "The greatest living poet in English." He adds that Lee "... sows everyday experiences with a timeless gravity and awe." *(Both quotations on John B. Lee's back cover of This is How We See the World, Hidden Brook Press, 2017)* I have little to add – and keep my promise to stop – except that I am more than honored for having read, understood, learned from and e-met this transcending "someone who writes poetry." Thank you, John.

Highway Lost; Highway Regained
A Comment on Four Poems by James Deahl in
Travelling The Lost Highway

(Poetry) (2019) Guernica Editions. Canada

I have read poets whose poetry has marked me forever and in many aspects influenced and channeled my own writing. During my youth, in Spanish, one name stood out, Pablo Neruda, the Chilean giant who wrote passionate love poems and impressive political ones.

Also in Spanish, a Cuban, my Carilda Oliver Labra, translated and published in The Ambassador, the official magazine of the Canada Cuba Literary Alliance. Carilda is my ultimate Muse; her poetry is lyrical *par excellence.* She was every inch an erotic poetess of unsurpassed caliber and mastery of the intricacies of the word.

In college, I read the English greats. It is hard to pick one name but I will make do with Shakespeare, and my favorite woman poet is Elizabeth Barrett Browning. On this side of the world, I studied the American classics. Edgar Allan Poe ranks first; the female icon for me is Emily Dickinson.

In 2017 I started a welcome journey through Canadian poetry. It is indeed difficult to choose names out of a vast number of fine poets I have been reading these past four years yet I will settle with John B. Lee, Richard Grove and James Deahl. The female poets I feel more identified with are Elana Wolff, Merle Amodeo and Eva Kolacz. Readers must keep in mind that I am talking about favorites, never claiming they are the only ones, the best ones, the definitive ones. I have many more favorites.

I want to share a few comments precisely about James Deahl's *Travelling the Lost Highway*, a 2019 Guernica Edition. In this same review book I approach Lee, Grove, Deahl (as editor) and Wolff (I also reviewed Lee, Grove and Deahl in my first book, *In a Fragile Moment: A Landscape of Canadian Poetry (Hidden Brook Press, 2020)* with other titles.

Travelling the Lost Highway is a superb compilation of poems, written from 2011 to 2018, which presents us a mature poet who is always growing, whose acumen in observing, noticing, decoding realities and souls and penning all those experiences with fresh imagery and level-headed layout, ranks him among the most representative Canadian poet-chroniclers of love, life, society and nature.

The book is a man's story told in poetic form. He offers his vision of things, his insights based not on supposition or instinct but on his determination to gain knowledge of his themes while travelling. In his words: "One got to know the nation… one got to know the people." He is primordially interested in finding ways that "might recapture the values that once animated the American and Canadian people." *(Both quotations taken from the book's introductory words by Deahl)* You get a taste of all that in the book.

David Haskins said that "There are meditations, eulogies and laments contained here, passionate love poems, poems that call upon national and generational history…" *(Taken from the book's back-cover comments by Haskins)*

With these assertions in mind we read his opening poem, "A Music Innocent Of Time And Sound." A somber pun comes in the first line, where Deahl seriously plays with the overlapping meanings of "dead": "No Jews visit their dead during the dead / of winter." Solemnity in wording and intention envelops this piece, with a full-grown visualization of death.

The last two lines struck a biblical passage in me, my hypothesis leaping back to Jesus´ lesson about a first stone being cast only by those without sin. In a way, Deahl's variation, "We, the living, are never so innocent / as to fearlessly watch that casket down," is evocative of the teachings and truth in that scene.

In the poem, innocence and fearlessness of the living must bow while they "watch that casket down." In my view, "casket" does not mean only the coffin. Contextually, it develops into extended metonymical shades referring to death or even final judgment of our acts in life.

A hymn to death and life – natural, human and societal – is heard in "Woodlot." The poet has no choice but to seek refuge in nature, elicit hope from eager line-wishes: "buds proclaim / spring might be near at hand," where spring is hope and buds are the slowly blooming evidence that hope will eventually crystallize.

Even when "All is born anew in this woodlot," the second stanza pierces hope with a crude reality: "last month the remains / of the young teacher were dumped, / whatever life remained / leaking from her forty wounds." If in the first stanza we read of "plague-struck elms," the second bares another kind of plague, a sadly social one.

The closing lines are ominously vibrant, "her blood, / as if to claim this land her own, / tried, but failed, to penetrate / this frozen soil," sending a message of a posthumous symbolic will of the teacher to claim a life that was prematurely stolen from her.

Another poem I want to comment briefly is "Bells That Beat Against The Heart." Metaphors surprise us in this piece, like the one emerging from the title and retaken in the lines: "trees stand frozen where / water will pool in spring; / they are bells beating / against a fragile heart."

The way the poem is structured, the poet returns "through darkness" from nature, depicted in stanzas one and two. Then his "fragile heart" leads him to refuge in his salvation, "the woman I love." He had previously emphasized her relevance in the line "This is my only life," where "only" does not cage the man; it voices a choice, a preference of being within nature and with his woman.

That was stanza three and line one in the next. Stanza four goes back to nature, and metaphors ("dawn summons heavy clouds"), as if he felt safe between stanzas and right in the middle with his beloved.

"A Book Of Snow" is actually a poem filled with warmth, beauty, passion and high-style imagery. We rejoice in Deahl's "… miles of buried fields awaiting spring's touch. / The sky's a cathedral of light, a place / where only the impossible happens." The poet speaks in wonder of nature's might: "What strength do we have before implacable / nature? Even the green thought of April / grows ever more distant, exiled by / winter's fierce grip, by snow's vast solitude."

He runs to his lover's arms and shivers at "… the sudden shock of your beauty, / of pleasure beyond all expectation." He knits a grand finale, breathtaking and unforgettable, "Waking beside you after our night of love, / I want to give you the gift of my life / and February's book of snow."

For my comments on "Sarnia By Starlight" and "Quince-bush In Winter" the reader may go to my essay "Architects and Epitomes. A Word about Three Canadian Poets: Richard Marvin Grove (Tai), John B. Lee and James Deahl. Comments on poetry they have published in The Envoy, the CCLA newsletter (Poetry) (2019)" in this same review book.

For my brief characterization of the significance of the poem "After Coming To The North," the reader may consult my essay "My College Canada; My Sentimental Canada. A Brief Reflection on Canada and its Influence on Canadians and Cubans," also in this book.

James Deahl once more strums the strings of feeling and stirs diverse emotions. He has been doing that in the fifteen books to his name I have in my bookshelf. No wonder he is one of my favorites. Thank you, James.

Canadian Poetry for the Millennium
A Reverence for
Tamaracks: Canadian Poetry for the 21st Century

(Poetry) (2018) Lummox Press. U.S.A. Edited by James Deahl

Perhaps being somehow hyperbolic in my title, I feel it reflects anyway my frank judgment of an anthology that has left an exceptional indentation on the literary map. My second review book cannot – won't – go to printout nor reach public domain without a few modest words about a transcendental book, *Tamaracks: Canadian Poetry for the 21st Century,* edited by James Deahl. I call it exceptional and transcendental comfortably shielded in three central arguments. The first one is based on the opinion voiced by one of Canada's most qualified and prolific scholars, Terry Barker, who stated:

"*Tamaracks: Canadian poetry for the 21st Century* serves a similar function in today's political *milieu* as the *Canadian Poets* anthology did just over one hundred years ago in 1916. While I am not qualified to comment on the literary merit of the poetry in *Tamaracks*, it seems to me that it fulfills its two chief goals, as set out clearly by its editor at the beginning of his "Introduction": (1) "to present readers with some fine poetry" and (2) "to show where Canadian poetry stands about one fifth of the way into the 21st century." *(Taken from "Tracking the True North," by Terry Barker)* Barker places the anthology in a position of privilege and impressively – deservedly – ranks it among the most representative works of this type in the last hundred years.

The second argument reflects what Bruce Meyer, a well-known Canadian poet, said about it: "This is the most solid, broad, astute, and engaging selection of poetry yet published in the US or outside Canada. It doesn't make its selection based on sneering favoritism: these are all tremendously readable, beautifully written, and entirely expansive poems that speak to the complexities and breadth of Canada. Deahl has presented us with a selection that shows the greatness of Canadian poetry from coast to coast. He is judicious in his choices, yet he is entirely open to the great range of expression that this country has to offer. This is not a dot on the map of a generation, but a geography of words and ideas unique and enlightening unto itself. If you want to experience Canadian poetry, start with *Tamaracks*. You won't be disappointed. It is a brilliant collection!" I need not explain this passionate, established, respected criterion.

The third argument is a more personal, modest one: mine. As a reader, I am entitled to have opinions about what I read. *Tamaracks* educated me in very much the same terms and grounds as Meyer expounds in his heartening words or Barker considers it enjoys in its role as a comprehensive anthology that has a national coverage, even if some fine poets did not submit their poetry for a variety of reasons.

In this respect, there is a Cuban saying to describe the still perfect essentialness and wholeness of a work where many were invited yet not all finally participated. In Spanish we say: "*No están todos los que son; pero si son todos los que están*" (Not all the best ones who ought to be are included; but all who were included are the best too in their own right").

It means that a list of authors in this case may be incomplete in terms of names of renown not included on it and should have been, given their prestige; but it must be clear that all those who are on the list and published are equally prestigious and deserve their presence in the book, they suffice to honor the book and confer a high status to it.

What can a Cuban professor, a reader of Canadian poetry and apprentice of its prominence, add to Meyer's or Barker's contribution? They have defined from their angles the significance of a book that was needed. On the book's back-cover comments, we read "It's the first book of its kind in decades." Above, Michael Wurster and Judith Robinson had posited "It is about time a contemporary anthology of Canadian poetry was published… and James Deahl… is the perfect choice as Editor," and William Oxley opened the comments by saying: "… is a valuable and much-needed collection… the anthology is both a delightful and intelligent survey of contemporary poetry in the Canada of today."

The criteria I have quoted here bring me to my personal approach to the anthology. In my humble view, eight pillars/factors sustain a brilliant anthology:

The caliber of the poets invited to submit their work.

The quality of the poems submitted and later short-listed for publishing.

The editor in charge of the oftentimes heavy work of inviting, encouraging, re-inviting, convincing, receiving, conceiving, organizing, gleaning, short-listing, arranging, explaining, creating, etc.

The Publishing House assuming the responsibility of pre-publication promotion, printing, publication and post-promotion.

The parallel critical phases of designing, layout, artwork, revision, proofreading, etc.

Potential readership.

Temporal-spatial-contextual scenario of publication: Pertinence and opportuneness. (Accounted for on the book's back-cover comments and the quotations by Barker and Meyer)

Fulfillment of the editor's objectives. (Accounted for in Barker's words)

While I am not an expert on any of these points – nor claim that these points are the only ones or *the* ones at all – I can certainly express my position in regards to most of them as a reader, as a convinced believer in the significance of poetry and arts in general for the salvaging of the most important resource: human beings – and their creation in the broad sense of the word. Without them there would be no language, no education and no literary/artistic patrimony to safeguard.

No wonder Margaret Atwood, a high Canadian icon, said: "The arts"–as we've come to term them–are not a frill. They are the heart of the matter, because they are about our hearts, and our technological inventiveness is generated by emotions, not by our minds. A society without poetry and other arts would have broken its mirror and cut out its heart. It would no longer be what we recognize as human." *(Taken from her words in Beyond the Seventh Morning (Poetry) (2013) SandCrab Books. From the essay "Why Poetry," The Anne Szumigalski Memorial)*

There should be no pressing aspirations for humanity higher than to honorably and harmoniously live and co-exist and be spiritually enlightened. Language, the arts and literature are central to attaining such goals. The patrimony – science, literature, arts – created, inherited and preserved by society to be enjoyed today and tomorrow, covers the former elements and the tangible and intangible heritage in and by which we live. It is the legacy that builds cohesion, sense, trajectory, purpose, and developing mode into our actions as humans.

A. F. Moritz (included in the anthology) was very thorough in an interview in reference to the role of poetry. He referred to a poet's "job" as "To write well: creatively, authentically, powerfully, beautifully.... poetry is partly self-development... is duty, belonging to a community... poetry's role is as the guardian and developer of language." *(Taken from an interview on the Web)*

James Deahl has played – and by stating this I am addressing factor 3 – his poet (he is in the book) and editorial roles flawlessly. He has been called "A champion of poetry and poets" by friends, and is considered one of the most knowledgeable scholars when it comes to Canadian poetry. His fervor in bringing this anthology to fruition made him a personal "overseer" of the eight pillars I suggest.

Insistent on the fact that I have no expertise on any of the above-mentioned pillars, I still want to make a point about some of them. Factor 1 is paramount in attaining quality levels beyond standards. Of all 113 poets, I am familiar with thirty-three, whose books and poems I have read and reviewed either in my first review book, *In a Fragile Moment: A Landscape of Canadian Poetry* or in this second volume. Statistically speaking, the number of poets I have reviewed plus those whose names are familiar to me and I had read prior to *Tamaracks*, forty-four, is quite representative of the total 113.

Factor 2 stands as a priority for both the editor and me. In fact, Deahl makes it very clear "... that this anthology is not about poets. It is solely about poems... Poets and reputations are neither accepted nor rejected, only poems are." *(Taken from Deahl's Introduction to Tamaracks)* That disclosed, I can add that I have read poets and poems in

Tamaracks and feel as happy and optimistic as Meyer on the solidity, broadness, scope and beauty of the poems, as well as the editor's judiciousness.

On a further note, I must say that the poetry included in *Tamaracks* (178 poems, though we can count more as some poets submitted more than one piece under a general title. For example, Elana Wolff with eleven and Henry Beissel with four plus two separate ones) is wide-ranging not just geographically but also in its register, style, themes, structure, presentation *and heart.* Deahl tells us that "There are many types of poetry written in Canada." There is an evident sense of nationhood in all of them, quantitatively and qualitatively cosmopolitan and multicultural in their expression and individuality.

To illustrate my point on poetry quality, and steering clear of favoritism, as Meyer warns, I will only quote fragments of my reviews about the first (coincidentally one of the poets I reviewed in this second volume) and the last poets in the book, Becky D. Alexander and Anna Yin (whom I also wrote about in my first book).

"Becky D. Alexander was published in *Tamaracks. Canadian Poetry for the 21st Century* (Lummox Press, 2018) with the poem "Buried Deep." She submitted a moving piece about Canadian soldiers thus deploying her broad poetic bandwidth, which I had already noticed in *Beyond the Seventh Morning* (2013) (Poetry) SandCrab Books, the book from where I took the two poems she included, "Myth-Morphosis" and "Seeking the Windigo," for analysis… These are Alexander's poems. Tall in the solemn poetry of "Buried Deep," she explodes too in a feat of artistic puissance, with a wide poetic register gripping the reader, tightening the grip to such lengths that we lapse into the mental labyrinth of desperately wanting to escape from the lurking darkness of the "northern woods."

"There must be something in Anna Yin's poetry that I only had to first read it to fall in love with her… She was contacted by the publisher to find out if she wanted to contribute her fine poetry to a project he and I were working on: publishing my literary reviews of Canadian authors, a tribute compilation of all my writings on their poetry or prose. Anna took no time to reply directly to me with a generous 'yes'… I have modestly analyzed six of them here… There is definitely something in the way Anna writes her poetry. A beholder of life – still or bustling – and thought – pensive or turbulent, Anna Yin embarks on her voyage into and from the depths of many faceted life and deposits it in her poems for us to feel, marvel and dream."

To end my comments, factor 4 is an asset here. Lummox Press has published myriad authors of stature. They say on their Mission Statement that "Over the past 24 years 150 titles have been published." *(Bottom of second page in Tamaracks)* I won't tell names of authors to avoid being partial and to help readers gain in interest. They also state: "The goal of the press is to elevate the bar for poetry." *(Idem previous quotation)* Indeed, the bar keeps getting higher, and *Tamaracks* has had a solid input in this.

While I reckon factor 5 to have been professionally accomplished (See artwork and design) and factor 6 to be a constantly moving figure, and a challenge Deahl dealt with in

Canada, the US and beyond, it must be declared as a major fact that *Tamaracks* is already a jewel as a book, and a success as a literary endeavor.

In my essay on Bernice Lever in this volume, I said: "The year 2018 brought to light through Lummox Press an unquestionably essential anthology of poetry, *Tamaracks: Canadian Poetry for the 21st Century*, edited by James Deahl. It was meant for Canadians but also, especially, for their neighbors to the south and a broader public interested in an update with "… an indication of where Canadian poetry finds itself in 2018 and … a hint of its possible future directions." (*Taken from Tamaracks: Canadian Poetry for the 21st Century, Lummox Press, 2018, Introduction by the Editor*)"

A word on the pictures, factor 4, that accompany many of the poems across the anthology's pages: they play a key part in the overall aesthetic proposal of the book, visually, culturally and spiritually speaking. This is valid too for the front cover, the maple leaf, one of Canada's symbols of nationhood – which alongside the suggestive initial part of the title, *Tamaracks* – embodies the most genuine Canadian spirit of a "True North." Interestingly, I have always praised Canadian poets´ intimate bond with nature, and the book's cover and title specifically emphasize one of its components, its flora.

James Deahl may make plans to send a second round of invitations to new poets, especially inclusive of those who did not appear in this first edition, with his mind specially set on a probable second edition of the anthology. The job he has done – plus all the factors herein discussed – deserves to transcend. This anthology is a treasure. Long live Poetry! Thank you, poets. Thank you, James.

Everywhere You Go Beauty Shows. A Review of *The Beauty Of Being Elsewhere*

(Poetry) (2020) Hidden Brook Press. Canada. Edited by John B. Lee

The Beauty of Being Elsewhere, edited by Canadian poetic gem, John B. Lee, is a wonderful book everyone should buy. Reading it will inevitably spark two effects. First, the desire effect: to travel and see, "live," places that the authors describe, miss and memorialize so warmly. Second, the learning effect: we are enlightened cognitively and touched affectively during our many journeys beside the poets.

Lee's summoning power groups more than a hundred poets, mostly Canadian, between the covers of this "*Elsewhere*" anthology. *The Beauty* unfolds with Lee's selection of an attractive, I´d say "exotic," leitmotif, travelling. Emily Dickinson speaks to us in the book´s opening quotations, "*Go travelling with us!... By routes of ecstasy.*" The quotation's page finishes with an excerpt from one of Lee´s poems, "… *a Cuban evening feeling the lovely melancholia of being elsewhere* …" Both are poignant and well-chosen epigrams to the book.

Reverence and flashback reflections are felt in the pieces included in the book, outlined in the editor´s preface, lines wherefrom the title was born: "… *inspired by the journey or the sojourn these poems were written and have been gathered here to honour the beauty of being elsewhere.*"

Every poet offers his/her experience, the wide-open hues of each pair of eyes enticed by what they perceive and breathe in. It is an entire anthology singing the marvels of learning, seeing, touching and safeguarding in the mind´s niche "*things of beauty*" dazzling like a rainbow, heart-touching as if an angel´s invisible soaring had sprinkled afterglow dust.

The spirit of the book echoes epigraphically in the lyrics from Ian Bell's song "I'll Fly Away" from his CD "Free Range." These poetic lyrics sing the book into the theme of travel: "*Geese in the stubble and a deer in the corn / Listen to the water as the stream rolls by / Smoke in the air on a frosty morning / I'm going to fly away / Light through the valley as the sun climbs higher / Listen to the water as the stream rolls by / Sumac setting all the hills on fire / I'm going to fly away…*" Poets flew away – and returned with a bagful of responsive poetry we are enjoying from here to the end of the book.

Marsha Barber is context-thrilled in "Las Vegas," where sights, music, dancing, glamour dazzle and baffle flash about, "*I am part of the glittering Eiffel Tower / find the Paris of Moulin Rouge / Cancan dancers perform high kicks and wild splits / as Bellagio's fountains dance / I linger at street cafes / feeding sparrows fresh baguettes / tour art galleries / filled with Impressionist paintings / ride gondolas in shallow canals by Piazza San Marco…*"

Particularly spiritual is Nancy Bell´s poem "Never Linger," Her haunting lines instantly drew me in; "*Never linger by the orphaned house near the slough / Lest the spirits of the past catch your hand / And draw you with them into a sunny summer past / When the apple trees were young and heavy with fruit…*" and markedly idyllic is the last stanza, "*Never linger under the old twisted trees of the orchard / You may find a sunny meadow and August sun / In the deep cold of a January day / The soft moo of the milk cow and the drone of honey bees*".

Consider these lines by Bronwen McRae, "*Sit on the dock, a breezy morning. / Watch momentary mountains climb from the lake. / Later the water is a living carpet rolled between shores. / So real you could walk across, your toes sluicing through silky fibres. / Know you have witnessed loon love, / listened to squirrel gossip…*" The poet has been able to involve me with nature, enthrall me as a reader and give me peace. In a string of film-like images rolling softly; kindling touch, sight, hearing, threaded into appealing metaphors, MacRae treats us as almost-guests sitting on that dock contemplating the beauty of a place in her poem aptly entitled "The Writing Retreat".

The magic of travelling descends upon us taking us close and far across sea and landscapes that defy the four points of the compass. It was Ireland in Lisa McGuire´s "Song 3" and "*The tiny, dark pub... alive at just 11:11 a.m.*" Suddenly, it is Rhonda Melanson´s journey in "Strong Women," "*… play penny whistles and drums / in Alaskan string bands / lilt their chords in clear Juneau air…*" or Bruce Meyer grasping the book´s concept in lines I quote only a few from. They epitomize the beauty of being elsewhere and back: "A Grace for Welcome": *You have been many places, / and the world that followed you… / Come in. Rest here as you wish… / Feel at home. If you have left / the comforts of the familiar, / look around... / You bring the gift of experience / from the places you have seen…*

Later, you are in Michael Mirolla´s "Juhu, Mumbai": "*Fingerling on Arabia's sea, Mumbai / vapours in the distance, sky / scraping*" and miraculously back in Ireland in Mary Ann Mulhern´s "Fishing Village in Ireland": "*In Porturlin, County Mayo, Ireland / I stand on a cliff / Overlooking the sea / My mother says when she was a child / Sheep sometimes perished / On rocks below…*" or waking up with Richard Grove´s "Without a Word."

The fragment I quote shows his unending allegiance to Cuba, his love for the simple things he finds in my country and leave him speechless: "*I had intended / to sit in the Cuban sun / and read the wisdom of José Martí… / but the longing call / of my rooster friend / drew me to the top / of the stuccoed wall… / I was instantly, / without a word / with you and Martí.*" Despite the wordlessness he writes about, expressive words flow in the poem!

John B. Lee himself becomes an agile stair-climbing tour guide roller-coastering us from sweet little Cuba in his "So, this is a place of places," "*we climb the four hundred steps / to the Cross of Holguin / and Manuel says / "So, this is a place of places ..." / and we stand /*

above the city..." to cyclopean China in "Climbing the Great Wall of China": "*I climb the stairs / to where the great wall / breaks its spine / along the grey-green ridge / of smoke and fog above the Yanshan mountains...*"

It is impossible to comment on every fine and eloquent poet that Lee has carefully, skillfully, chosen. I have tried to capture the essence of this book by simply sharing ideas that came to me as I ponderously pored through the pages and lingered long enough to celebrate. Readers will appreciate and rejoice in this journey that Lee has laid before us. I found familiar names – some I have written reviews about or recognized from the many books I have reviewed – and I also ran into new voices that I will keep an eye open for in the future. Mostly, I have partaken in the stirred nostalgia of my own travelling, which has been limited but experiential; short but indelible.

As to *The Beauty*, it is unlimited in scope, widely experience-based, warmly long, and absolutely indelible for poets, editor and readers. Let´s end this review with Lee´s own elucidation of what travelling may mean, an excerpt from his poem "I Too Can Show the Way": *Where would you lead me friend? / into what future / and from what past / and by what light guide / and for what purpose go / and to what end / and with what faith ...*

In travelling we meet with the past and savor it; we envision our many tomorrows, lean hopefully on them pedestaled on our present. In travelling we grow and become informed humans, we are invested with the gift of constructive comparison and contrast, we forge purpose, seek end and stand trustfully on faith. In travelling our individuality waxes as universality that we lacked as "locals," and we learn to appreciate "thereness" and otherness in geographies we had at our fingertips and encounters we embraced.

And after our Ulysses ventures, we value more our *home sweet home*, where we sit before a desk and thank *Calliope*, *Erato* and *Terpsichore* for the blessing of poetics. Let´s thank John B. Lee too for this new chapter of fine poetry, sceneries, people and engaging aesthetics. Thank you, John.

Afterword

Even when as a reader I may enjoy the right to comment on other people's work, poets and prose writers in this case, I will always feel uncomfortable if I write without getting valuable feedback from them. Thus I have invariably tried to reach most of the poets I review. The response of those I have succeeded in contacting has been overwhelmingly big-hearted and significantly instructional culturally speaking.

As I did in my previous review book, I include some of those replies. Thank you, my friends, for your generosity and your contribution to improve my work and my knowledge of Canadian literature.

I quote what I said in my Afterword to *In a Fragile Moment: A Landscape of Canadian Poetry*: "Here is my humble tribute to you, my dear poet friends. After all, this book is not really about my modest words at all: it is fully about you and your ability to craft words into poetry. You and the Canadian poetry movement are the ones who made it possible. Thank you."

Ed Woods: "Dear Miguel; I find your review so enlightening that I may be walking on air for days. It is so beautiful that I would not know where to start upon any change as it would be difficult to improve upon your poetic review perfection. Thank you and have a great year. Ed."

Elana Wolff: "Thank you so much for your extra-attentiveness—in expanding and deepening your review of poems in *Birdheart*. And thank you in advance for this most thoughtful new year's gift! I truly appreciate your reading and sensitivity to my earliest work. I am indeed happy with your assessments. Best wishes, Elana."

Hugh Hazelton: *(first email)* "Hi Miguel, Thanks for sending along your essay: I'm delighted you like my work. I'll read it over carefully and send you my comments in a couple of days. One thing I can tell you is that I wrote "communiqué" several decades ago, before the use of "dis" appeared in slang, so the primary word play at the time was simply by separating "dis" and "information." However, your interpretation of a triple play involving slang expression "to dis" is a great example of the evolution of meaning adding an unexpected and complementary aspect to the text! Best wishes, Hugh."

(second email) "Just a note to tell you how much I enjoyed your analysis of my poems. You really get what my poetry is about, both in terms of technique, content and vision. It was great to follow your insights and your understanding of the "misty maelstrom" of my words… Best wishes for the holidays, Hugh."

Eva Kolacz: "Good afternoon Miguel: What a delightful surprise to receive the excellent essay concerning my book *Whatever We Are*. I'm very happy that I followed James Deahl's suggestion to send you my book, along with my husband's Laurence Hutchman, whose book, *The House of Shifting Time* for potential reviews... I would like to personally thank you for taking interest in Canadian literature, especially poetry. This task requires a lot of time and an intense study of the subject. I'm pleased to learn that you enjoy the works of Canadian women poets and I noticed that you wrote essays on their works which will be part of the upcoming book, first volume *In a Fragile Moment: A Landscape of Canadian Poetry*. And I'm glad that you will include your essay on my book on the second volume of "Fragile Moment." In your review you skillfully interpreted the poems that you have chosen to discuss, going deeply into the matter. These five poems are expressing our personal search to find balance in life, shattered by events that we encountered that were unavoidable. They are full of existential questions so difficult to answer. Thank you for this marvelous appreciation of my work. It is the first time that a critic has found resemblances in my poems to that of Pablo Neruda, Al Purdy, and Milton Acorn. I'm gratified that you understood the philosophical nature of my poetry and its various levels. I found your precise analysis of my metaphors and ideas very perceptive. You were able to see the various possibilities of my work and its essential optimism. Greetings from Canada Eva Kolacz."

Laurence Hutchman: "… I found your commentary of my four poems concerning time and travel very perceptive, especially with "Travel," the way you presented the past and present time by using the quotations from the poem to effectively support your ideas. I also liked your sensitive reading of the poem "Resonance." This poem represents important reflections on my Irish childhood. I liked the questions you pose"." Why does history record such progress . . .? Why was humanity compelled to transform reality?" Thank you for such an illuminating and in-depth reading of four of my poems. Your analysis of "Autumn Afternoon" was brilliant. Thank you again. Eva and I wish you and your family a Merry Christmas and a healthy, productive new year. We look forward to meeting you when we come to Cuba. Kind Regards, Laurence."

Bernice Lever: "Greetings, Miguel Olive Iglesias: I eagerly read your fine academic review of my 2 poems when I came home for my evening meal. I am delighted with your publishing plans with CCLA, to include me. … This weekend I will respond more clearly to your fine article on my poetry. With much appreciation and good wishes for You and Yours in Cuba. Bernice Ann Lever."

April Bulmer: "Hello Miguel, We are having winter rain here in Cambridge, Ontario, Canada where I live, but your email and article brought light to this rather dismal day. Thank you so very much for your sensitive reading, reflecting and writing on two of my poems. I remember sending work to *Beyond the Seventh Morning…* You are a very fine critic and academic, indeed, and my work was in good hands as you analyzed it. All the best with your future essays. Tai Grove has published two of my books through Hidden Brook Press. He has been so kind to me, and I respect his efforts in forging an alliance between Cuban and Canadian writers. Many thanks for your work with the CCLA. Sending holiday wishes to you, April Bulmer."

James Deahl: "Because of his deep understanding of such Canadian poets as Milton Acorn, Margaret Atwood, John B. Lee, and Al Purdy, Miguel Ángel Olivé Iglesias is able to write about any Canadian poet with an insight into his proper context. His grasp of prosody and the Canadian poetic tradition is excellent."

John B: Lee: "I forgot to mention that I read your two essays and I am impressed with your scholarship and your erudition. I've always suggested that the job of a reviewer involves finding and recommending work to a potential audience, since you can't read every book, see every movie, listen to every cd, etc. You need the guidance of someone with whose judgment and taste are reliable. The job of a critic on the other hand involves illuminating the art in such a way as to enlighten the recreator… So, you my friend, are the light we carry with us when we go into realms beyond the light on the surface, and like the limpid waters of deep wells, the water need not be murk, it only needs that we carry a light where we go… all good things, your admiring friend, John B."

Brian T. W. Way: *(first email)* "Hello Miguel, Thank you so much for deciding to do a literary essay on my work. I was very impressed, and flattered, by the things you had to say. Very insightful and well said. I think it makes my work sound much grander than it is… Anyway, once again, many thanks for your kind and insightful words. To steal from Wordsworth, I must say that your comments make 'my heart leap up'… All the best. Brian"

(second email) "Dear Miguel, Let me echo the ending of your essay — 'Thank you, Miguel.' I am humbled by your words and your positive analysis of my poems in *redirection…* What you say is clear and insightful and, I think, makes my writing seem better than it probably is. And any comparison to Al Purdy is an honour, I can assure you… So thank you for your excellent work — I know how much time and effort gets poured into writing an essay such as this… Until we talk again... Brian"

Antony Di Nardo *(His assessment after reading the reviews in this book)*: "I've enjoyed these reviews, Miguel... the passionate intensity of your writing and the clarity you bring to your subject. You are most definitely knowledgeable about the roots of Canadian poetry and how that poetry has branched out into some of our contemporary voices, voices you understand with remarkable insight..."

Henry Beissel *(General reference made to my reviews): (first email)* I've now read a couple of your reviews and I must congratulate you on the sensitivity and intelligence with which you undertake the task. What I like most is that you go very concretely to the text of the poems, instead of waffling abstractly about a work… Thanks and congrats! Take it easy. Henry

(second email) I've read some more of your reviews and it's remarkable how easily you feel yourself into the voice and perspective of very different poets. Congrats.

John Di Leonardo: Dear Miguel, I am honoured and delighted that you chose to review my book *Conditions of Desire…* Thank you for the insightful analysis on my work and ekphrastic poetry in general, it is an enjoyable and informative read regarding the genre… Wishing you all the best in your new project, Warm regards, John Di Leonardo

Comments about

A Shower of Warm Light

As both a reader and an academician, I want to acknowledge Professor Miguel Olivé´s tour-de-force new review book. *A Shower of Warm Light* is a continuation of a previous book, *In a Fragile Moment: A Landscape of Canadian Poetry*, he published with Hidden Brook Press in 2020 about Canadian poets and prose writers. He is loyal to his style, which remains flowing and captivating. The book is easy to read, engaging and adheres to valid standards of text analysis we make in our English major. Olivé studies the authors, places them in context, offers examples and arguments, and brings pleasure to the act of reading his reviews and the poems. Canada visits us in his words that stand as poetic as the pieces he chose; however, he does not compromise the essayistic character of his work. Quite the contrary, there is passion convincingly harmonized with reliability in his coherent assertions and conclusions. We welcome this new book, and its appealing angle, into our university studies of Canadian literature.

PhD Julio Rodríguez
Associate Professor
Chair of the Foreign Languages Department
Holguín University, Cuba

I had the pleasure to read Professor Olivé´s first review book, *In a Fragile Moment: A Landscape of Canadian Poetry*. He surprises us now, and enriches our curricular goals, with this second volume, *A Shower of Warm Light*. In my forty years in academia, I do not recall a similar compilation of essays about a specific country or group of poets, so comprehensive and accessible to general readers, English major students and faculty in our universities. Besides, we must mention that it was written in English, an extra challenge for any Spanish speaker. A nation´s literary heritage records for posterity the best of its intellect and heart. Canada is safeguarded in this creation, and Olivé stands as its passionate contributor and "curator" beyond Canadian seas. The book puts poetry and prose in our hands, with a view that is fresh, well founded, respectful and an encompassing analysis of Canadian literature broad in time, geography and style.

PhD Pedro Machín
Full Professor
Head of the English Major Studies
Vice-chair of the Foreign Languages Department
Holguín University, Cuba

I welcome this new review book by Professor Olivé, *A Shower of Warm Light.* I teach History of the English Speaking Cultures in our Holguín University. Both Olivé´s first book, *In a Fragile Moment: A Landscape of Canadian Poetry*, and this one are a major contribution to our syllabi and to the Cuban State´s endeavors towards the formation of cultivated students. Olivé proves beyond doubt how powerful, legitimate and appealing Canadian culture is, centering on literature, especially poetry. Reading the books, one cannot avoid wanting to access the sources he based his studies on, it also helps in bringing quality education to our minds and nourishment for the soul.

BEd Katherine Mora Chacón
History and Literature Professor
Teacher Education English Major Studies
Foreign Languages Department
Holguín University, Cuba

To my knowledge, few critics outside the country have traveled the landscape of English-Canadian literature with such verve, scope, and sensitivity as Miguel Olivé Iglesias. His itinerary, from writer to writer, poet to poet, champions both an elevation of their work as well as his own unique and personal understanding of their craft and aesthetics.

With writing that is crisp, incisive, even casual, he takes us on a deliberate journey beyond borders, to where poetry can be either a detour or a main attraction. Professor Olivé Iglesias is the consummate traveler and reader—eager to make sense of his destinations, seriously engaged with the work on the page, passionate about his encounters. Not only is there an unabashed appreciation of the poetry he reviews, but there is evidence throughout this book that his insights into the broken line and the Canadian idiom speak of a genuine scholarship that stems from an intimate reading of the poets in question.

Iglesias goes back to the very roots of Canadian poetry, applauding the work of Bliss Carman and Pauline Johnson, and recognizing the role that later luminaries such as Souster and Purdy play in shaping our present, contemporary idiom. He never shies away from saying what he thinks or feels about the poetry that moves him; and he is just as comfortable in providing technical, analytical justification for his responses. These reviews certainly serve as a traveler's guidebook to a discovery of recent Canadian writing and, as he admonishes the reader in one of those pieces, you're best not to leave home without it.

Antony Di Nardo
Canadian poet and professor

Authors reviewed in this book:

Becky D. Alexander

Canadian poet. Bachelor of Arts degree at Wilfrid Laurier University and took post-graduate studies in education through the University of Western Ontario. Her writing has won hundreds of awards. She operates Craigleigh Press, which has published the works of over thirty local writers. Published in *Tamaracks. Canadian Poetry for the 21st Century*, an anthology edited by James Deahl and conceived to offer readers home and abroad a panorama of contemporary Canadian poetry where 113 poets where featured.

Donna Allard

Canadian poet Donna Allard is the founder of Sojourner Literary Festival and past President of the Canadian Poetry Association. She was recently published in *Tamaracks. Canadian Poetry for the 21st Century*, an anthology edited by James Deahl and conceived to offer readers home and abroad a panorama of contemporary Canadian poetry where 113 poets where featured. Email: donnaallard@live.ca.

Henry Beissel

Canadian poet recently published in *Tamaracks. Canadian Poetry for the 21st Century*, an anthology edited by James Deahl and conceived to offer readers home and abroad a panorama of contemporary Canadian poetry, which included 113 poets. Beissel has published over forty books, among them twenty-two poetry collections. His *Cantos North*, a formidable epic – and Beissel's *magnum opus* – is considered by by F. R. Scott as the first to see Canada and the North "... in its entirety, as a matrix which binds the whole together in a national mythology."

Nancy M. Bell

A Canadian poet from Alberta. She lives near Balzac, Alberta, with her husband and various critters. She works with animals. Nancy is a member of The Writers' Union of Canada and the Writers' Guild of Alberta. She has publishing credits in poetry, fiction, and non-fiction. For the past three years she has been invited to read her poetry at the Stephan G Stephansson House event Poetry. She was included in *Tamaracks: Canadian Poetry for the 21st Century* (Lummox Press, 2018), anthology edited by James Deahl, bringing together Canadian contemporary poets.

Stella Body

Born in Africa, the poet currently lives in Canada. Body has a Master's degree in Canadian Poetry thus certified to teach at college level. She has been publishing poetry for years and writing about Canadian poetry. Her key themes are nature and conservation issues. She has won numerous awards and is actively involved in preserving nature.

Heide Brown

She started writing when she was 11, producing plays for her Girl Guide friends. Since then, she has filled her file-cabinet with multiple drafts of stories, memoirs and poems, and her bookshelf with journals. Since 1990, she has lived on Gabriola Island, B.C. She loves writing, painting, hooking rag-rugs, her family life, friends, and The Gabriola Commons, which she co-founded. Email: heidebro@telus.net

Ronnie R. Brown

U.S. born Canadian poet who steps into the night, dreams and wandering thoughts, taking them as favorite themes for her poetry. She explores with underlying sensuousness those dark realms we enter when we close our eyes, and pulls us in through words and images that will stay with us. She has published with Black Moss Press and was included in *Tamaracks: Canadian Poetry for the 21st Century* (Lummox Press, 2018), anthology edited by James Deahl, bringing together Canadian contemporary poets.

April Bulmer

Canadian poet who has published with Hidden Brook Press and SandCrab Books. She holds Master's degrees in religious studies and theological studies, as well as creative writing. She was included in *Tamaracks: Canadian Poetry for the 21st Century* (Lummox Press, 2018), anthology edited by James Deahl, bringing together Canadian contemporary poets. She lives in Ontario. april.poet@bell.net

Bliss Carman

Canadian poet who was born in 1861 and died in 1929. He actually lived for most of his life in the United States and it was here that he became known worldwide. He was never forgotten in Canada though and they made him their Poet Laureate in his later years. He was a lyrical poet who was numbered amongst the so-called Confederation Poets in Canada and shared this status with the likes of Duncan Campbell Scott and Archibald Lampman. Carman stood out from some of his contemporaries in that he dedicated himself to poetry, occasionally writing critical commentaries on philosophical or literary topics. Others often chose to diversify into journalism or writing novels.

Leonard Cohen

Canadian artist born in Montreal in 1934. His artistic career began in 1956 with the publication of his first book of poems, *Let Us Compare Mythologies.* He has ten books of poems and made seventeen albums. He is considered one of the most influential artists in Canada and abroad.

James Cockcroft

Bilingual award-winning author of 50 books, including, Why? Por Que? Pourquoi? Poetry & Poesia published by Hidden Brook Press, 2009, 2nd ed. 2013, Canada and Mexico's Revolution Then and Now, NY: Monthly Review Press, 2010, now in 5 editions and 3 languages. Email: jcockcro@yahoo.com

Dorothy Cox Rothwell

A Spiritualist Minister, Writer, Poet and works in healing arts. Her work has appeared in Portraits, by Peterborough Area Women Past and Present, the Otonabee Tapestry, Poetry Box, Parachute, Sacred Encounters with Mary, Grandfather, Father and Me and The Link Magazine. She is member of the Writer Group, 7ish. Email: dotcox@cogeco.ca

James Deahl

Born in 1945 in the U.S., Deahl is a Canadian poet and publisher. He has been described as "one of the ten or twenty finest poets writing in the English language today." He is a founding member of the Canadian Poetry Association and is a Canada Cuba Literary Alliance Ambassador, Editor and contributing poet. He has many poetry titles and essays to his name. He has edited important poetry books, among them one dedicated to Milton Acorn, In a Springtime Instant. He has been – and continues to be – a very active and indispensable figure in the Canadian literary world.

John Di Leonardo

A graduate of McMaster University, where he earned an Hon. BA in Fine Arts. He subsequently taught Visual Arts for thirty years, and is currently a full time artist who divides his time between writing, painting, and travel. John's poetry has received recognition in numerous poetry competitions. He is the recipient of the Ted Plantos Memorial Award 2017. He is member of The Canadian Authors Association, and is an associate member of The League of Canadian Poets.

Antony Di Nardo

Poet born in Montreal. Professor. Post graduate degree in English from the University of Toronto. Initially a journalist. His work has been translated into French and Italian and has been anthologized in several collections of poetry in Canada and abroad. He has many titles to his name. Previously reviewed in *In a Fragile Moment: A Landscape of Canadian Poetry*, Hidden Brook Press (2020).

Graham Ducker

Oshawa resident, a published author, a poet, retired Principal, primary Methods Specialist and former Kindergarten Teacher. Mr. Ducker has received National and International awards and recognition for his writing. He had the esteemed title of being the Poet Laureate of Oshawa for five years. His published memoir book entitled, Don't Wake the Teacher, is an integral part of the University of Holguin's Teacher Education English Major. He has had two poetry books published: Observations of the Heart and Mind, and Where Warm Hearts Blend.

Andreas Gripp

Canadian author with twenty-three poetry books to his name and three books of fiction. His book *Anathema* was shortlisted for the Acorn-Plantos Award for People's Poetry in 2010. Published in *Tamaracks. Canadian Poetry for the 21st Century*, an anthology edited by James Deahl and conceived to offer readers home and abroad a panorama of contemporary Canadian poetry where 113 poets where featured.

Richard Marvin Grove (Tai)

Richard Grove is a man of the 7 Ps – Poet, Publisher, Photographer, Painter, President, Public Speaker, and Potter. Richard has been going to Cuba, once or twice a year for over 25 years now. He is the president of the CCLA – Canada Cuba Literary Alliance founded in 2004. Find the CCLA at www.CanadCubaLiteraryAllicnac.org. He takes groups of Canadian authors to Cuba on reading and writing tours and then publishes their work. He has given readings, interviews and talks on publishing and writing around the world including Germany, New Zealand and Cuba. He has had poems and prose published in many different periodicals around the world as well as having been published in over 50 anthologies. He is the artist and author of over 15 books. He lives in Presqu'ile Provincial Park with, his freelance editor/writer wife, Kimberley Sherman Grove. At their Presqu'ile home they run a B&B called Presqu'ile Point B&B.

Don Gutteridge

Author of more than fifty-five books: poetry, fiction and scholarly works in educational theory and practice. He was born in Sarnia, Ontario and raised in the nearby village of Point Edward. He graduated from Western with an Honours English degree, taught school for seven years and then joined Western's Faculty of Education. There he taught English methods for twenty five years and is now Professor Emeritus. He won the 1972 UWO President's Medal for the best periodical poem of that year, "Death At Quebec." His poetry collection Coppermine was short listed for the 1973 Governor General's Literary Award.

Hugh Hazelton

Poet, translator, and editor, who lives in Montreal where he is Professor Emeritus of Spanish translation and Latin American civilization at Concordia University. He translates from Spanish and French into English and specializes in works by Latin American authors living in Canada, as well as in the poetry of Québec. His fourth book of poetry, *Antimatter*, was republished with CD by Broken Jaw Press in 2010; a Spanish version, *Antimateria*, came out with Split Quotation/La Cita Trunca in 2009. He performs his poems in several languages and believes that poetry should bite, caress, laugh at, confront, lament, name, envision, remember, invoke, oppose, and reflect.

Laurence Hutchman

Canadian author. Professor and poet who has published in Canada and abroad. He has received awards and public recognition. He has a PhD and has taught literature in Canadian universities. Recently published the book analyzed here with Black Moss Press in 2019. Was published in *Tamaracks. Canadian Poetry for the 21st Century*, an anthology edited by James Deahl and conceived to offer readers home and abroad a panorama of contemporary Canadian poetry where 113 poets were featured. His poems have been translated into several languages.

I. B. Iskov

Maturely existential and deeply reflective, Iskov is a Canadian poet who addresses her own life in her poetry, her roots, how far and high those roots can make her grow towards the future. Iskov molds fresh metaphors that elevate yet do not miss nor forget their down-to-earth duties. The poet has a strong will, she intends to survive, and shares with us one way to do it. She has been published in the CCLA formats, such as The Envoy and The Ambassador.

Emily Pauline Johnson

Also known in Mohawk as Tekahionwake –pronounced: dageh-eeon-wageh, literally: 'double-life.' Canadian writer and performer popular in the late 19th century. Johnson was notable for her poems and performances that celebrated her First Nations heritage; her father was a Mohawk chief of mixed ancestry, and her mother an English immigrant. Her poetry was published in Canada, the United States and Great Britain. Johnson was one of a generation of widely read writers who began to define a Canadian literature. Since the late 20th century, Johnson's writings and performance career have been reevaluated by literary, feminist, and postcolonial critics. They have appreciated her importance as a New Woman and a figure of resistance to dominant ideas about race, gender, Native Rights, and Canada.

Eva Kolacz

Canadian author. Professional artist, contemporary painter, poet who has published and exhibited her work in Canada and Poland, her homeland. She has received many awards and public recognition in both countries. Published her book *Whatever We Are* with Hidden Brook Press in 2019. She was recently published in *Tamaracks. Canadian Poetry for the 21st Century*, an anthology edited by James Deahl and conceived to offer readers home and abroad a panorama of contemporary Canadian poetry where 113 poets where featured

Laurie Kruk

Canadian writer with a Ph.D. and a postdoctoral degree. She has taught English at the Nipissing University, North Bay. She specializes in Canadian Literature. Her poetry is emotion-stirring, to-the-point, epigrammatic and unleashed in terms of syntax, bringing to the spotlight the maelstrom of living and loving with a bared and breath-taking singularity.

John B. Lee

Author and poet who is Poet Laureate of Brantford, Ontario. He is the only Canadian to be a Poet Laureate in two locations simultaneously. He is also the poet Laureate of Norfolk County. He has received more than sixty prestigious international awards for poetry. He has been named to the Ridgetown District High School Hall of Excellence along with other distinguished alumni. In 2010 he received the UWO Alumni Award of Merit for Professional Achievement in recognition for his career as a poet/author/editor/performer/mentor. Lee is the author of thirty seven published books and ten published chapbooks and he is the editor of nearly ten published anthologies. Lee has also been a visiting professor at University of Western Ontario, University of Windsor, Canador College, and a guest speaker at the University of the

Witwatersrand in South Africa, and many universities throughout Canada and the United States. He was named Member of the President's Circle of McMaster University and his personal collection of Canadian Poetry was donated to the City Library where it is available for circulation under the title "The Poet Laureate Collection."

Bernice Lever

Canadian poet, founding Editor of WAVES, a literary magazine. She has published ten books of poetry and a teaching English text, *The Colour of Words*, and short prose too. She has a BA and an MA in English. She has four Lifetime Achievement Awards. She is focused now on international peace poetry. She appeared in *Tamaracks. Canadian Poetry for the 21st Century*, an anthology edited by James Deahl and conceived to offer readers home and abroad a panorama of contemporary Canadian poetry where 113 poets where featured.

Stella Mazur Preda

Stella Mazur Preda has been published in numerous Canadian anthologies and some US, most notably the purchase of her poem My Mother's Kitchen by Penguin Books, NY. She has released two previous books, Butterfly Dreams and The Fourth Dimension and is currently working on her third book, Tapestry, to be released in 2018. She was recently published in *Tamaracks. Canadian Poetry for the 21st Century*, an anthology edited by James Deahl and conceived to offer readers home and abroad a panorama of contemporary Canadian poetry where 113 poets where featured. Email: star.preda@cogeco.ca.

Michael Mirolla

A well-known author of novels, short stories and poems, co-owner and editor-in-chief of Guernica Editions literary press. He describes his writings "as a mix of magic, realism, surrealism, speculative fiction and meta-fiction." Entering his poetry is entering a grid of images, those that may well hand us a key to a post-realm of words and syntax, a semiotic pathfinder that challenges – and hooks.

A. F. Moritz

Born in Niles, Ohio, in 1947, A. F. Moritz has written more than 15 books of poetry. He has been a finalist for the Governor General's Literary Award and he has won the Award in Literature of the American Academy and Institute of Arts and Letters, a Guggenheim Fellowship, the ReLit Award, Poetry magazine's Bess Hokin Prize, and the Griffin Poetry Prize. A. F. Moritz lives in Toronto and teaches at Victoria University at the University of Toronto. Published in *Tamaracks. Canadian Poetry for the 21st Century*, an anthology edited by James Deahl and conceived to offer readers home and abroad a panorama of contemporary Canadian poetry where 113 poets where featured.

Marion Mutala

Ukrainian by birth, Canadian by choice, this poet enraptures us with her musical poetry. It is all motion, hues, pain, hope, refuge in nature; close images neatly and sincerely outlined for us. A world of movement, sound, colour reverberates in her poetry, alongside the deeply-rooted sense of belonging to her traditions, and her will to honor and remember, all of which float intensely and wondrously.

K. V. Skene

Her work has appeared in Canadian, U.K., U.S., Irish, Indian, Australian and Austrian magazines – most recently in Scintilla (UK,) FreeFall (Canada) The Stony Thursday Book (Ireland), Poetry News (The Poetry Society Newsletter (UK). Tower Poetry (Canada) and The Frogmore Papers (UK). A winner in the 2018 erbacce prize contest, her latest collection, *Unoriginal Sins*, was published this year by erbacce-press (UK). Also, a winner in the 2018 Cinnamon Press pamphlet contest, her new chapbook The Love Life of Bus Shelters, appeared in March 2019. She was featured in *The Dream The Glory and The Strife* in 2018, a Hidden Brook Press CCLA members anthology.

Raymond Souster

Born in Toronto on January 15, 1921. He spent his entire life in Toronto except for the years during which he saw active duty with the Royal Canadian Air Force during World War II. The principal aspects of his literary life fall into eight areas: Poetry, Fiction, Editing, Book Publishing, Organizing Readings, the League of Canadian Poets, Mentorship and the Souster Legacy. He can be placed, according to James Deahl, "among the most important dozen poets of 20th century Canada."

Robert Sward

Poet Laureate of Santa Cruz County, 2016-2018, Robert Sward has taught at Cornell University, the Iowa Writers' Workshop, and UC Santa Cruz. A Fulbright scholar and Guggenheim Fellow, he was chosen by Lucille Clifton to receive a Villa Montalvo Literary Arts Award. His 30 books include: *Four Incarnations* (Coffee House Press), now in its second printing; *Heavenly Sex*; *The Collected Poems (1957-2004)*; and THE TORONTO ISLANDS, a bestseller. Widely published in traditional literary magazines and anthologies, Sward has served as contributing editor to "Web Del Sol," "Blue Moon Review," and other online publications since 1995. Born and raised in Chicago, Robert Sward served in the U.S. Navy in the combat zone during the Korean War (1951-1953) and later worked for CBC Radio and as book reviewer and feature writer for *The Toronto Star* and *The Globe & Mail.*

John Tyndall

Canadian writer. His poetry has been presented in magazines and anthologies like *Canadian Author*, *Windsor Review*, *Window Fishing: The Night We Caught Beatlemania* (Hidden Brook Press, 2013), edited by John B. Lee, and on Cornelia Hoogland's blog *Crow*: https://crow2011.wordpress.com/blog/. *Listen to People* was also edited by B. Lee.

Brian T. W. Way

Canadian poet who holds degrees from Queen's (B.A. Hons; B.Ed.) and Western (MA; PhD) and worked as a professor at Western in the Departments of English and Education. He also taught English and Media Studies in various secondary schools across the province and at Loyalist College. He has served as a member of the Board of Governors for the Royal Military Colleges of Canada, the Al Purdy A-Frame Association, and the Prince Edward County Libraries and Archives. He is author of: The Prince of Leroy; redirection; County Time; Bee; and Print Preview in addition to poems and stories published in a variety of magazines over the years including, recently, The Ambassador.

Elana Wolff

Canadian poet. Her poetry speaks highly of her artistry and style, of her devotion and love for life, of her joy and constancy above pain. Also a teacher, she has dedicated her life to others. She is a full giver who now visits our magazine. She has been a regular author, poet and essayist, in the Guernica Editions publications since her first book appeared, *Birdheart*, in 2001. Her book *Swoon* came out in 2020.

Ed Woods

Canadian poet who knows the world, has tasted land, sea and air, has held their essence in his hands and carried them in his heart. Such experiences combined with his insight and gave him one-of-a-kind material and motivation to start writing poetry. A pilot by profession, Woods has performed all sorts of jobs and crafts. He has published in mags, websites, anthologies, etc. A direct, uncomplicated, open and handsome style underscores his work that limns nature, creation and everyday things influenced by his experiences.

Donna Wootton

Canadian author who has published with Hidden Brook Press. Member of the Canada Cuba Literary Alliance. Her style is based on a graceful depiction of people and places, of circumstances and fate that she delineates in her characters.

About the Author

MSc Miguel Ángel Olivé Iglesias

Editor-in-chief of the Canada Cuba Literary Alliance (CCLA) magazine *The Ambassador*, also Assistant Editor of The Envoy newsletter, and CCLA President in Cuba. He does translation, proofreading and revision, along with compilation and anthologizing, and writes prose, poetry and literary reviews.

He is a member of the Mexican Association of Language and Literature Professors, VP of the William Shakespeare Studies Center and member of the Canadian Studies Department of the Holguín University in Cuba.

Born in 1965 in Bayamo, Cuba, he travelled to Holguín City in 1977 for his Junior, Senior High and College studies. Today he is an Associate Professor at the University of Holguín, with a Bachelor's Degree in Education, Major in English, and a Master's Degree in Pedagogical Sciences.

He has been teaching for over thirty years and writing reviews, poems and stories in Spanish and in English. Miguel has written and published numerous academic papers in Cuba, Mexico, Spain and Canada. So far he has published over one-hundred poems, four short stories and more than forty critical reviews of poetry and prose in different issues: *The Ambassador*, official flagship of the CCLA; *The Envoy*, official newsletter of the CCLA; The Bridges Series Books, published by Hidden Brook Press and SandCrab Books; Adelaide Group, New York and Lisbon (an essay on a Maltese poet); and other anthologies by Hidden Brook Press and SandCrab Books.

Hidden Brook Press published his first solo full length book of poems, in English and Spanish, *Forge of Words* (2019). SandCrab books also published the ebook he edited, *These Voices Beating in our Hearts: Poems from the Valley* (English-Spanish), where his poems and haiku appear together with other ten Holguín poets.

His most prominent work is *In a Fragile Moment: A Landscape of Canadian Poetry*, published by Hidden Brook Press in 2020, with one essay on the CCLA and thirty-five reviews on thirty-one Canadian poets and prose writers. The present material is that book's second volume.

He is currently involved in many other CCLA projects, which include his second solo book of poetry, *This Pulse of Life, These Words I Found.* He works at the Teacher Education English Department of the Holguín University as a professor of English and English Stylistics. He is also Head of the English Language Discipline.

He uses his academic papers, essays, stories and poems in class for reading, debating and practicing the language, adding a didactic and formative element to his scientific and literary production. He also does book presentations and donations, and poetry reading in co-curricular on-campus and community activities.

CanLit Revealed

A Series of Review and Essay Books on Canadian Literature.

Title: *In a Fragile Moment: A Landscape of Canadian Literature*

ISBN – 978-1-927725-92-4 – Softcover
ISBN – 978-1-927725-93-1 – epub
ISBN – 978-1-927725-94-8 – mobi

Publisher: QuodSermo Publishing

In a Fragile Moment is an insightful collection of essays and reviews, written from the poetic heart of Professor Olivé. The authors covered in this astute critical study are treated with heart felt respect. Professor Olivé has the uncanny ability to portray his incisive observations in a poetic and perceptive manner.

Title: *A Shower of Warm Light: Reviews and Essays on Canadian Literature*
Author: M.Sc. Miguel Ángel Olivé Iglesias

ISBN – 978-1-989786-55-0 (softcover)
ISBN – 978-1-989786-56-7 (ebook)

Publisher: QuodSermo Publishing

A Shower of Warm Light follows in the footsteps of *In a Fragile Moment* as a profoundly insightful collection of reviews and essays by M.Sc. Miguel Ángel Olivé Iglesias on Canadian Literature. Professor Olivé continues to open the readers eyes to the warm light of contemporary Canadian Literature.

Title: *On the Breeze of Canadian Literature: International Reviews and Essays*
Editor: M.Sc. Miguel Ángel Olivé Iglesias

ISBN – 978-1-989786-20-8 (softcover)
ISBN – 978-1-989786-21-5 (ebook)

Publisher: QuodSermo Publishing

On the Breeze of Canadian Literature follows in the tradition of In a Fragile Moment and A Shower of Warm Light but this time as an international collection of reviews and essays by scholars, professors and academics from around the world. Through these well written and accessible essays Professor Olivé brings us an enlightening perspectives on Canadian Literature.

Title: *Ploughing the Home Ground: Essays on Canadian Literature and Poetics*
Author: Don Gutteridge

ISBN – 978-1-989786-59-8 (softcover)
ISBN – 978-1-989786-60-4 (ebook)

Publisher: QuodSermo Publishing

Ploughing the Home Ground is a collection of republished essays on Canadian Literature and Poetics by Don Gutteridge including two essays about Don and his work.

Title: *Five Canadian Poets: Analytical Essays on, James Deahl, John B. Lee, Don Gutteridge, Glen Sorestad, A. F. Moritz*
Author: M.Sc. Miguel Ángel Olivé Iglesias

ISBN – 9781989786369 (softcover)
ISBN – 9781989786376 (ebook)

Publisher: QuodSermo Publishing

Here you will find outstanding essays on both the biographical history as well as the literary history of five of Canada's top poets. This collection of essays brings literary life to Canadian poetry in the making. Examples of each poet's work are critiqued, examined and observed gently and sympathetically. They have been described as "well-researched love letters to poetry and the poetic spirit." These essays will open your eyes to poetry.

Title: *The Canadian Poet Who Wrote Himself Whole: Revealing the Poetics of Don Gutteridge*
Author: M.Sc. Miguel Ángel Olivé Iglesias

ISBN – 978-1-989786-57-4 (softcover)
ISBN – 978-1-989786-58-1 (ebook)

Publisher: QuodSermo Publishing

The Canadian Poet Who Wrote Himself Whole is a fine collection of essays and reviews by scholar and essayist Miguel Ángel Olivé Iglesias on the poetry and prose of world class Canadian poet Don Gutteridge.

www.ingramcontent.com/pod-product-compliance
Lightning Source LLC
Chambersburg PA
CBHW080255030726
47593CB00009B/2500